52 WAYS TO

NATURE

WASHINGTON

52 WAYS TO
NATURE
WASHINGTON

YOUR SEASONAL GUIDE
TO A *Wilder* YEAR

Lauren Braden

SKIPSTONE

Published by Skipstone, an imprint of Mountaineers Books—an independent, nonprofit publisher

Skipstone and its colophon are registered trademarks of The Mountaineers organization.

Printed in China

25 24 23 22   1 2 3 4 5

Copyeditor: Amy Smith Bell
Design and Illustration: Melissa McFeeters
Cartography by Lohnes+Wright and Melissa McFeeters
All photographs by Lauren Braden unless credited otherwise.
Photos on pages 82, 86, 112, 148, 184, 186, 214, 222, 226, and 242 from unsplash.com.

Library of Congress Cataloging-in-Publication Data is on file for this title at https://lccn.loc.gov/2021039972 and ebook record is available at https://lccn.loc.gov/2021039973.

Printed on FSC®-certified materials

ISBN (paperback): 978-1-68051-313-4
ISBN (ebook): 978-1-68051-314-1

Skipstone books may be purchased for corporate, educational, or other promotional sales, and our authors are available for a wide range of events. For information on special discounts or booking an author, contact our customer service at 800.553.4453 or mbooks@mountaineersbooks.org.

Skipstone
1001 SW Klickitat Way
Suite 201
Seattle, Washington 98134
206.223.6303
www.skipstonebooks.org
www.mountaineersbooks.org

LIVE LIFE. MAKE RIPPLES.

To my husband, Brian, for his endless support and love. To my son, Isaac, for his sense of adventure and inspiring curiosity for the natural world. To Mom and Dad, for everything.

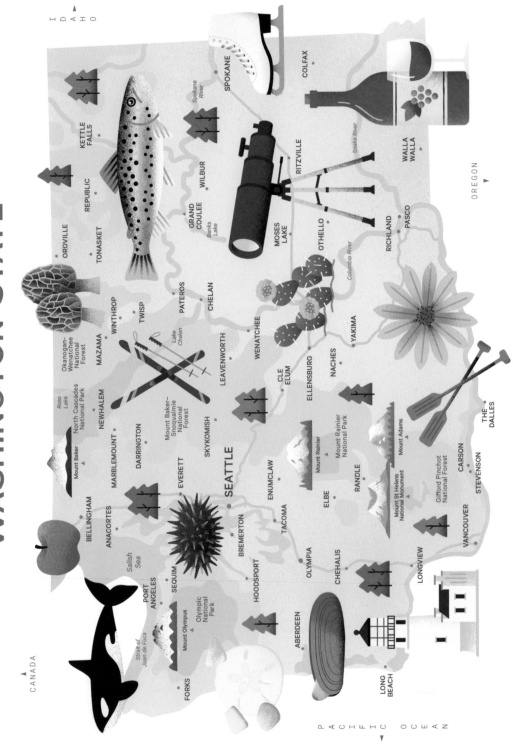

WASHINGTON STATE

CANADA

IDAHO

OREGON

PACIFIC OCEAN

KETTLE FALLS
SPOKANE
COLFAX
Spokane River
REPUBLIC
WILBUR
RITZVILLE
Snake River
WALLA WALLA
OROVILLE
TONASKET
GRAND COULEE
Banks Lake
MOSES LAKE
OTHELLO
RICHLAND
PASCO
Columbia River
PATEROS
CHELAN
WENATCHEE
YAKIMA
Okanogan-Wenatchee National Forest
WINTHROP
MAZAMA
TWISP
Lake Chelan
LEAVENWORTH
CLE ELUM
ELLENSBURG
NACHES
Ross Lake
North Cascades National Park
NEWHALEM
Mount Baker-Snoqualmie National Forest
SKYKOMISH
Mount Rainier
Mount Rainier National Park
Mount Adams
THE DALLES
Mount Baker
MARBLEMOUNT
DARRINGTON
EVERETT
SEATTLE
ENUMCLAW
ELBE
RANDLE
Gifford Pinchot National Forest
CARSON
STEVENSON
BELLINGHAM
ANACORTES
BREMERTON
TACOMA
Mount St Helens National Monument
VANCOUVER
Salish Sea
SEQUIM
OLYMPIA
CHEHALIS
LONGVIEW
PORT ANGELES
Strait of Juan de Fuca
Olympic National Park
Mount Olympus
HOODSPORT
ABERDEEN
LONG BEACH
FORKS

CONTENTS

INTRODUCTION

Paradise at Mount Rainier National Park

THIS IS A BOOK about things you can do to bring more nature into your life. It offers a year's worth of ways to deepen your connections to Northwest nature in every season. These fifty-two adventures will help you discover the marvels of the natural world while unearthing your place in it.

Washington is a wonderland of nature, from our neighborhood greenspaces to the state's spectacular national parks. We're lucky to live in a place so rich with natural beauty and public access to it—42 percent of Washington's land is in public hands. There are rocky and wild seashores, rain forests with ancient trees and cool critters, and glacier-flanked volcanoes that remind us of the region's geologic past as well as its future. We venture to these spectacular places to learn about them, enjoy them, and also to protect them from harm. These special places hold the power to teach us more about ourselves. Nature feeds our souls and restores our mental health the way nutritious food fuels our bodies.

Some adventures in this book may be familiar and already part of your life exploring the great outdoors, while other activities may compel you to try them for the first time. This guide shows you how. If you're new to the Northwest or to outdoor adventure, I hope these ways to nature capture your curiosity and rouse you to indulge. If you're looking for fresh ideas, you're likely to find your next favorite outdoor hobby in these pages. You might feel a few of the activities are outside your comfort zone or beyond your current abilities, but keep an open mind: all fifty-two adventures have been created for beginners, and the steps for an absolute novice are provided.

Combine these activities to pack even more nature into your year-round, all-weather outings. Add berry-picking to any spring hike. Let geocaching lead you to a little-explored corner of your favorite city park. Once you've learned to paddle a kayak, learn the names of the diving ducks alongside you. Nature and signs of wildlife can be found everywhere. Look for ways to incorporate everyday experiences with nature into your life, even during a morning stroll to the bus stop: a hole in the ground might be a chipmunk's house, or a blue and black feather in the grass may have been lost by a Steller's Jay.

I grew up in the Midwest, where public land was scarce and not particularly wild. My parents were more into rock and roll than nature, but I've always been drawn to wild places. They sent me to summer camp in the Ozarks, where I rode a horse and learned to build a campfire. I kept a journal then and wrote about snacking on lichen (it's not very tasty). In high school I took to birdwatching in local parks and fishing out of an old, leaky canoe. During my college years I learned to cross-country ski in northern Wisconsin and camped in tents across the Rockies. The mountains cast a spell on me, and I uprooted myself to go west.

Soon after moving to Seattle, I took my first backpacking trip and tasted a ripe huckleberry straight from the bush. I hiked to alpine talus every summer in search of the White-tailed Ptarmigan (I finally found one at Hannegan Pass in the North Cascades). I learned to kayak in Puget Sound and found out that a lot of those small islands have patches of poison oak. All the while, I discovered new ways to explore nature and deeper ways to connect. I was creating this book, but didn't yet know it.

HOW TO FIND NATURE

Go slowly and use all your senses. Don't rush through the landscape. Listen and stay alert.

Pause now and then. Notice the rich textures and interesting patterns in nature—from snowflakes to sand dunes, the bark on a tree, and the veins of a leaf. If you hear birdsong or see movement in the brush, be still and have patience. It can take critters a while to stop noticing you so that you can then notice them.

Be prepared. Bring the Ten Essentials (see later this section) on all outings. Dress for the weather, but be prepared for it to change. Wear comfortable shoes and clothes. Stay dry. Eat protein-rich snacks and stay hydrated. Eat only plants you are certain are edible. If you explore alone, tell someone where you're headed and when to expect your return.

Leave no trace. Don't feed wild creatures. When you encounter wildlife, keep a respectful distance. Don't pick wildflowers. If you turn over a rock to see what lies beneath, place it back just as it was. You can gather a few mementos (like leaves from the ground, pebbles from a beach, seashells, or a walking stick) as long as they are in abundance.

NATURE OUTINGS CHECKLIST

Turn any walk in the woods or stroll on the beach into a nature adventure by packing these key items.

- ☐ Nature journal
- ☐ Sketchbook
- ☐ Pencil
- ☐ Magnifying glass
- ☐ Binoculars
- ☐ Nature field guide
- ☐ Nature app (such as iNaturalist)
- ☐ Camera
- ☐ Garden gloves (for handling sharp objects)

KEEPING A NATURE NOTEBOOK

All of the adventures in this book include accompanying prompts—and even space—for nature journaling, should you keep one. Here are some tips for making the most of a nature notebook, be it on these pages or somewhere else.

Record basic information, and more. For future reference, include details about the outing such as time, date, location, and weather. Translate the information you take in through your senses onto the paper. What does the stream sound like? How does a caterpillar feel on your skin as it crawls up your arm?

Doodle away. Give yourself permission to sketch plants and animals without judging your artistic skill.

Make lists. Whether it's the wildflowers you noticed on a walk, or the trails you hope to hike next year, creating a simple list is an easy way to process information or make a plan.

Notice changes. Observe and make note of changes in nature over time. Note the date the cherry blossoms bloom or when you first spot a tulip opening its petals.

Write often. Collect and transcribe nature quotes that inspire you. As you write about your experiences in nature, you'll notice more when outdoors, as if someone turned up nature's volume.

HIKING SAFETY

Washington offers some of the world's most spectacular terrain and scenery for outdoor adventures. Take these precautions to help ensure your safety out there.

Choose the right adventure. Pick a hike that matches your expectations and current abilities. For instance, if you're not comfortable with stream crossings or talus scrambles, make sure there aren't any on your route.

Check trail conditions. Is the access road open? Is there ice on the trail? Find out if there are any trail washouts, large downed trees, or lingering snowfields to cross. There are a few ways to do this—through reading hiker trip reports on Washington Trails Association's website, checking the land agency's website, or calling the ranger station directly.

Confirm the weather forecast. Will the day be sunny and hot? Rainy and windy? Is there a chance of snow? Knowing the forecast gives you a heads-up on just how much sunscreen or raingear to pack, but be prepared for changes in the weather too.. Find the forecast at the National Weather Service; in the winter check the avalanche danger at the Northwest Avalanche Center.

Tell a friend. Let someone know exactly where you are going, who you will be hiking with (or whether you're going alone), and when you'll be back. Also important: the make of your car, the license plate number, and whom to contact should you not return when expected. And don't forget to call your friend when you return.

THE TEN ESSENTIALS

A time-tested list of items to bring along on your hike no matter how short or familiar the trail may be, the Ten Essentials can help you to stay safe should things go wrong in the backcountry. If you sprain an ankle or take a wrong turn, you may end up spending an unexpected night in the woods, and you'll be so glad to have extra clothes, food, and a flashlight. Chances are you won't need to use these essentials, but in case of an emergency, they could help save your life.

1. **Topographic map.** Carry a detailed topographic map of the region you'll be exploring. I like Green Trails Maps, which you can buy individually or in regional packs at your local outdoor store.
2. **Compass.** What good is that map if you can't determine where on it you are? That's where a compass comes in, and you'll need to know how to use it before you're at the trailhead. Learn basic navigational skills through a class at The Mountaineers or your local outdoor store, or watch a tutorial from a trustworthy source online.
3. **Sunglasses (and sunscreen).** Shades with polarized lenses will reduce glare so you can spot dangers like big tree roots or cliff ledges, even in bright sunlight. Pack and apply sunscreen, even in winter.

Use caution when crossing snowfields.

4. **Extra clothing and raingear.** When it comes to clothing, think layers for versatility. Weather on a mountain is not always the same as down at the trailhead; you could ascend up to a windy ridge or get stuck in an unexpected downpour. Avoid cotton, and instead opt for wool or polypropylene fabrics. Always keep a raincoat in your pack, even in sun-drenched summer.

5. **Headlamp or flashlight.** If you linger too long over lunch at the viewpoint, you might find yourself hiking in the dark back to your car. Always have a good light source in your pack, just in case.

6. **First-aid supplies.** First-aid supplies are essential in the backcountry. Buy a pre-packed hiker first-aid kit, or assemble your own. A host of things could happen out there: a bee sting, a twisted ankle, a punctured leg, or a migraine. In other words, supplies should include much more than a few little bandages. If you are prescribed an EpiPen, bring it along with any other medications you might require. Increase your knowledge of how to deal with more significant injuries by taking a backcountry first-aid course at your local outdoor store.

7. **Firestarter and matches.** Pack the tools to start an emergency fire—like matches in a waterproof container. In wet conditions you may not be able to find dry kindling on the ground, so bring a candle, compressed wood balls, or dryer lint as a firestarter.

8. **Water and purification.** Fresh water is abundant on many trails, but don't dip and sip. Backcountry water needs to be purified first so it doesn't make you sick from *Giardia*. Always carry extra water and purification tablets or a water filter.

9. **Knife or multitool.** A trusty pocketknife comes in handy—it slices your cheese, clips your blister bandages, and helps you repair your gear.

10. **Extra food.** In case you need to spend an unexpected night in the backcountry, pack a few extra trail bars and some gorp. Make sure the stash doesn't require any cooking.

In addition to the Ten Essentials, the following items provide more assurance of safety should something go wrong.

- **Emergency shelter.** This could be a lightweight tent or bivvy sack, or in a pinch, even a heavy-duty garbage bag.
- **Whistle.** It's lightweight and cheap, so there's no reason not to carry one. Better yet, pick up a six-function whistle at your local outdoor store that includes a compass, LED light, thermometer, and more.
- **Bug repellent.** Very few trails are bug-free, and in the high lake country midsummer, mosquito repellent is undoubtedly an essential!
- **Miscellaneous.** Other key items depend on where you are hiking and in what season. Do your homework before any outing.

ROAD TRIP CHECKLIST

To explore the nooks and crannies of Washington, you have to hit the road. Have fun and stay safe with this road trip checklist.

☐ **Plan your route and itinerary.** Use an app like Google Maps to plan ahead by saving the route, detour options, and snack stops.

☐ **Check the passes.** If you'll be crossing the Cascades anytime but summer, make sure your highway is open and know the snow conditions at the passes. Visit the Washington State Department of Transportation's website.

☐ **Drive the right vehicle.** If you have a low-clearance vehicle, you'll need to steer clear of some Forest Service roads. The easiest way to check conditions is to call the local ranger station and ask.

☐ **Prevent theft.** When parking at hiking trailheads, take steps to keep prowlers out of your car. Lock all doors and don't leave any items visible inside the car; stash them in the trunk out of sight.

☐ **Gear up for winter road trips.** Carry chains for your car tires (and know how to put them on), a scraper, a small shovel, and de-icer spray.

☐ **Keep cool and comfy in summer.** Bring a sunshade for your windshield and put it up during long stops. Wet wipes and a stocked first-aid kit are road trip essentials. Pack the cooler with water, drinks, and snacks.

☐ **Gas up before you leave town.** Vast areas of Washington's national forests, national parks, and Bureau of Land Management (BLM) lands have no gas stations.

☐ **Make the journey fun.** Play classic road trip games like Road Trip Bingo, Color Car, I Spy, or Twenty Questions.

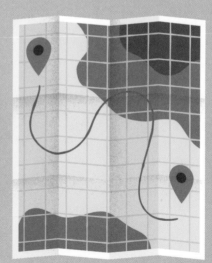

WINTER

- ○ Go Ice Skating
- ○ Sled Down a Hill
- ○ Hike Through History
- ○ Ski Like a Nordic
- ○ Snowshoe with a Ranger
- ○ Bask in the Rain Shadow
- ○ Go Animal Tracking
- ○ Find Razor Clams by Moonlight
- ○ Bag a Peak
- ○ Watch Storms Roll In
- ○ Camp in a Yurt
- ○ Go Birding
- ○ Bathe in a Forest

At first glance, winter is the season of nature's dormancy—a drab stretch of quiet, scant sunshine, and inclement weather before the burst of bright blooms and birdsong of spring. But if you're curious enough to brave the weather, you'll find nature to be very much alive during winter. Where do snowshoe hares find food in all that snow? Do most birds fly south for the winter? Why is each snowflake unique? If you wonder about such things and want to discover the answers, these winter adventures are for you.

What good is the warmth of summer, without
the cold of winter to give it sweetness.
—John Steinbeck, *Travels with Charley: In Search of America*

To appreciate the beauty of a snowflake, you have to be out in the cold. Dress to stay warm, dry, and (above all) avoid hypothermia, caused by exposure to cold and aggravated by moisture and wind. That means no cotton; bundle up head to toe in moisture-wicking layers. Choose polyester or wool fabrics close to your body, then add insulating layers like fleece or down, and cover all with a waterproof shell. Don't forget a hat, scarf, and gloves. Warm wool socks and waterproof boots are a must. Pack a thermos of hot chocolate or tea for frequent warm-up breaks, and bring lots of energy-packed snacks.

Before you head out, check the mountain forecast and avalanche conditions at NOAA Washington Mountain Weather and the Northwest Avalanche Center. Driving in winter requires extra precautions. If you're headed into the mountains or over passes, always carry tire chains. Stock your vehicle with a shovel to dig your car out of snow, a first-aid kit, blankets, extra clothes, food, and water. Consider taking an avalanche awareness class or the more extensive Avalanche Safety Course from The Mountaineers—indispensable education for anyone participating in backcountry winter activities.

GO ICE SKATING

SKATE AL FRESCO THIS WINTER

Skating at
Winthrop
Ice Rink

photo by Holly Rikhof

IF YOU GREW UP in the Upper Midwest or New England, frigid winter days might have been spent wearing skates, carving shapes or scraping hockey sticks on the murky gray ice that capped your neighborhood pond. Skating on natural ice is the sound of blades sweeping across the glassy surface, cold air on your cheeks, a waft of woodsmoke drifting from a nearby chimney. There's nothing else quite like it.

Pond skating is ubiquitous in some places and unheard of in others—it requires long cold snaps, at least three full days with temps below 32° F so ice forms on lakes and ponds, reaching at least four inches thick to walk or skate on. Ice fishermen and skaters use augers to drill holes and measure thickness of the ice for safety. With experience comes knowledge of the telltale signs of thin ice, such as color, cracks, or bubbles under the surface. As the climate warms, frozen ponds are in jeopardy: even states like Minnesota and Vermont are recording fewer days each winter with skateable ice.

As anyone who lives west of the Cascades will tell you, it's rare that we get a deep freeze that lasts long enough to freeze anything much bigger than a sidewalk puddle. Mountain lakes in the Cascades and Olympics freeze over in winter, but they're usually covered in snow and not accessible to skaters (though hardcore alpine ice skaters will pack their skates and search out snow-free frozen lakes by snowshoe). Maybe you're lucky enough to live beside a shallow pond in Eastern Washington that freezes over each winter. If not, grab some skates and head to an open-air ice rink.

Never been on ice skates? The wobbles you feel upon gingerly stepping onto ice for the first time feel hopeless at first, but with a few tips or a short lesson (many rinks offer

them—just ask), you'll get your ice legs. Hold on to the side rail or use a device called a skate helper until you're standing and gliding on your own (first on two skates, then one). Bend your knees a little and stay low to maintain balance. When you fall (and you will), come to all fours like a cat to get back up, one skate at a time.

If you don't own a pair of ice skates, no worries—you can rent them at most outdoor ice rinks. Some offer skate rental packaged with the price of admission. Ice skates fit stiffly around your ankles to stabilize them, and they can feel uncomfortable without a little extra padding, such as doubled-up socks. Bundle up in layers because it's cold out there on the ice, but you'll warm up as you exercise. Wear a bike or ski helmet (some rinks require them), knee pads, and elbow pads for protection. Flexible clothing like leggings may feel more comfortable than jeans.

WHERE TO GO

Skate on ice in the fresh, frosty air throughout Washington on these rinks. Each charges a modest admission (usually under $10 per person) and offers skate rentals.

WINTHROP ICE RINK
208 White Avenue, Winthrop
winthroprink.org, (509) 996-4199
Trek over to the gorgeous Methow Valley where the open-air Winthrop Ice Rink sits

against a backdrop of craggy, snowy peaks. It's hands-down the state's most scenic rink. Usually open from mid-November to March, the rink offers open skate sessions six days a week.

SKATE RIBBON AT RIVERFRONT PARK
507 N Howard Street, Spokane
spokanecity.org, (509) 625-6601
The first skate ribbon on the West Coast, this 16-foot-wide, 650-foot-long looped ribbon of ice, plus an attached 3500-square-foot

pond, is in the heart of downtown Spokane's vibrant riverfront. After a bit of open-air gliding, warm up by one of the cozy fire pits with a mug of hot cocoa. Open mid-November through mid-March.

KAHLER GLEN ICE RINK AT LAKE WENATCHEE
20700 Club House Drive, Leavenworth
lakewenatcheeinfo.com, (509) 763-4025
This ice rink is a real frozen pond on the golf resort's driving range, offering unique, natural ice skating on 14,000 square feet. Hockey

NATURE NOTEBOOK

Location: _____   Date: _____

Co-naturers: _____

Trying something new like ice skating for the first time can be hard. Describe a time you took on a new challenging activity in the great outdoors. How did you deal with fear and overcome doubt while trying this novel adventure? Think of a way to honor this personal growth.

_____

_____

_____

_____

_____

_____

_____

_____

AFFORDABLE WINTER FUN

It can seem like winter recreation requires a whole new wardrobe and gear closet. Here are some ways to spend less while getting out more.

RENT SNOW GEAR.
This lets you sample a new snow sport before you commit. Find rentals at your local outdoor shop.

BUY USED GEAR.
Scour online swap boards for deals, and check the inventory of secondhand shops.

HUNT FOR DEALS.
Some local ski areas offer affordable "learn to ski" packages that include instruction, equipment, and admission or lift tickets (for example, the Summit at Snoqualmie has a "New to Nordic" package). The website Liftopia aggregates deals from Washington's winter recreation areas.

SKIP THE CHAINS AND TAKE A SHUTTLE.
Seattle Ski Shuttle offers transport from several Puget Sound–area locations to the mountain passes.

and figure skates in all sizes are available, no charge, although donations are appreciated. Skating the rink is free courtesy of the Lake Wenatchee Winter Recreation Association whose volunteers maintain it.

BELLEVUE DOWNTOWN ICE RINK
NE 1st Street and 100th Avenue NE, Bellevue
bellevueicerink.com, (425) 453-1223

Bellevue's Downtown Park hosts the Seattle area's best pop-up ice-skating rink from late November through late January. The rink has a tent roof to protect skaters from Western Washington's winter drizzle but is entirely open on one side and partially open on the others. The rink's calendar will point you to special stroller skate hours and free beginner skating lessons.

SLED DOWN A HILL

LOVE WINTER LIKE A KID

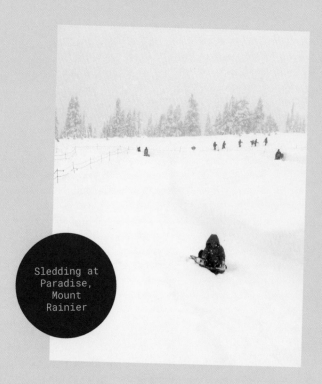

Sledding at
Paradise,
Mount
Rainier

SNOW HAS THE power to evoke strong feelings and memories. We recall epic blizzards from childhood in extraordinary detail, make wishes under the fall of winter's first flurries, and still get a thrill forming a snowball in our bare hands and throwing it at . . . anything. No matter your age, nothing screams excitement like careening down a powdery hill on a sled. It's low-tech and high fun, a throwback to simpler times when all you needed for a perfect winter day was a flattened cardboard box and a snowy hill.

These days most people sled on affordable plastic toboggans or saucers with ropes attached for towing them behind you back up the hill. Inflatable snow tubes common at groomed tubing hills and mountain resorts have also gained steam as personal sleds because they're fun and fast, though a bit hard to steer and inflating them takes time (you'll need an air pump—make sure the nozzle fits the tube's valve before you leave for sledding). Retro runner sleds, like the iconic Flexible Flyer steerable wooden sled with red steel runners, are heavier on nostalgia than usefulness: they don't work well in wet snow and are prohibited on some sledding hills. Sleds, saucers, and toboggans seem to fly off the shelves when snow starts falling in the lowlands, so buy your "vehicle" at the start of winter for best selection. Note the weight limit, as some are made for kids.

Take basic precautions to stay safe while sledding. Stick to designated snow play areas, or pick a hill free of trees, posts, fences, boulders, and other obstacles. Make sure your hill doesn't end in a drop-off, road, or pond. Wear a helmet and sunglasses. Don't tow a sled behind a vehicle or snowmobile. Sit upright and face forward—do not sled headfirst down a slope. Avoid steep, icy hills; soft snow is best. Sledding hills are open dependent on

MAKE SNOW ICE CREAM

Did you know you can make ice cream from snow? Just take eight or so heaping cups of fresh, clean snow and add to a whisked mixture of half a cup of sugar, a cup of milk, and 1 teaspoon vanilla extract. Then dig in!

snow conditions, so check the status before you head out.

Sledding gives you an exhilarating taste of downhill skiing without the expense or steep learning curve. Old-school sledding gets you outside into nature in the season it can be hardest to leave your warm, comfy couch. So grab your toboggan, pack a thermos of hot cocoa, and pile on some warm layers for this wondrous adventure.

WHERE TO GO

Every city has a favorite sledding hill where lucky kids off school flock on snow days, like Gas Works Park in Seattle or Underhill Park in Spokane. If you can't access good snow in your own neighborhood, try these spots.

HURRICANE HILL, OLYMPIC NATIONAL PARK
17 miles south of Port Angeles
nps.gov/olym, (360) 565-3130
NATIONAL PARK PASS
400 inches of snow per year, 5242 feet elevation
Hurricane Hill is probably the most scenic sledding hill in the state, short and sweet as it is. This traditional sledding area by the visitors' center is perfect for newbies, and

there's plenty of room for snow angels and snowball fights. Après sled, warm up by the fire in the visitors' center and gawk through the window at the sparkling glaciated peaks that surround you. Hurricane Ridge Road opens during daylight hours Friday–Sunday in winter, weather permitting. Vehicles must carry chains.

PARADISE, MOUNT RAINIER NATIONAL PARK

SR 706, 24 miles east of Ashford
nps.gov/mora, (360) 569-2211
NATIONAL PARK PASS
643 inches of snow per year, 5400 feet elevation
There are no tubing lanes, tow rope lines, or paid time limits at Paradise, just a couple of groomed runs on the hill above the Jackson Visitor Center, where you can sled to your heart's content. Bring your own flexible sleds, snow tubes, saucers, or cardboard boxes—sleds with metal runners or wooden toboggans are not allowed. Depending on snow conditions, the runs are open winter weekends, school breaks, and holidays. Pop into the Jackson Visitor Center whenever you need a bathroom break or snack. After a frigid day sledding, warm up and repose by the crackling fire at the rustic National Park Inn at Longmire, which offers reduced room rates in winter.

HYAK SLEDDING HILL, SNOQUALMIE PASS

I-90 at Exit 54, parks.state.wa.us
SNO-PARK PERMIT + GROOMED PERMIT
400 inches of snow per year, 2726 feet elevation
It's wintertime and the sledding is easy at Hyak Sno-Park at Snoqualmie Pass. This long, gently graded hill is regularly groomed, the walk back up is gradual, and there's a warming hut with heated restrooms. The Sno-Park doubles as a popular destination for cross-country skiers. If you want more thrill on your hill, the nearby Summit at Snoqualmie's Tubing Center is a primo spot to bomb down one of eight groomed powder chutes and then catch a ride back up to the top.

LAKE WENATCHEE SLED HILL, LEAVENWORTH

21588 SR 207, parks.state.wa.us, (509) 763-3101
SNO-PARK PERMIT + GROOMED PERMIT
150 inches of snow per year, 1873 feet elevation
Get ready to be transported to the Swiss Alps! Glacier-fed Lake Wenatchee, ringed with snowy peaks, sits on the drier eastern slope of the Cascades. That means snow here is less heavy and more powdery compared to the western slope's "Cascade Concrete." This sledding hill is a long, gradual, easy slope on what is actually a snow-covered road that's

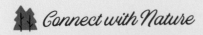 *Connect with Nature*

Snowflakes form in clouds from microscopic water droplets that collide, freeze, and build ice crystals, the start of a snowflake that will grow more intricate and complex as it attracts more ice crystals. When it's snowing, wear dark gloves and use a hand lens to see different patterns and shapes in the snowflakes that land on your hand. Then sketch the different patterns you see.

NATURE NOTEBOOK

Location: _____   Date: _____

Co-naturers: _____

Snow holds the power to evoke strong memories. Did you play in the snow as a child, throwing snowballs with your friends or carving snow angels in fresh powder?

_____

_____

_____

_____

_____

_____

closed to traffic in winter. When you tire of sledding, the groomed Nordic ski trails here are delightful.

OFFBEAT SLEDDING SPOTS

LOUP LOUP SKI BOWL LUGE RUN
Off SR 20 east of Twisp
skitheloup.com, (509) 557-3401
If you've watched the Winter Olympics, you've seen the luge—a lightweight toboggan with runners that is ridden in a sitting or supine position. In Washington's beautiful Methow Valley, this Olympic sport has gone recreational, sans the extreme banked curves. Flying down the side of a mountain on this special groomed luge chute is kind of like a roller coaster, only you have to steer, swerve, and stop. Fortunately, your first session begins with an hour of instruction on how to

do those maneuvers, and beginners are welcome. This luge run is one of just a few in all of North America. Luge sleds are included in the price, as is a ride up the mountain on a snowcat. Reservation required; bring your own ski helmet.

DOG SLEDDING

FISH LAKE, NEAR LEAVENWORTH
Off SR 207, northwestdogsledadventuresllc.com
If you have mushing dreams of the Iditarod Trail Sled Dog Race, start with the microversion—a ride through the snow with a dog team called the Flying Furs. Captain Larry with Northwest Dogsled Adventures steers the 13-foot sled with room for one or two passengers—one in front and the other standing on the back—around Lake Wenatchee and Fish Lake. Reservations are required for the one-hour tours.

HIKE THROUGH HISTORY

DISCOVER TRACES OF WASHINGTON'S PAST ON ITS TRAILS

History hike at Fort Flagler State Park

ARE YOU A CURIOUS hiker who ponders what hidden history lies beneath your boots? The Pacific Northwest isn't known for storied battlefields or ancient ruins, yet the rich past of people who shaped this region surrounds us. Stories of Washington's past are inextricably linked with its bountiful landscape—from the abundance of food and wood enjoyed by Salish Sea tribes, to settlers drawn here to farm, log timber, fish, mine, and explore. History helps us understand ourselves and our place in the world. It brings into focus the legacies we have inherited from those here before us: tending to the land and water, enjoying the bounty with gratitude, protecting wild places for the future.

WHERE TO GO

These history hikes connect you to the people of the past, whether they were here to celebrate at a potlatch, mine for gold or limestone, or plant an orchard. Some trails are historically significant because of an event that took place there, while others harbor artifacts from days gone by.

NORTH HEAD

Cape Disappointment State Park, 244 Robert Gray Drive, Ilwaco, parks.state.wa.us, (360) 642-3078

DISCOVER PASS

4.2 miles round-trip, 300 feet elevation gain

⭐ *Explorers were here*

Washington State's modern history began when the Lewis and Clark Expedition reached the mouth of the Columbia River, hiked up this 700-foot towering basalt headland, and spotted the Pacific Ocean for the first time. Traverse through a misty coastal Sitka spruce forest with peekaboo views to the churning sea. You'll come to a parking lot and the lighthouse keepers' residences, then head to the 1898 North Head Lighthouse—one of two in

LEARN MORE

Hiking Washington's History, by Judy Bentley and Craig Romano, is the history buff's trail guide and the hiker's history book.

the park that guide mariners into the river to prevent history from repeating itself. Frequent shipwrecks once earned this infamous stretch of coast the nickname "Graveyard of the Pacific." The Lewis and Clark Interpretive Center offers stories of the journey.

CAPE FLATTERY, OLYMPIC COAST

Just outside Neah Bay, makah.com

MAKAH RECREATION PASS

1.5 miles round-trip, 200 feet elevation gain

⭐ *Makah ancestral land*

Bundle up for rain and wind on this short walk through spruce and cedar forest with the thunder of waves in your ears to the most northwesterly tip of the contiguous United States. This wild and rugged headland belongs to the "people of the cape," as the Makah are called, sustained for thousands of years by the bounty of the ocean that surrounds them: clams, crabs, halibut, salmon, and, most famously, whales. A mix of trail, steps, and boardwalk leads you to three unique lookouts around the cape, places where the Makah people stood and watched explorer's ships just off the coast in the late 1700s. The Makah called them "houses on water" and carved images of the ships in stone.

FORT FLAGLER STATE PARK, MARROWSTONE ISLAND

10541 Flagler Road, Nordland

parks.state.wa.us, (360) 385-1259

DISCOVER PASS

5 miles round-trip, 150 feet elevation gain

⭐ *Coastal military fort*

At the tip of Marrowstone Island east of Port Townsend is the largest of five US military installations built more than a century ago to protect Puget Sound from invaders during wartime. All five installations were converted to state parks in the 1950s, giving the public access to thousands of near-shore acres, miles of saltwater shoreline, and all the history embedded in their historic buildings and bunkers. The 5-mile loop hike starts on the stony beach, with views of the surrounding sea, islands, and mountains. Leave the beach behind after a few miles and follow the trail up a bluff and around a wildlife-rich lagoon, passing historic buildings and bunkers along the way. A small museum on-site tells stories of the park's wartime past.

LIME KILN, ROBE CANYON HISTORIC PARK

East side of Granite Falls on Waite Mill Road
(425) 388-6600
7 miles of trails, 625 feet elevation gain
⭐ *Limestone mining*

This easy trail follows the south fork of the Stillaguamish River through a lush, mossy canyon along the long-gone Everett & Monte Cristo Railway, built in the 1890s. Look for artifacts of the limestone mining era along the trail, from moss-cloaked saw blades to old bricks and rotting boots left by workers from the distant past. The well-signed trail starts in quiet forest and joins the Stilly about 1.5 miles in. From there it's one more mile to the 20-foot-tall old lime kiln, the highlight of the hike. This kiln is where calcium oxide was extracted from limestone for use in Everett factories. Turn around here or continue another mile to the trail's end where a riverbank vantage point invites you to look for spawning salmon.

WIND MOUNTAIN, COLUMBIA GORGE NATIONAL SCENIC AREA

Off SR 14 east of Carson, (541) 308-1700
2.8 miles round-trip, 1230 feet elevation gain
⭐ *Indian rock pits*

The steady switchback climb through mixed fir and maple woods to the scenic summit of Wind Mountain leads to more than a vista into the heart of the Columbia Gorge; the talus slope is a sacred archeological preserve. Hundreds of years ago, Wind

NATURE NOTEBOOK

Location: _____   Date: _____

Co-naturers: _____

If you had a time machine, what era in Washington's history would you visit?

_____

_____

_____

HIGH HIKES FOR HISTORY

These mountain trails for history buffs must be saved for summer when they'll be snow-free.

IRON GOAT TRAIL.
Hike up to 12 miles on the old railroad grade that once carried Great Northern trains as they slowed around shoofly curves and switchbacked down the craggy Cascades toward Seattle. Lots of interpretive signs guide you to snowsheds, artifacts, and tunnels you'll encounter. The easternmost stretch of trail traverses the site of the 1910 Wellington avalanche, one of the worst railroad disasters in US history.

MONTE CRISTO.
The promise of gold and silver lured thousands of men to this mountain mining camp east of Everett in the 1890s, but the dream was washed away with the river's frequent washouts. Reach the ghost town in an easy 4 miles and look for artifacts like a railway turntable that still spins, dilapidated cabins, and rusty mining tools.

Mountain was a Spirit Quest site for youth of local tribes questing for their guardian spirit. It's believed they hiked up here, entered constructed rock pits large enough to hold a person, fasted, and awaited visions from their guardian spirits. The rock pits are three- to five-foot deep depressions made by rearranging the rocks. Don't enter them; maintain respect for both their cultural and archeological significance.

SACAJAWEA HISTORICAL STATE PARK
2503 Sacajawea Park Road, Pasco
parks.state.wa.us, (509) 545-2361
DISCOVER PASS
1.2 miles round-trip, no elevation gain
⭐ *Explorers were here*

Tour the Sacajawea Interpretive Center and hike the adjacent trail to learn the remarkable story of this land that sits at both the confluence of two rivers and for a brief moment, the confluence of two cultures. Sacajawea, a Lemhi Shoshone woman traveling with the Lewis and Clark Expedition as a scout and interpreter, arrived at this site with her fellow explorers on October 16, 1805. The group camped and hunted for the next three days, repaired their gear, and mingled with about two hundred Sahaptin-speaking Native Americans—a meeting that wouldn't have been possible without Sacajawea, whom Clark described in his journal as a "token of peace."

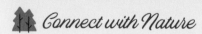 *Connect with Nature*

Each lighthouse, stream, mountain pass, and fire lookout has a tale to tell. As you hike, look for clues hidden in the terrain that reveal stories about each place's history.

SKI LIKE A NORDIC

FIND YOUR WINTER BLISS ON A SNOWY GROOMED TRACK

Nordic skiing in the Methow Valley

photo by Jodi Connolly

CROSS-COUNTRY SKIING—with its quick learning curve, simple gear, and affordable trail access (no pricey lift tickets!)—is winter's best-kept secret. Just a few hours into your first outing on cross-country skis, you might glide along on a groomed trail through the glistening snow at a comfortable pace, feeling crisp air on your face and freedom to roam in your heart.

"Nordic" refers to a few different styles of skiing. The most common are classic cross-country (slim, lightweight skis with grippy scales on the bottom that travel on two parallel groomed tracks of compacted snow) and skate skiing (even slimmer skis on a wide groomed corduroy-like surface using a technique much like ice skating). Groomed Nordic ski trails usually have a skating lane and one or two classic lanes. All Nordic skis have a free-heel binding system; boots clip onto the skis only at the toes. Rent boots, skis, and poles your first time out, and buy them later if you take to the sport.

Washington State Parks manage dozens of Sno-Parks with groomed Nordic ski trails. Your vehicle needs a one-day or seasonal Sno-Park Permit. Eight Sno-Parks (Cabin Creek, Chiwawa, Crystal Springs, Hyak, Lake Easton, Lake Wenatchee, Mount Spokane, and Nason Ridge) require an additional Groomed Permit. Buy permits online at parks.state. wa.us or call (360) 902-8684 for vendors. There are a few privately managed Nordic areas throughout the state, and some downhill ski resorts have Nordic trails as well.

WHERE TO GO

Try these spots, or head off the beaten path on ungroomed trails by breaking track over untouched snow, trading the extra work for more wild and solitude—and the meditative

rhythm as you glide through a snow-flocked forest.

LAKE KEECHELUS / HYAK SNO-PARK, SNOQUALMIE PASS

Exit 54 off I-90, parks.state.wa.us, (509) 656-2230

SNO-PARK PERMIT + GROOMED PERMIT

Never been on skis? Start here. There are four Sno-Parks along I-90 east of Snoqualmie Pass with fantastic groomed ski trails; Hyak is the closest to Seattle, followed by Crystal Springs, Cabin Creek, and Lake Easton. Choose a weekday morning to learn the ropes sans crowds on 7.5 miles of flat, groomed tracks that hug the shore of frozen Lake Keechelus. This easy grade was once the Milwaukee Railroad line through the Cascades, now a segment of the Palouse to Cascades Trail.

LAKE EASTON SNO-PARK, SNOQUALMIE PASS EAST

Exit 70 off I-90, parks.state.wa.us, (509) 656-2230

SNO-PARK PERMIT + GROOMED PERMIT

Uncrowded and small, Lake Easton's 5 miles of groomed tracks with skate lane have some gentle rolling hills and winding curves, so come here to perfect your snowplow and turns. The east slope of the Cascades typically has drier powder than the west slope, so try out both and decide which type of snow you prefer to ski on. You won't share a trail with the snowmobiles here, but you may hear their roar.

SALMON RIDGE SNO-PARK, MOUNT BAKER

Mount Baker Highway (SR 542)

SNO-PARK PERMIT

There's a trail here for every level, a classic skier's buffet. The most-used track is Razor Hone—flat terrain and gentle hills for 3 miles through beautiful woods along the north fork of the Nooksack River. Not so gentle is Cougar Loop, rated difficult for its big climb and descent. Directly across the highway begins another easy groomed track, Anderson Creek, with open turns and gradual slopes.

MOUNT SPOKANE STATE PARK, SPOKANE

SR 206 northeast of Spokane
spokanenordic.org, (509) 238-4025

SNO-PARK PERMIT + GROOMED PERMIT

Set in the Selkirk Mountains, this expansive Nordic area with a staggering 37 miles of groomed trails (easy, moderate, and difficult) sits within Washington's largest state park. If you're feeling old-school, you'll find a handful of ungroomed roads and routes to venture off-piste. This is one of the few places you can rent skis, boots, and poles at a snow park, and there are two woodstove-heated warming huts off the trails.

OLDMAN PASS, KOSHKO, MCCLELLAN MEADOWS SNO-PARKS, UPPER WIND RIVER

Wind River Road, 25 miles north of Carson
(509) 395-3400 • **SNO-PARK PERMIT**

Tucked in a remote corner of the Gifford Pinchot National Forest, these three non-motorized Sno-Parks are clumped together with about 40 miles of easy and moderate groomed and ungroomed trails that can be looped. The terrain is lush forest mixed with open meadows, offering gorgeous views of Mount St. Helens and Mount Adams. Keep an eye out for deer and elk that overwinter in the Wind River Valley.

BACKCOUNTRY SKIING HUT TO HUT

Have you dreamed of touring the Alps on skis from one cozy hut to the next? Good news—you can skip the flight to Europe and ski hut to hut at a few choice Cascades locales. In the Methow Valley, book your stay in the Rendezvous Huts, rustic ski-in-only cabins along the Methow Trails. On the southwest side of Mount Rainier, the Mount Tahoma Huts are three chalet-type huts and a yurt, each fully furnished and with a kitchen, free with a modest reservation fee. About half of the 50 miles of ski trails in the network are groomed.

NATURE NOTEBOOK

Location: _____   Date: _____

Co-naturers: _____

Fresh snow quiets the world. The hush that falls over a snowy landscape isn't your imagination, it's science. Snow crystals are porous, so they absorb sounds. Some studies have found silence relieves tension and stress. Did you notice the quiet in the snow? How did your body and mind feel in the silence?

_____

_____

_____

_____

_____

_____

Can you draw a map of your route, and some highlights you saw along the way?

Skiing
in the
Methow
Valley

photo by Jodi Connolly

METHOW TRAILS, WINTHROP

SR 20 (N Cascades Highway) northwest of Twisp,
methowtrails.org, (509) 996-3287

ACCESS TICKET

Once you've fallen in love with Nordic skiing, find your new winter paradise in the Methow Valley surrounded by snow-capped peaks of the North Cascades. The nation's largest cross-country ski area sprawls across rolling hills and quiet pastures from Mazama to Winthrop, totaling more than 120 miles of groomed and ungroomed trails. To access you'll need a ticket available for sale at businesses across the valley, sold for one, three, or ten days. Many of the valley's lodgings have ski trails passing right outside your door. Rent skis and ski gear at your local outdoor store, or locally in Winthrop.

CROSS-COUNTRY SKIING 101

The elementary techniques can be covered in a single lesson or online video, and practiced on groomed tracks. Cross-country skiing is known for being great exercise—you'll get a full-body workout, although the skis do a lot of the work so it doesn't demand much exertion. Here are the basics:

Get in the tracks. Place your skis on the ground parallel to the groomed tracks. Clip your boots into each ski and loop your poles over each wrist. Step your skis into the groomed tracks one at a time.

Stay low and loose. Skiing will be awkward if you keep your body fully upright. Instead, slouch a little and keep knees loose.

Step, step, glide. Step the skis like you're walking, using poles alternately. Then add a glide after every two steps. When you feel ready, transition to all gliding. Now you're doing the . . .

Diagonal stride. On flat land this is your only move! Shift your weight from ski to ski, pushing off one ski then gliding on the other. Remember: push, kick, glide. Use your left pole for stability when you glide on your right ski, and vice versa.

Rise from falls. Get your skis parallel on the ground, crouch over them, and slowly stand back up.

Snowplow to descend hills or stop. Some Nordic runs have real hills, and you'll need control going down them. As you start the descent, go into the snowplow by making an upside-down "V" with your skis, tips together, pushing down on the inside edges like you're shaving snow off the trail. Practice on gentle hills first.

Herringbone up hills. On steeper hills turn the tips of the skis out to a wide "V" shape, walking up the hill with knees and ankles rolled in so the skis' inside edges dig into the snow.

SNOWSHOE WITH A RANGER

MAKE YOUR OWN FRESH TRACKS ON A GUIDED WINTER HIKE

Snowshoeing in the North Cascades

photo by Kim Brown

IN THE DEPTHS of winter, when the lowlands are socked in with drizzle and fog, remember what sits up there above the marine layer, blanketing the valleys and peaks: SNOW. Each winter, snow renews our sense of wonder. Pretty as it is, snow beckons us to do more than admire it; sometimes we must get out and play in it. While the snowy wonderland may look off-limits to casual hikers, it's not. A pair of snowshoes, a set of poles, and a little know-how are your access pass to the winter backcountry.

You may have heard, "If you can walk, you can snowshoe," and that's true. Snowshoeing is a lot like walking, as long as you don't try to walk backward! No special skills are required, so most anyone can do it. The gear is simple and affordable, just a pair of snowshoes that strap on to a regular pair of waterproof hiking boots or snow boots. Snowshoes are adjustable to your boots and generally come in just one size for adults, though some higher-end brands offer women's snowshoes that are a tad lighter and narrower in the frame. A good pair of snowshoes will run between $150 and $250 new, or you can rent them from your local outdoor store. Ranger-guided snowshoe hikes usually provide snowshoes free. Many people use trekking poles for added stability.

Having the right clothing for the winter backcountry makes the difference between a cold, miserable day or a comfortable day snowshoeing. This is especially true in the Pacific Northwest, where our snow trends toward heavy and wet rather than dry and powdery. Dress in layers, and avoid cotton because it doesn't wick moisture or dry easily (wet clothing can lead to hypothermia). Top it all with a waterproof outer layer, like a rain jacket. A pair of gaiters will prevent snow from finding its way into your boots.

Snowshoes require at least five inches of snow on the ground, since it's in deeper snow that the flat surfaces of snowshoes do their job: keeping you afloat on top of the snow instead of postholing through. If you'll be snowshoeing without a guide, choose a trail with little to no potential for avalanches, then go when avalanche danger in the backcountry is low. Some wonderful summertime hiking trails with treeless slopes are notorious for avalanches and should be avoided altogether by wintertime snowshoers. If snowshoeing becomes a regular hobby, take an avalanche safety course so you can enjoy some epic snowshoe hikes like Artist Point on Mount Baker or Mazama Ridge on Mount Rainier.

WHERE TO GO

If you're new to snowshoeing, start with a ranger-guided snowshoe hike (free, donation suggested) offered on low-risk trails throughout Washington on weekends from January through March, snow depending. Rangers provide snowshoes and poles, and combine a hike on snowshoes with a winter ecology lesson and a talk on avalanche safety. The exact trail the rangers choose for any given day may vary with the snow level and avalanche conditions. For National Forest outings, find exact dates, times, and how to make reservations at Discover Your Northwest (discovernw.org).

HEATHER MEADOWS, MOUNT BAKER
10091 Mount Baker Highway SR 542
(360) 599-2714
Snowfall here is legendary, setting the world record at 95 feet in a single year. On this half-day excursion you'll learn to snowshoe in gobs of it blanketing the valleys and slopes above the north fork of the Nooksack River, surrounded on all sides by arresting craggy

peaks of the North Cascades. Meet at Glacier Public Service Center.

SOUTH FORK STILLAGUAMISH RIVER, MOUNTAIN LOOP

33515 Mountain Loop Highway, (360) 436-1155
Experience the serenity of the Mountain Loop in winter. Rangers guide you along the south fork of the Stilly—the route once carried the former Everett and Monte Cristo Railway. Now the valley is wild once again and home to a number of birds, fish, and mammals. Watch for Bald Eagles in the riverside tree branches, waiting for a migrating salmon to scoop up for a snack. Meet at Verlot Public Service Center.

NATURE NOTEBOOK

Location: _____   Date: _____

Co-naturers: _____

What are a few ways you've observed that wildlife and plants have adapted to winter life in frigid temps and heavy snowfall in Washington's mountains?

_____

_____

_____

_____

_____

_____

_____

_____

_____

_____

_____

COMMONWEALTH BASIN, SNOQUALMIE PASS

69805 SE Snoqualmie Pass Summit Road
(425) 434-6111

Ranger guides lead this gentle climb through towering old-growth into a wide, open basin, all the while pointing out signs of the diverse wildlife that call this basin home, such as wolverines, bobcats, ravens, and martens. Meet at Snoqualmie Pass Visitor Center.

WENATCHEE RIDGE, BLEWETT PASS

US 97, 22 miles north of Cle Elum
(509) 852-1062

SNO-PARK PERMIT

Want to spot tracks of a snowshoe hare, or glimpse a Northern Goshawk soar overhead? A forest ranger naturalist will lead you through this frozen landscape in search of animal tracks and birds, sharing how wildlife carries on in the Cascades in winter, pausing for beautiful views of the Stuart Range. Meet at the Swauk Campground Sno-Park.

PARADISE, MOUNT RAINIER NATIONAL PARK

SR 706, 24 miles east of Ashford
nps.gov/mora, (360) 569-2211

NATIONAL PARK PASS • *carry tire chains*

Snowshoe to the open snowfields and meadows above the lodge with stunning views of the mountain looming above you on a clear day. Knowledgeable rangers explain how the plants and animals of Mount Rainier—from hoary marmot to White-tailed Ptarmigan—adapt to the colossal snowfalls. Sign up one hour in advance of the scheduled time inside the Jackson Visitor Center near the information desk.

HURRICANE RIDGE, OLYMPIC NATIONAL PARK

17 miles south of Port Angeles
nps.gov/olym, (360) 565-3130

NATIONAL PARK PASS • *carry tire chains*

Make a ridgetop traverse at tree line on snowshoes. Covered in snow, the Olympic peaks are so close you can almost touch them. Walks happen weekend afternoons and some holidays. Sign up at the Hurricane Ridge information desk thirty minutes before the walk. Note: Unlike other locations, there is a modest per-person fee for this guided snowshoe walk.

BASK IN THE RAIN SHADOW

THE OLYMPIC MOUNTAINS CAN TURN RAIN CLOUDS TO SUNSHINE

Ebey's Landing on Whidbey Island

photo by Craig Romano

YOU MIGHT ASSUME winter in Western Washington is synonymous with months of mist, drizzle, and the occasional downpour. For the most part, you'd be right. But there's a sunny sanctuary in that cloud cover, a place where persistent showers give way to dry air and clear skies. This "blue hole" exists thanks to a special mix of weather and topography, creating a local climate phenomenon—the Olympic Rain Shadow.

Here's how it works: Warm winds roll off the Pacific Ocean onto the coast from the southwest, carrying water vapor like a soaked sponge. The Olympic Mountains are a barricade, forcing the air up the west slope as it cools and condenses. Lowering the temperature on a cloud system is like wringing out a sponge, so it starts to rain and then snow as the air climbs to the summit. On the flip side of the mountain range, the air mass warms and dries as it sinks.

Over millennia, this weather pattern created some fantastically damp temperate rain forests on the peninsula's southwest side, and a dramatically different rain shadow ecosystem on its northeast corner. While the Hoh Rain Forest enjoys around 140 inches of rain each year, Sequim gets just 16, shaping a drier climate that hosts prairie bluffs of native grasses and stands of trees like oak and madrone.

The Cascades create a rain shadow effect as well, creating the dry ponderosa pine belt on the range's eastern slope to the sagebrush country of the Columbia Basin.

WHERE TO GO

The Olympic Rain Shadow encompasses Port Angeles, Sequim, and Port Townsend on the Olympic Peninsula, the San Juan Islands, and Whidbey Island. Here are some places to bask in it.

AMERICAN CAMP, SAN JUAN ISLAND NATIONAL HISTORICAL PARK
4668 Cattle Point Road, Friday Harbor
nps.gov/sajh, (360) 378-2240

Perched on the southern tip of San Juan Island is a bluff overlooking brackish ponds and untamed beaches. Consult a map and you'll see this protected national park unit sits in the middle of the Olympic Rain Shadow. Pack your binoculars and hop on a ferry from Anacortes. Two distinct units on opposite ends of the island comprise the park, both remnants of the joint military occupation here by England and the United States in the Civil War era.

Several miles of easy trails amble through tallgrass prairie and along the water; combine a few for a full day of exploring. An easy loop down to South Beach and back passes the Officers' Quarters and interpretive signs that tell the land's history. At the windswept beach, use binoculars to scan for passing whales and sea lions. Take the short jaunt to salty, sheltered Jakle's Lagoon, where you might spot a river otter or a diving loon. Pick up a map of the park's walking trails at the visitors' center. On the north end of the island, stop by English Camp for a hike to Young Hill that traverses another rain shadow habitat, a Garry oak prairie.

EBEY'S LANDING NATIONAL HISTORIC RESERVE, WHIDBEY ISLAND
Ebey's Landing Road, Coupeville
nps.gov/ebla, (360) 678-6084

On the windy edge of Whidbey Island, Ebey's Landing is loaded with drama—crashing surf against a high bluff, emerald grassy fields, a wild beach strewn with driftwood, and a coastal lagoon—all of it overlooking Puget Sound and snowy Olympic peaks.

NATURE NOTEBOOK

Location: _____ Date: _____

Co-naturers: _____

Describe five things you observed on your rain shadow adventure that are clues of a drier climate.

_____

_____

_____

_____

_____

_____

_____

_____

_____

_____

_____

_____

More than 17,000 acres comprise this preserve—a patchwork of state, national, and private lands used for centuries by the Skagit peoples to harvest the roots of camas and bracken fern. Homesteader Isaac Ebey laid claim here in 1851. Today, this rain shadow prairie draws hikers to traverse the Ebey's Landing Loop Trail, which climbs to a green bluff. Be sure to look up, as the sight of a soaring Bald Eagle is all but guaranteed. The

LEARN MORE

Best Rain Shadow Hikes: Western Washington, by Michael Fagin and Skip Card, features trails from all of Washington's rain shadows—from the Teanaway to the South Cascades.

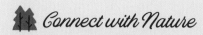 Connect with Nature

Add some Olympic Peninsula towns (like Forks and Sequim) to your smart-phone's weather app. Over a few weeks you may see a pattern: Forks likely scores high for rainy days, while Sequim enjoys more sunshine. How does your own city compare? Sometimes weather systems move onto the Washington Coast directly from the west; notice how the rain shadow shifts, creating a "blue hole" over Seattle.

footpath steeply descends the bluff to encircle Perego's Lagoon, a large coastal wetland that sustains migratory birds all winter long. The beach walk that returns you to the trailhead is over wobbly pebbles in places, so wear sturdy shoes.

OLYMPIC DISCOVERY TRAIL BY BICYCLE
Sequim to Port Angeles
olympicdiscoverytrail.org

Mount your bicycle and pedal the uberscenic, mostly paved Olympic Discovery Trail. This rail-to-trail project launched in 1988 when a group of cyclists dreamed of a public access path along the Olympic lowlands from Port Townsend to La Push, eventually totaling 130 miles of off-road cycling. For a day trip, plan your route from Sequim Bay State Park to downtown Port Angeles, a flat 26 miles of rain shadow cycling with periodic views across the Strait of Juan de Fuca. One of the highlights is the 410-foot-long Johnson Creek Trestle near John Wayne Marina, towering 100 feet over the creek. A good stop for a picnic is also a birdwatching hot spot: Railroad Bridge Park on the west side of Sequim.

GO ANIMAL TRACKING

FIND CLUES THAT TELL THE STORY OF LOCAL WILDLIFE

Bird tracks on the Washington Coast

YOU COULD HIKE IN the Cascades countless times and not encounter a black bear or spot a red fox; the woods are full of remarkable fauna who excel at hiding from us. Discover their habits and secrets by playing nature detective, solving the mystery of who lives in the forest by following clues left behind. Animal tracking is a fun way to connect with even the most bashful critters living in the woods all around you.

From a trail of paw prints in snow to piles of scat (that's poop—a reliable clue!), signs of animal activity are everywhere; we just need to look. In your own garden you might notice a freshly spun spiderweb or ribbon of slime from a long-gone banana slug. When you come upon a clue, imagine what transpired when no human was there to witness it. Some signs tell a story of a particular event in the animal's life, like discarded antlers from a bull elk or downy feathers on the forest floor that are remnants of a Sharp-shinned Hawk's dinner. Tracks are often fleeting (like the footprints of a vole atop the snow), but others endure the change of seasons and might remain long after the animal is gone, like the neatly patterned holes of a sapsucker in a deciduous tree trunk or a bobcat den under a fallen log, littered with old bones from its prey.

TIPS FOR TRACKING ANIMALS

Get a good tracking guidebook, or join an animal tracking field trip. "Tracks" refer to prints in the snow or dirt from an animal, as well as scat. "Signs" are disturbances in the environment created by an animal's activity, like nests, dens, dams, gnawed branches, deer trails, or food caches.

See tracks? Look at the overall shape— count the number of toes, check for claws, measure the track's length. Study the animal's stepping or trotting gait. Some tricky challenges will present themselves (moose or deer? muskrat or raccoon? mouse or chipmunk?). All mammals poop, and scat is a key clue to an animal's presence. Note its size, color, and shape. Scat from an herbivore (shrew, vole, chipmunk, hare, moose) will be small and uniform, in small or large piles. Carnivore and omnivore scat, from black bear to bobcat, will be larger, with bone fragments, fur, seeds, or berries.

Winter's snow and bare trees help in spotting signs of wildlife. Shorter and colder days force animals that don't hibernate into action as they search for their next meal. Critters are most active at dawn and dusk. Look for wildlife tracks in snow or dirt at first light when they're fresh. Tracking sometimes leads you to an animal! Hunters use tracking to find deer and bear, as do wildlife photographers. If you encounter an animal, maintain a safe and respectful distance.

WHERE TO GO

The great thing about animal tracking is you can add it on to any nature outing—from a walk in your city park to a snowshoe hike. Here are a few suggestions.

Urban parks. Look for "whitewash" of owls on and around tree trunks (it looks like splattered white paint and indicates an owl roost), a tangled ball of a squirrel nest in a tree, or tracks in mud by a creek. Head to your favorite urban forest (like Seattle's Lincoln Park, Issaquah's Cougar Mountain, or Bellingham's Sehome Hill Arboretum), and look up—is there an owl perched on an upper branch close to the tree trunk? Check the ground below the roosting spot for owl pellets—clumps of regurgitated hair and bones, the indigestible parts of prey. Break them apart with a pencil to see what the owl had for breakfast.

In the snow. Look for various mammal tracks, piles of scat, burrows, scraped or gnawed bark. Venture out early in the morning when tracks are fresh and easier to spot. An easy place to start is Trail of the Shadows at Mount Rainier, across from the National Park Inn at Longmire. This flat interpretive loop (under a mile) wends through old-growth cedar and fir. Look for tracks from the industrious beaver, which constructs dams and lodges around ponds like the cedar marsh here. There's a conspicuous beaver-gnawed tree trunk just off the trail. In the Methow Valley pull on some snowshoes and head to the Cedar Creek Trail (Highway 20 west of Mazama), which starts along FS Road 200, closed to cars in winter. Tracks are common and easier to spot on the wide road. Look for trails etched in the snow from critters like weasels, red squirrel, snowshoe hare, deer, coyote, and red fox. You might even see tracks in fresh snow in your own backyard.

NATURE NOTEBOOK

Location: _____ Date: _____

Co-naturers: _____

Use the space below to draw the tracks you see. Taking photos or making sketches of what you spot in the field can help you figure out which animal made them.

ANIMALS & THE CLUES THEY LEAVE BEHIND

Look for these wildlife signs to turn an ordinary hike into an adventure.

Beaver. Tree stump with bite marks, or a dome-shaped lodge built from mud and logs for their home.

Barn swallow. Nest is a half-cup made of mud pellets the swallows collected in their beaks, built under the eaves of a shed or barn.

Black bear. Piles of scat full of berries.

Cougar. Round tracks with four toes, 4 inches across, no claws.

Coyote. Tracks are 2 inches long, four toes, claws clearly visible.

Moose. Scat is oblong, 1.5 inches long, in large piles.

Pileated woodpecker. Large excavated holes, often rectangular, in dead snags made to uncover carpenter ants.

River otter. Tracks in the mud about 3 inches across, five toes and claws visible, with webbing between back toes.

Snowshoe hare. Distinctive tracks, with larger hind feet (5 inches long) in front of small forefeet. If snow is not powdery, you may see the four toes.

LEARN MORE

The indispensable book for tracking in Washington is *Wildlife of the Pacific Northwest: Tracking and Identifying Mammals, Birds, Reptiles, Amphibians, and Invertebrates*, by David Moskowitz. Take a tracking course to sharpen your skills and meet other trackers at Alderleaf Wilderness College or North Cascades Institute.

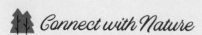 Connect with Nature

Join a tracking club. Wilderness Awareness School, based in Duvall, hosts guided monthly outings for free.

FIND RAZOR CLAMS BY MOONLIGHT

HARVESTING THIS FAVORED MOLLUSK IS A NORTHWEST WINTER TRADITION

Razor clamming on the Washington Coast

photo by Bruce McGlenn

IF SOMEONE TOLD you the fun of razor clamming is being cold on a rainy beach in the dark with a few hundred other people digging in the sand by headlamp, would you still try it? Some clamming veterans swear the suffering endured to score the region's most-beloved bivalve is the secret ingredient to the best Northwest clam chowder. Perhaps, but it's definitely an ingredient to a fun off-season weekend.

So what's the catch? You'll drag yourself out of bed well before the crack of dawn (these clam digs happen very late at night or first thing in the morning) and wear more layers than an onion—it's pretty darn cold on those beaches.

The meaty Pacific razor clam lives low in the intertidal zone of surf-pounded sand. Harvest them at designated beaches during very low tides in cool-season months; state restrictions help keep clam populations healthy. The digs are announced a few weeks in advance by the Washington Department of Fish and Wildlife (usually during low minus tides from November through April; find dig dates and obtain a clamming license at wdfw.wa.gov/fishing). Beaches may close to clamming if toxicity tests show high levels of domoic acid—call the Shellfish Safety Hotline at (800) 562-5632.

Razor clamming is pretty simple—the only equipment you need is a shovel or clam gun (a special suction tube that unearths a pile of sand and the clam hiding within), a mesh bag or bucket to put your clams in (one per person), a headlamp or lantern for night digs, and your shellfish license. Good raingear is essential, including tall boots or waders. Time your dig to start two to three hours before low tide. Each digger can take up to fifteen razor clams per day. If you find a clam, you must count it, even if it's small or cracked. Have fun, savor the experience, and if you love it, make a pilgrimage to the coast for razor clamming an annual winter tradition.

WHERE TO GO

Washington allows razor clamming during scheduled digs at five coastal beaches.

LONG BEACH

From the Columbia River north to the mouth of Willapa Bay

In the summer this sandy stretch is all kites and saltwater taffy, but some winters it's clams, clams, clams. If you strike out, you'll see razor clams on nearly every restaurant menu in town. Find camping and yurts to rent at Cape Disappointment State Park. The region hosts a Razor Clam Festival in early spring.

TWIN HARBORS BEACH

From Willapa Bay north to the south jetty at the mouth of Grays Harbor

This beach comprises three nice oceanfront state parks—Westport Light and two camping parks, Twin Harbors and Grayland Beach. Twin Harbors has yurts and cabins to rent. The fishing village of Westport has a few marine supply stores to pick up clamming gear, and good chowder can also be found there.

COPALIS BEACH

From the north jetty at the mouth of Grays Harbor to the Copalis River

Ocean Shores or Ocean City make a good base and have plenty of beachy motels with kitchenettes to cook up your catch. Camping can be found at Ocean City State Park with 140 standard sites and 29 full hookup sites. The tidelands at the mouth of the Copalis River, at Griffiths-Priday State Park, conceal big, juicy razor clams.

RAZOR CLAMS 101

HOW TO DIG FOR RAZOR CLAMS

Look for a "clam show"—a telltale dimple in the sand that indicates a submerged razor clam. These form when a clam withdraws its neck or starts to dig, leaving a small hole on the sand's surface. Stomping around or smacking your shovel on the sand can provoke a clam to show and spurt water. Larger dimples usually indicate bigger clams. Once you've settled on a clam show, face the ocean to keep an eye out for sneaker waves while you dig it out. There are two methods.

Clam gun method. Center the tube of the clam gun over the dimple. Slant the top of your tube back slightly toward you. Next, use a gentle twisting motion to work the tube into the sand until the tube is about 6 to 10 inches below the surface. Place your thumb over the air vent, bend your knees, then pull up on the handles. There—you've just brought up a core of sand. Is the clam in there? You have to check—it may be concealed within the sand. If the clam does not come up in the core of sand, reach into the hole for it.

Clam shovel method. Insert the blade vertically into the sand about 4 inches from the clam show on its seaward side. Face the blade away from the clam and start removing sand by lifting and twisting the shovel. You're not digging up the clam, but instead digging a hole right next to the clam, eventually exposing it. Then, you can reach down and remove the clam by grasping the neck or shell. Dig quickly to catch the clam before it burrows away, but take care to not hit the clam with the shovel—this could shatter its porcelain-like shell.

HOW TO PREPARE RAZOR CLAMS

Keep your clam haul in a bucket with a little seawater until you get to your campfire or kitchen. Wash each clam under running water to get sand off, then put some water to boil. One at a time, use tongs to submerge the clam in the simmering water until the shell pops open, then quickly transfer it to a bowl of iced water to cool. At this point you'll be able to coax the clams from their shells easily.

The last step before cooking is to separate the white meat of the clam from any dark parts. Slice off the dark tip of the siphon, then cut the clam open lengthwise along the zipper from foot to both tubes of the siphon, opening it flat and cutting off the tan gills, guts, and removing the stomach. What you're left with are pieces of sweet clam meat, a Northwest delicacy.

One of the tastiest ways to eat them is panko-coated, fried, and topped with a squeeze of lemon and dipped in tartar. Or sauté them in a hot pan with butter, minced garlic, and a pinch of crushed red pepper. Chop up the rest and use the sweet, tender meat for yummy clam chowder. Take care to not overcook razor clams, as they'll go from buttery to chewy.

MOCROCKS BEACH

From the Copalis River to the south boundary of the Quinault Indian Reservation

Miles of sand blanket meaty bivalves just waiting to be unearthed. If you want to pitch a tent, Pacific Beach State Park has beachfront camping sites—twenty standard sites, forty-one with hookups, and two yurts. The cute town of Moclips offers some fine places to stay, some just steps from the beach and possibly even offering a fully loaded outdoor clam-cleaning station.

KALALOCH BEACH

From the South Beach Campground north to ONP Beach Trail #3

Mix in some Olympic National Park hiking with your razor clamming adventure on this northernmost dig beach, at least when you can; low razor clam populations here mean it's included in dig dates less frequently in recent years. Stay in one of the oceanfront cabins with kitchenettes at Kalaloch Lodge, or find a campsite at Kalaloch Campground (they have 170 to choose from).

NATURE NOTEBOOK

Location: _____   Date: _____

Co-naturers: _____

How many clams did you find, and how did you cook them? What do you think your life would be like as a hunter-gatherer, living off the land and sea?

_____

_____

_____

_____

_____

_____

_____

_____

_____

BAG A PEAK

GET TO THE TOP YEAR-ROUND ON THESE SUMMIT HIKES

Hiking up
Dog Mountain

photo by Sarah Lynch

Climb the mountains and get their good tidings.
—John Muir, *Our National Parks*

IN THE SEASON of verdant river walks and easy beach strolls, hiking to a peak may seem out of place. The snowmelt is months away on favorite summits like Granite Mountain or Desolation Peak. But why should summer hikers have all the fun?

Surprisingly, slogging up to a mountain summit can feel like an exhilarating achievement. The killer views are a motivating reward for your hard work, and your aching leg muscles are a testament to your own strength and endurance. Fortunately, peaks in the lowlands can keep you in summit-seeking shape through the winter and provide regular training for all those much higher summit hikes next summer. These summits don't require glacier travel or technical climbing skills, but that doesn't mean they're easy. Here are some tips for hikers in pursuit of great heights:

- **Pace yourself.** Sometimes the climbing starts right from the trailhead and continues all the way to the top. Pack lots of water and high-protein snacks, and stop to rest often.
- **Protect your knees.** To reduce knee pressure when you descend the mountain, go slow and steady. Keep the knees slightly bent. Use trekking poles to reduce impact.
- **Be careful on mountaintops.** They can have steep drop-offs and loose rock.

WHERE TO GO

In love with summit hikes? Take your skills to the next level with mountaineering training. Some outdoor organizations, including The Mountaineers, offer courses that teach how to navigate off-trail to a summit over steep rocks and snowfields, as well as rappelling, snow climbing, glacier travel, and more. Not ready for that? Try these spots:

GREEN MOUNTAIN, KITSAP COUNTY
398 Gold Creek Road W, Bremerton
dnr.wa.gov, (360) 825-1631
DISCOVER PASS
5.2 miles round-trip, 1100 feet elevation gain,
1639 feet elevation
It's a moderate climb to the top of the Kitsap Peninsula's second highest point (Gold Mountain to the southeast is taller but protected for the local water supply, so there are no trails). Clear skies mean great views from the summit—westward across Hood Canal to Olympic peaks, and eastward to downtown Seattle against a wall of snowy Cascades. The hike is on a year-round multiuse trail, so be prepared to share it with mountain bikes, especially on weekends.

DOG MOUNTAIN, COLUMBIA GORGE
Off SR 14 east of Carson
fs.usda.gov/crgnsa, (541) 308-1700
NORTHWEST FOREST PASS
7.3 miles round-trip, 2900 feet elevation gain,
2945 feet elevation
In a nutshell, Dog Mountain is a hard hike with a huge reward—the best views in the Columbia Gorge. It straddles the misty west side and the arid east end of the Gorge, so the steep ascent takes you from green forest to wide-open slopes that come spring are carpeted in colorful purple lupine and yellow balsamroot. Check the snow level before your hike: the upper reaches of this trail see snow periodically in winter.

WEST TIGER MOUNTAIN, ISSAQUAH

High Point Trailhead off I-90 exit 20
dnr.wa.gov/WestTigerMountain
DISCOVER PASS
5 miles round-trip, 2100 feet elevation gain,
2522 feet elevation

This hike up Tiger Mountain is like a favorite pair of jeans—familiar, comfortable, and a staple for after work and weekends. Located in the "Issaquah Alps" (a chain of small mountains that face I-90 between Bellevue and North Bend), the climb up to the West Tiger #3 summit makes a great conditioning hike or quick foray into nature. Winter brings a higher chance of snow near the summit and of wildlife sightings—prepare to be serenaded by hungry Canada Jays and keep an eye out for deer.

BADGER MOUNTAIN, TRI-CITIES

525 Queensgate Drive, Richland
friendsofbadger.org
3.25 miles round-trip, 1195 feet elevation gain,
1579 feet elevation

Local activists made it a goal to preserve 650 acres of this mountain and build a trail to the top, and that's just what they did. The Canyon Trail leads through the subtle beauty of the Columbia Plateau, where jackrabbits hop through sage and coyotes dwell in deep ravines. From the dual-peaked summit, you'll bask in the sun (bring plenty of water) with the Blue Mountains to the east and a whole bunch of Cascade volcanoes to the west.

OYSTER DOME, BELLINGHAM

Chuckanut Drive (SR 11)
south of Larrabee State Park
DISCOVER PASS
6.5 miles round-trip, 1900 feet elevation gain,
2025 feet elevation

Ascend a mountain in ocean air; Blanchard Mountain is the only Cascade peak that rises directly from the Salish Sea. Most of the mountain (atop which Oyster Dome sits) has long been off-limits to logging, so the huge stumps and snags you see are ancient remnants of giants from centuries past. This summit is small but scenic, with views to Salish Sea islands, Canadian peaks, and sparkling waters.

MOUNT CONSTITUTION, ORCAS ISLAND

3572 Olga Road, Moran State Park, (360) 376-2326
DISCOVER PASS
7.81 miles round-trip, 1640 feet elevation gain,
2409 feet elevation

Hike to the highest point in the San Juan islands, where steps in a Civilian Conservation Corps–era stone observation tower take you even higher to a view of the scenic straits and mountain ranges in every direction. You could drive to the top of Mount Constitution, but that would defeat the purpose.

NATURE NOTEBOOK

Location: _____   Date: _____

Co-naturers: _____

What does reaching a summit mean to you? Do you need to reach the top to feel
you've met your goal, or is the journey the destination? Reflect on how your
perspective on hiking up peaks might mirror your approach to other life goals.

_____

_____

_____

_____

_____

_____

_____

_____

_____

_____

_____

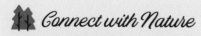 *Connect with Nature*

A map and compass are part of the Ten Essentials (see the introduction), but
have you ever actually used them for navigation? Practice on your summit hike:
locate landmarks using a topo map for the area you're hiking in, get your
bearings, and find true north. A step-by-step map and compass tutorial on
YouTube will help you become a navigation ninja.

WATCH STORMS ROLL IN

BE ON THE COAST WHEN THE WEATHER GETS WILD

Watching the weather at Chito Beach

THINK OF THE Washington Coast in winter and two words come to mind: fog and drizzle. Clouds settle in like a melancholy mood, beckoning you to turn inward for some reflective down time. If the quiet season is your thing, book a seaside getaway. Off-season solitude and the rhythm of the ocean help reset the tempo of a hectic life. It's not always mist and tranquility on the coast though; each winter brings a dozen or so wind storms. A few of these are big: gusts over 40 miles per hour, surly swells, gnarly surf crashing into shore, toppled trees, and gobs of rain. If you're by the sea when a storm hits, hunker down for an experience in nature you'll not soon forget. Just make sure you pack head-to-toe raingear!

Winter storms were no mystery to the Coast Salish tribes who inhabited the continent's edge. In their legends, wind storms were the work of Thunderbird, a giant creature hailing from high in the Olympic Mountains who would come down to the sea in search of orca whales. When Thunderbird flapped his enormous wings, it produced massive winds and stirred up torrents of rain.

Meteorologists have their own theories for how the biggest storms come about. Cool waters of the north Pacific don't favor hurricanes, but the region occasionally gets strong midlatitude tropical cyclones with wind roughly the speed of a Category 2 hurricane. The Hanukkah Eve Storm of late 2006 was a notable monster, with winds gusting to 90 miles per hour on the coast and record-breaking rainfall around Puget Sound. Spend a little time in Northwest storm-watching circles and you'll hear all about the Columbus Day Storm of 1962, the Hood Canal Storm of 1979, and the Inauguration Day Storm of 1993.

WHERE TO GO

Storm-watching is really just "watching"—from inside. There's a whole industry on the Washington and Oregon coasts devoted to storm-watching, where cabins and inns have huge picture windows facing the ocean. Venture out before or after with caution, as sneaker waves are always possible in winter. Beachcombing is fantastic at low tide after a big storm. If a storm is in the forecast, chances are it'll be on the smaller side (20–40 mile-an-hour gusts with gobs of rain). That's plenty big enough to enjoy watching a 20-foot ocean swell pound itself against a basalt headland. Book an ocean-view cabin or hotel room (a fireplace is a plus), pack a few good books and some hot cocoa, and settle into a cozy chair by the window. Outside, it's raining horizontally and winds are howling off the ocean, bringing the spray of salt along for the ride. Inside, you are warm and dry, enjoying the show.

KALALOCH BEACH
Kalaloch Lodge, 157151 US 101
thekalalochlodge.com, (360) 962-2271

For some high-drama weather book a lodge room or bluff cabin with kitchenette and wood stove (ask for an open ocean view). It rains buckets here, about 17 inches per month in winter. After a storm at low tide, miles of Olympic National Park beach trails await your exploration in both directions from the lodge. Watch your footing when crossing piles of driftwood, as logs can be unstable after a storm.

FIRST BEACH, LA PUSH
Quileute Oceanside Resort
330 Ocean Front Drive, La Push
quileuteoceanside.com, (360) 374-5267

NATURE NOTEBOOK

Location: _____   Date: _____

Co-naturers: _____

Recall the Salish legend of Thunderbird. Then create your own mythical legend for how storms form in the Pacific Ocean and pound the Northwest coast.

_____

_____

_____

_____

_____

_____

_____

_____

_____

_____

The storms of La Push are legendary. This low-key resort has spacious cabins with kitchenettes and motel rooms, some with outstanding ocean views. At low tide, several short hiking trails await—the trailhead to beautiful Second Beach is a stone's throw down the road.

COPALIS BEACH

Iron Springs Resort, 3707 WA-109 in Copalis Beach, ironspringsresort.com, (360) 276-4230
These revamped cabins on a small bluff were originally built in the 1940s as a place for

LEARN MORE

The Weather of the Pacific Northwest, by Cliff Mass, mixes meteorological science and eyewitness stories to explain the region's unpredictable weather. Follow Washington Weather Chasers on social media for exciting chatter and forecasts on winter storms off the coast and around the state.

WINTER BEACH SAFETY

You'll want to stay safely indoors during a big winter storm. When you venture out to the beach before or after, though, follow these tips.

- **Don't walk along the surf.** Wave heights are unpredictable before, during, and after a storm, and "sneaker waves" can occur, pulling you out to sea.

- **Never turn your back on the ocean.** Keep an eye on the surf to anticipate large waves that may be headed in.

- **Check the tides.** You'll want to know when low tide is if you want to comb the beach for treasure after the wind has died down.

- **Dress for downpours.** It often rains relentlessly on the coast even before and after a storm, so if you're out exploring, you'll want a rain coat, rain pants, and tall rubber boots.

- **Bring a lantern.** Power outages are common in storms, and most seaside accommodations stock flashlights for guests, but bring one just in case.

families to unwind, gather clams, and wander beautiful beaches. Each adorable cabin has a full kitchen, wood-burning fireplace and deck. Cozy chairs and blankets await near floor-to-ceiling windows that overlook the ocean—a perfect perch for when the wind picks up and wild waves roll in.

CAPE DISAPPOINTMENT
Cape Disappointment State Park
244 Robert Gray Drive, Ilwaco
parks.state.wa.us, (360) 642-3078
Perched on the edge of the earth, where the Columbia River meets the Pacific Ocean, Cape Disappointment is famous for shipwrecks, history, and relentlessly pounding waves against the steep cliffs below the

historic Cape Disappointment Lighthouse. The yurts and cabins don't have ocean views (though some of the campsites do, if you have a storm-worthy RV or camper), but they're affordable, furnished, and heated, and you're just steps from the beach.

CHITO BEACH, STRAIT OF JUAN DE FUCA
Chito Beach Resort, 7639 SR 112, Sekiu
chitobeach.com, (360) 963-2581
Perched on a basalt outcrop between Clallam Bay and Neah Bay, this is a sweet location for catching the brunt of storms that stir up frothy waves. Every cottage is waterfront, but The Rock House is special as it sits beside its own sea stack.

CAMP IN A YURT

COZY CAMPING IN WINTER WILDLANDS

Yurt at Cape Disappointment State Park

DOES CAMPING IN winter sound about as fun as cuddling with a snowball? Maybe this will warm you to the idea: heated yurts! These green canvas domes are an overnight option at many state park campgrounds throughout Washington, along with rustic cabins and a few platform tents, beckoning you to try cold-season camping in comfort.

Rustic rentals are a fairly new phenomenon in Northwest campgrounds—not so long ago they could be found only at Oregon's Cape Lookout. They were such a hit that a few county and state parks in Washington replicated the idea around 2005. Ten years later, the little domes and cabins were seemingly everywhere.

Felt- and fur-covered yurts were traditional shelters for nomadic people in Central Asia for thousands of years. The modern versions are like domed tents, walled with sturdy, weatherproof canvas on wooden platforms and simply furnished with a table, bunk beds, and a futon (just bring a sleeping bag and pillow). They have electricity, heat, screened windows, a skylight, and locking doors. The rustic cabins that are also found at some state parks are similarly furnished. Both sleep up to six people. This is still camping, though—the bathroom is a short walk away, and cooking is outside on a camp stove or campfire; state and county park cabins and yurts have a picnic table and campfire ring. Advance reservations aren't required for Washington State Park's yurts and cabins, but they are strongly recommended.

Off-season camping is loaded with perks. Bees and mosquitoes are long gone. You'll have plenty of solitude—no lines for the restroom, for example, or teenagers partying in the next campsite. The same uncrowded feeling carries over to hiking trails and beaches, too, especially in the morning or evening. Wildlife may be easier to spot in winter as creatures move around in search of food in the short days and cooler weather. The yurt or cabin keeps you warm and dry inside, and when you're outside, the crisp, fresh air reminds you why you ventured out.

The packing list for camping in a yurt or rustic cabin is similar to the summer camping list (see the summer section of this book), with a few changes. You don't need a tent or sleeping pad. Pack a few extra comforts that will keep you warm: lots of layers, cozy blankets, down booties, and plenty of hot cocoa. Consider bringing a canopy for the cooking area to keep it dry in the rain, or rig your own using nearby trees with a tarp and rope.

WHERE TO GO

Here are five particularly awesome spots for winter yurt or rustic cabin camping.

WASHINGTON COAST
Yurts at Pacific Beach State Park
49 2nd Street S, Pacific Beach
This area is known as the North Coast, a remote stretch north of Ocean Shores popular for razor clamming, beachcombing, kite-flying, and storm-watching. The yurts at Pacific Beach are a perfect refuge on blustery days, and within walking distance of the beach. Outside you'll find a picnic table and small covered porch.

CENTRAL CASCADES
Cabins at Wallace Falls State Park
14503 Wallace Lake Road, Gold Bar
After a night in one of the cozy private cabins at Wallace Falls State Park, wake up and hike to a plunging waterfall. The park has trails for every level—flat interpretive nature trails

NATURE NOTEBOOK

Location: _____   Date: _____

Co-naturers: _____

Try to identify the trees around your winter campsite (an app like iNaturalist can help). Deciduous trees will have shed most of their leaves in winter, so the bark and overall shape of the tree may be your main clues. List all the species of trees you can ID within a twenty-yard radius of your yurt.

_____

_____

_____

_____

Draw the pine needles, pine cones, or any leaves you can spot:

through woodland, switchbacks through forest to tiered falls, and a more challenging trail to Wallace Lake. The five cabins (two are pet-friendly) are nestled within the park's lush forest along the Wallace River.

SNOQUALMIE VALLEY

Yurts or a shipping container at Tolt MacDonald Park, 31020 NE 40th Street, Carnation

Here's a unique rustic retreat—this King County park in the Snoqualmie Valley has a

BUILD A CAMPFIRE

Build a campfire and make s'mores. Chilly winter air summons the cozy warmth from a campfire, and toasty, gooey marshmallows really hit the spot. Knowing how to build a campfire is an important outdoor survival skill, and telling great campfire stories is an underrated life skill! Bring cash to purchase firewood and kindling from your campground host, or gather your own, using only downed wood collected from the forest floor.

In your campfire ring, start with a loose pile of tinder (twigs, needles, dry leaves). Next comes the kindling, or sticks that are no bigger than one-inch diameter, formed into a pyramid or log cabin over the tinder. Light the tinder with a match, letting it burn. Blow lightly at the base of the fire to stoke it if needed. Next comes your fuel logs—one or two larger pieces of wood, which should catch fire and burn slowly.

Add kindling and fuel to keep the fire going as long as you like. Keep the fire small and under control. To put out the fire, slowly pour water over it from a bucket. Stick to established campfire rings, never leave a campfire unattended and—of course—always make sure the fire is fully extinguished before you leave.

WINTER CAMPING: YURTS AND CABINS

Keep this list handy to find yurts and rustic cabins to rent in the off-season. To reserve one at state park campgrounds, go to washington.goingtocamp.com or call (888) 226-7688. Snohomish County yurts can be reserved at snohomishcountywa.gov, and King County yurts at kingcounty.gov or call (206) 477-6149.

 YURTS

1. Cape Disappointment State Park
2. Grayland Beach State Park
3. Kanaskat-Palmer State Park
4. Kayak Point, Snohomish County Park
5. Pacific Beach State Park
6. Seaquest State Park
7. Twin Harbors State Park
8. River Meadows, Snohomish County Park
9. Tolt-MacDonald, King County Park

 RUSTIC CABINS

10. Battle Ground Lake State Park
11. Bay View State Park
12. Belfair State Park
13. Cama Beach State Park
14. Camano Island State Park
15. Cape Disappointment State Park
16. Dash Point State Park
17. Deception Pass State Park
18. Dosewallips State Park
19. Fields Spring State Park
20. Ike Kinswa State Park
21. Kitsap Memorial State Park
22. Potholes State Park
23. Rasar State Park
24. Riverside State Park
25. Steamboat Rock State Park
26. Twin Harbors State Park
27. Wallace Falls State Park

shipping-container-turned-camping-vessel set along the river. It features a full-sized bunk bed, table, and multipurpose cabinet made from reclaimed materials. Other signs of sustainability include used soccer goals that were converted into a green wall and an old door that is now the kitchen table. The park also has six yurts.

HOOD CANAL
Platform Tents at Dosewallips State Park
US 101, Brinnon
Play pioneer while camped near the shores of Hood Canal in one of the wooden platform canvas tents at Dosewallips State Park. Dosewallips is a favorite for off-season exploring because of the variety of forested trails and saltwater beaches, including one of the region's best clam beds. The modern platform tents set in a maple forest are 14 by 16 feet inside, furnished just as the yurts are, and comfortably sleep five.

EASTERN WASHINGTON
Cabins at Steamboat Rock State Park
51052 SR 155, Electric City
In the heart of Washington's Grand Coulee desert country is an island-like hunk of rock that resembles a steamship and juts like a finger into Banks Lake. Hike all the way up to its sagebrushy summit (bundle up in winter—it's windy!). Settle into one of their three heated cabins after your hike, but don't fall asleep yet—the sky is wide open, dark, and usually clear here, so it's a popular spot for gazing at stars and gawking at the Milky Way.

GO BIRDING

BIRDS HELP YOU FIND NATURE EVERYWHERE

Song Sparrow in a marsh

photo by Kelly Hill

TO BECOME A bird watcher, just go outside. You don't need binoculars (although the experience is better with a pair) or even a field guide—a free smartphone app called Merlin will get you started. Make a list of the birds that you encounter over the course of the day, from your backyard to your lunch break at work. Note every bird species you see or hear; the app will help identify any mystery birds. Watching a bird's behavior can also help with identification. Is it alone, with a mate, or in a flock with other birds? Is the bird on the ground like a robin, or hopping along a fence like a Steller's Jay? Is it foraging for little bugs on a tree limb like a chickadee, or hunting for seeds on the ground like a junco?

When you've finished your list, you may notice three things: there are many different types of birds, there are great numbers of birds, and birds are everywhere. When it comes to birds, Washington State is pretty special. We boast an outstanding diversity of bird species; more than five hundred on the state bird list. The reason? The state's variety of habitat types and geography, from 3000 miles of saltwater shoreline at sea level up through coniferous forests to mountains that reach over 14,000 feet at Mount Rainier, then back down again to desert plateaus bisected by two mighty rivers and dotted with freshwater marshes. From migrating shorebirds and wintering waterfowl to resident songbirds and owls, the smallest western state has one of the biggest state bird lists.

WHERE TO GO

There's no right or wrong way to be a bird watcher, as long as you're respectful. Keep it casual and do some backyard birding now and then, or look for birds on all your hikes and travels. You can bird by sight, by ear, or do a little of both. Keep a detailed birding journal if you like, or just a list in your head of birds you've seen. If you love spotting birds, by all means, get yourself a pair of binoculars and take it to the next level. Here are some prime spots to check out around the state.

UNION BAY NATURAL AREA
3501 NE 41st Street, Seattle

⭐ *Great Blue Herons, Red-winged Blackbirds, Red-tailed Hawks*

For a quick birding stroll in the city, this marshy preserve at the University of Washington is a top spot. Set on a large wetland complex on Lake Washington, more than two hundred bird species have been seen here. In winter you're likely to see a variety of waterbirds, native sparrows, and raptors. This place is affectionately known as "the Montlake Fill" to old-timer bird watchers.

UPPER SKAGIT RIVER
SR 20 from Sedro Woolley to Marblemount

⭐ *Hundreds of Bald Eagles*

Wintering eagles congregate on tree branches right along the banks of the Skagit River, waiting for a tasty passing salmon. Eagles feed in the early morning—your best chance to spot them. On cloudy days, they will roost in trees along the river throughout the day. On sunny days, look for them soaring over the valley. There are many places to stop and spot eagles, including Howard Miller Steelhead Park in Rockport, Mile Post 100 Rest Area, and the Marblemount Fish Hatchery.

SAMISH FLATS
12161 Samish Island Road, Bow

DISCOVER PASS

⭐ *Swans, Snow Geese, falcons, shorebirds, and Short-eared Owls*

This fertile delta is prime stomping grounds all winter long for birders, and a haven for

NATURE NOTEBOOK

Location: _____ Date: _____

Co-naturers: _____

Every bird watcher has one—the bird that got them hooked. What was your "gateway bird"? Describe what it was, where you saw it, and why it inspired you to look for more birds.

_____

_____

_____

_____

_____

_____

_____

_____

wintering Snow Geese, Trumpeter Swans, and migrating shorebirds (and the owls, hawks, and falcons that hunt them). Some folks challenge themselves to have a "five falcon day," spotting a Peregrine Falcon, Gyrfalcon, Prairie Falcon, Merlin, and American Kestrel—all in one day. Shorebirds like Dunlin and Black-bellied Plovers just in from breeding in the tundra congregate in flocks where they number in the thousands, flying in aerial coordination as they evade an incoming falcon—an incredible sight.

BILLY FRANK JR. NISQUALLY NATIONAL WILDLIFE REFUGE

100 Brown Farm Road NE, Olympia

⭐ *Waterfowl, falcons, Bald Eagles, and owls*

Walk slowly and quietly to absorb winter's symphony of birds here. A loop hike on boardwalk trails over wetlands and through deciduous woods offers close-up peeps of dabbling ducks, herons, and maybe even a family of nesting Great Horned Owls in February.

WHIDBEY ISLAND

⭐ *Seabirds and shorebirds*

Puget Sound is wintering habitat for dozens of species of dabbling ducks, diving ducks, and seabirds, many of which breed in Alaska and the Arctic. Work your way up or down the island stopping at public shorelines and viewpoints to scan just offshore for waterbirds and onshore for shorebirds. Some great stops are Deception Pass State Park (Rosario Beach is good for Marbled Murrelets, various species of gulls, sea ducks, cormorants, and loons), Libbey Beach County

LEARN MORE

Get Merlin, the free birding app for your smartphone by the Cornell Lab of Ornithology. A wonderful field guide for beginners is *Sibley Birds West: Field Guide to Birds of Western North America*. For birding locations, get *A Birder's Guide to Washington*. Download and print the free bird checklist from the Washington Ornithological Society. Attend a local bird walk or bird talk. All Audubon chapters host bird walks, usually free to members of the organization.

Walk the Oaks to Wetlands Trail through 2 miles of majestic, centuries-old Oregon white oak trees, fir and cedar woodlands, cottonwood and willow stands, and wetlands teeming with wildlife. The rounded, azure heads of California Scrub-Jays are distinct from the pointy crests of our common Steller's Jays. Red-shouldered Hawks flap over their winter wetland hunting grounds here, noticeably smaller than Red-tailed Hawks. Leave time to distinguish the elegant Tundra Swans from the Trumpeters in famously large flocks here. A drive on the 4.2-mile loop through the refuge's River S Unit might reveal some Black-crowned Night Herons roosting in trees, or Great Egrets stalking prey in the marshes.

Park (Harlequin Ducks, Pigeon Guillemots, Horned Grebes, and Black Oystercatchers), and Crockett Lake (by the Keystone ferry dock, look for Short-eared Owls, Northern Harriers, terns, and lots of shorebirds). This is a lovely winter birding road trip where binoculars are essential and a spotting scope is nice to have.

RIDGEFIELD NATIONAL WILDLIFE REFUGE

Off I-5 exit 16, south of Longview
fws.gov/refuge/Ridgefield

MODEST FEE PER VEHICLE

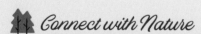 *California Scrub-Jays, Black-crowned Night Herons, Great Egrets*

COLUMBIA NATIONAL WILDLIFE REFUGE

SR 26 to Othello, fws.gov/refuge/Columbia

MODEST FEE PER VEHICLE

⭑ *Sandhill Cranes*

In late winter, thousands of lesser Sandhill Cranes stop over in the wildlife refuges of the lower Columbia on their way from California to their breeding grounds in Alaska. These large, gray, heron-like birds gather in huge flocks to feed in the fields and shallow marshes. They engage in some elaborate courtship displays, which you can see during their migration—graceful jumps and lovely dancing. Spot them from mid-February through early April.

Connect with Nature

Make your birding count as a citizen scientist! Record your bird sightings during the Great Backyard Bird Count (see Resources) along with thousands of other bird watchers around the world, and scientists will use the data to learn more about and protect birds.

BATHE IN A FOREST

IMMERSE YOUR BODY AND SOUL IN A LOCAL SWATCH OF NATU

Walking in a coastal woodland

IMAGINE A DOCTOR prescribing a restful afternoon in the woods for your back pain or anxiety. In Japan, they do. It's called *shinrin-yoku,* which translates to "forest bathing." A form of nature therapy, there's no actual bath involved, although you can slip off your shoes and wade into a cold, rushing stream if you want. In fact, that would be right in line with this therapy.

Forest bathing is the practice of immersing yourself in nature, engaging all of your senses in the present moment. Notice the sounds, scents, colors, and textures all around you, the breeze against your face that rustles leaves on the trees. Sit against a tree, stand in a clearing, lie on a carpet of moss. Wander along a trail, across a creek, or through the understory—unlike a hike, there's no destination and no goal.

There's real science to back up the therapeutic claims of forest bathing that have prompted Japanese doctors to recommend it for decades. Benefits include reducing anxiety, anger, inflammation, and depression while improving creativity and concentration. The most essential reasoning behind *shinrin-yoku* is simple: humans evolved outdoors. These days, we spend over 90 percent of our time indoors, scrolling, texting, watching screens, and reading—sometimes to a point of mental exhaustion. Soaking up the forest through sensory immersion heals us.

Forest bathing can be structured or unstructured: there's no instruction manual. Whether you practice daily for a short time or for a three-hour session one morning a month is up to you. Solo or with a friend? Up to you. This is an opportunity to slow down, take some time out of your hectic routine, and connect with nature. Just like a talk therapy session, do it as often as you need. In the dark damp of a Northwest winter, you might find you need it a lot. A forest bathing session that lasts about an hour might look like this:

- **Disengage from your regular routine.** Find a large rock to sit on or a tree to lean against. Practice deep breathing. This transitions your mind into connection mode.
- **Engage in nature connection.** Quietly focus your attention on the moment through your five senses. Feel the mist, smell the cedar, hear the rustling of a critter in the brush. Notice movement, like the way dappled sunlight dances on the forest floor.
- **Take off your shoes.** Feel the earth under your feet. Let your toes sink into the mud on a streambank, and plunge your hands into a cold creek—yes, even in the chilly winter months.
- **Discover texture.** Pick up a stone and hold it in your hand, cool and smooth and heavy. Run your hands over the bark of a tree and wrap your arms around its trunk.
- **Take a walk.** Wander without going anywhere in particular. Let the sound of a distant birdsong or the scent of a plant draw you near. Let your childlike curiosity lead you.
- **Transition back into your daily life.** Notice how you feel. Pour yourself a cup of tea from a thermos, read a nature poem, or write in a gratitude journal.

WHERE TO GO

Choose a spot for forest bathing close to your home; if you make it a regular practice, you can visit the special site often. Returning to the same location is recommended, as if you're adopting a swatch of nature as your own. That way, you'll witness nature change slowly through the seasons. Try a few places to find one that feels right, and don't feel limited to deep woods—wetlands or more open meadows might resonate more with you. Here are some extraordinary swaths of nature.

SCHMITZ PRESERVE PARK

5551 SW Admiral Way, Seattle

This nice remnant stand of old-growth forest in a lush West Seattle ravine is one of a kind. Paths meander through the huge ancient trees with rich layers of native undergrowth and onto stepstones across a lovely stream. It's quiet in here, lightly visited on weekdays, and a delight to the senses.

SNAKE LAKE

1919 S Tyler Street, Tacoma

This oasis in the city features a nature loop trail with plenty of quiet corners to sit still in before wandering across a footbridge over wildlife-rich wetlands.

HAZEL WOLF WETLANDS

24739 248th Avenue SE, Sammamish

An easy trail and boardwalk lead you through boggy forest and wetlands, where songbirds serenade you and Great Blue Herons silently stalk their prey.

EVANS CREEK PRESERVE

4001 224th Avenue NE, Redmond

Up to 3.5 miles of mostly easy trails that can be looped take you through diverse habitats for birds, butterflies, frogs, and other critters (perhaps even a black bear), from open meadow to upland forest.

JAPANESE GULCH

4407 76th Street SW, Mukilteo

You won't see many people but may come upon some lovely waterfalls as well as forest creatures in Japanese Gulch, an emerald canyon and urban oasis that abuts the sprawling Boeing complex in Everett.

WHATCOM FALLS PARK

1401 Electric Avenue, Bellingham

A cascade in the city, this 240-acre park offers a shady forest, a tumbling creek, and a lagoon that provides habitat for dabbling ducks. Wander to the four cascading waterfalls on Whatcom Creek.

GRAND FOREST PARK

9752 Miller Road NE, Bainbridge Island

This forest preserve is crisscrossed with looping, quiet trails that skirt alongside verdant ponds and old homesteads, over bridges and across a meadow.

RIVERSIDE STATE PARK, BOWL AND PITCHER

4427 N Aubrey Lane White Parkway, Spokane

DISCOVER PASS

Immerse your senses in beautiful hues of basalt formations, a turbulent river, and

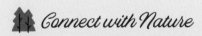 *Connect with Nature*

Record a nature soundscape. Use your smartphone to record a few minutes of your forest bathing session, capturing the cacophony of the woods. Take this piece of your practice home and replay it when you want to be transported back to a tranquil state in harmony with nature.

LEARN MORE

Certified forest bathing guide Melanie Choukas-Bradley wrote about connecting to nature through this practice in every season: *The Joy of Forest Bathing: Reconnect with Wild Places & Rejuvenate Your Life*. Find more close-to-home green spaces with the Urban Trails series from Mountaineers Books. There are guidebooks for Seattle, Tacoma, Eastside, Kitsap, Bellingham, Olympia, Vancouver, and Spokane.

fragrant ponderosa pine at this nature landscape.

BLACKBIRD ISLAND, WATERFRONT PARK
Off Commercial Street, Leavenworth

Stroll along a 2-mile loop trail around an island oasis in the middle of the Wenatchee River (a footbridge gets you safely across the water). Enjoy the sound of water and rustling of trees, and the feel of cold air coming off the snowy Cascades.

NATURE NOTEBOOK

Location: _____   Date: _____

Co-naturers: _____

What are your intentions for your forest bathing practice? Write them down and check in with them every so often.

_____

_____

_____

_____

_____

_____

_____

SPRING

- ○ Volunteer for Trail Maintenance
- ○ Hike to a Waterfall
- ○ Paddle a Canoe
- ○ Detour to the Desert
- ○ Gather Wild Edibles
- ○ Spring to a Wildflower Trail
- ○ Fly a Kite
- ○ Dig for Your Dinner
- ○ Watch Wildlife
- ○ Create a Haven for Wildlife
- ○ Cycle Around an Island
- ○ Raft Down a River
- ○ Work on a Farm

The transformation of the winter landscape to early spring is dramatic and sudden, like nature sounding an alarm clock. Wake up! Get outside! Hear the birds! Plant some seeds! Smell the flowers!

Spring unlocks the flowers to paint the laughing soil.
—Reginald Heber, "When Spring Unlocks the Flowers"

Spring announces itself, sometimes quite loudly. One morning before dawn you awaken to the quick, cheery notes of an American Robin, calling you out of a slumber to the start of a new season. You step outside and the air feels a bit warmer, the days a tad longer. New buds festoon tree branches that were bare just yesterday, catching the attention of busy acrobatic Bushtits as they gobble up tiny insects. Signs of the new season in the lowlands portend melting snow on the mountain slopes in the backcountry, opening up trails and surging waterfalls. There are many fun adventures ahead.

The season also requires a few special precautions in the backcountry. Trails may have winter storm damage not yet reached by trail crews. Always check Washington Trails Association's Trip Reports (wta.org/tripreports) for your destination before you head out. If you encounter washouts or downed trees, use caution making your way through or, if necessary, turn around. Then, write your own report to alert land managers and other hikers of the conditions. Spring sunshine can melt snow quickly, making streams more challenging to cross; a creek you crossed effortlessly on bare stones in the morning may be gushing and require great caution during the afternoon hike out. If too dangerous to cross safely, don't do it. Be flexible with your trip planning: if your chosen trail isn't accessible, find somewhere else. And always pack the Ten Essentials (see the introduction).

Springtime rouses a sense of wonder— the season of new life and renewal, of desert blooms and waterfalls, of clam digs and kites.

VOLUNTEER FOR TRAIL MAINTENANCE

PITCH IN TO GIVE BACK

Volunteers repair the Middle Fork Snoqualmie Trail.

photo by Susan Elderkin

THE NEXT TIME you go on a hike, really examine the trail. Notice the log bridge as it carries you across a creek, the puncheon (wooden plank boardwalk) that keeps your boots dry in a swamp, and rock steps that ease a steep grade for your ankles. Switchbacks lead gently up a steep slope, and rocks lined up across the trail divert water to the side. How did all this get here?

Whether you're deep in the Hoh Rain Forest or making your way up Quartz Mountain in Eastern Washington, the trail under your boots was built by someone, probably several people. Then, after a windstorm blew down trees and hard rain washed away a swath of trail, someone restored it. With nearly ten thousand miles of trails in Washington State, this is no small feat. Fortunately, many hikers give back to the trails they love as volunteers, wielding shovels and grub hoes and wearing brightly colored hardhats as they construct and maintain the hiking trails. And you can join them.

Volunteers with the Washington Trails Association (WTA) log more than one hundred thousand hours each year building and maintaining hiking trails on public lands. The WTA is the country's largest state-based hiking organization and a trail maintenance powerhouse. A handful of other organizations also host trail work parties.

You don't need trail work experience to volunteer, and the rules are pretty straightforward: be safe, have fun, and get some work done. You'll be provided with all the tools and training you need. There's always some physical exertion involved, but you can work at your own pace and there are many options for light work. Trail maintenance happens year-round: Fall and winter work parties focus on frontcountry maintenance and new trail projects in the lowlands. Spring and summer work parties follow the snowmelt, repairing winter damage in the backcountry by logging out blowdown or constructing new bridges, puncheons, turnpikes, and other trail structures.

Volunteering is a tangible way to give back to hiking trails that provide so many opportunities to explore nature. Other incentives sweeten the deal: it's a great workout, the teamwork builds camaraderie, and you'll be thanked profusely by the crew leader and passing hikers. Put in a few days and you'll earn a Northwest Forest Pass or Discover Pass. Finish five days on trail, and you'll secure your own personalized green hard hat.

VOLUNTEER OPPORTUNITIES

DAY WORK PARTY

These one-day trail work sessions are hosted year-round for maintenance and building new trails all over the state. To join one, review the work party calendar at wta.org /volunteer and find a date and location that fits your schedule. Day work parties are posted about six weeks in advance and you can sign up within forty-eight hours of the work party, provided it's not full. Bring a lunch, wear hiking boots, pants, and a long-sleeved shirt, and work or gardening gloves. The crew leader meets volunteers at the trailhead at 8:30 A.M. for a safety talk and describes the day's project with a quick tutorial on using provided tools. Then you'll hike together up to the site and get to work maintaining trails! Day work parties last about six hours, and end with candy, a cool drink, and camaraderie back at the trailhead.

VOLUNTEER VACATIONS

Reward your soul by spending a whole week in beautiful nature tending to local hiking

VOLUNTEER FOR TRAIL MAINTENANCE

NATURE NOTEBOOK

Location: _____ Date: _____

Co-naturers: _____

After a day of trail maintenance, you'll never forget the hard work that goes into a trail. Describe your experience. What was the day's trail project, and how did you contribute? What did you learn?

_____

_____

_____

_____

_____

_____

_____

_____

_____

_____

_____

_____

_____

_____

_____

_____

LEARN MORE

Washington Trails Association hosts one-day work parties year-round, and Volunteer Vacations in summer. Volunteers for Outdoor Washington manages work parties as stewards of particular trails, such as Robe Canyon and the Iron Goat Trail. The Student Conservation Association tackles projects in national parks across the US for youth and young adults.

trails. Volunteer Vacations are trail work parties that span a several days, tackling trail projects deeper in the backcountry than one-day trips can reach, or they may focus on a specific project that takes several days, like building a new bridge across a river or restoring a trampled alpine meadow. You'll find them from the dry, fragrant woods around Lake Chelan to the moss-cloaked forests of the Olympics, starting in late March through September, each year. Midweek, volunteers get a free day to hike, explore, or relax by the campfire.

Wondering where you'd sleep? Most Volunteer Vacations take place deep in the scenic backcountry with a primitive base camp, so you'll pack in your own camping gear in your backpack. Some trips get help from llamas to pack in gear, and a few Volunteer Vacations are pretty cushy, with cabins or other rustic lodging as the base camp. For a week's vacation, the experience is inexpensive—a modest fee covers all your meals and logistics. In exchange, you'll form some friendships with kindred spirits and make memories that last a lifetime.

HIKE TO A WATERFALL

PLUNGE INTO THE MESMERIZING WORLD OF CATARACTS AND CASCADES

Christine Falls at Mount Rainier National Park

FALLING WATER beckons the spirit and soothes the soul. A giant plunge waterfall is an invigorating five-senses experience, while a gentle cascade tumbling down rock steps lulls you to a tranquil rest. Choose your own adventure depending on your mood. Waterfalls have moods as well. Their demeanor can change in a matter of days depending on the sun, recent rain, the time of year, and the amount of snow that fell the previous winter.

The Cascade Range is named for them— hundreds of waterfalls, big and small, that cascade down streams and plunge over boulders, carrying impressive amounts of water from spring rains and melting snow. The Olympics are full of them, too. Both mountain ranges have the rugged terrain ideal for the formation of waterfalls, get lots of rain and snow, and are capped with glaciers. Some run year-round, while others slow to a trickle or disappear entirely in late summer. In winter, a frozen waterfall is a striking sight. But it's in the spring that waterfalls are at their most spectacular.

Waterfalls come in many forms, and as you get to know them, you'll want to see them all. Cataract falls are the gushers, enormous with tons of water. Horsetail falls skirt down a cliff face while partially maintaining contact with it. A plunge waterfall hurtles off the edge of a cliff and falls mostly uninterrupted. In a block fall, water flows in a sheet that is wider than it is tall, distinct from a curtain waterfall where the sheet of water is about as wide as it is tall. Segmented falls are created when water finds more than one path over a ledge. Tiered falls send water down a series of distinct falls. In cascade falls, water tumbles over many irregular rock steps. In a fan waterfall, the spill starts thin then spreads horizontally as it descends down bedrock. Waterfalls can be more than one form, and may change forms through the seasons.

WHERE TO GO

Before you go chasing waterfalls, understand their hidden dangers. It's risky to venture into the direct stream of a large waterfall, as loose rocks often tumble down in water. Don't climb up waterfalls, or jump from high rocks into a waterfall's pool. With safety in mind, explore these majestic spots.

SOL DUC FALLS, OLYMPIC NATIONAL PARK

US 101 west of Port Angeles
nps.gov/olym, (360) 565-3130
NATIONAL PARK PASS
1.6 miles round-trip, 100 feet elevation gain
⭐ *Waterfall form: segmented*

Set in the heart of Olympic National Park's temperate rain forest, enveloped by a mossy canyon, the swollen Sol Duc River splits as it spills with thunder beneath your feet. The stunning 30-foot plunge into a narrow gorge is uniquely viewable from above on a high wooden footbridge and other rustic platforms, offering different angles onto the enthralling torrent. Bring your good camera and a tripod, as photographers fancy Sol Duc to be one of the region's most beautiful waterfalls to shoot.

MARYMERE FALLS, OLYMPIC NATIONAL PARK

US 101 west of Port Angeles
nps.gov/olym, (360) 565-3130
NATIONAL PARK PASS
2 miles round-trip, 200 feet elevation gain
⭐ *Waterfall form: plunge*

Take a well-trodden trail up steps and over bridges fashioned from old-growth logs in search of the 90-foot falls. Falls Creek drops from a notch in a high, sheer cliff into a moss-ringed pool surrounded by a fern-laden ravine. Be sure to look up once in a while—trees here are giants. Take stairs to the right of the falls for a fantastic view near the upper portion.

FRANKLIN FALLS, SNOQUALMIE PASS

I-90 east to exit 47

fs.usda.gov/mbs, (425) 888-1421

NORTHWEST FOREST PASS

2 miles round-trip, 360 feet elevation gain

⭐ *Waterfall form: tiered plunge*

The forested path hugs the south fork of the Snoqualmie River and ends with a short, rocky ascent up to the base of the impressive falls, which spill from the top of a sheer rock face into a shallow pool, sending fine mist into the air. Watch from the observation area or make your way to the pool's rocky edge, keeping away from the fall's direct stream. The 70-foot plunge is the final of three tiered drops, 135 feet in all.

LEARN MORE

Waterfall Lover's Guide: Pacific Northwest, by Gregory Plumb, features trails to waterfalls throughout Washington, Oregon, and Idaho. The Northwest Waterfall Survey is an impressive online database of waterfalls in the Pacific Northwest—an essential tool for waterfall obsessives.

WALLACE FALLS, CENTRAL CASCADES

US 2 east to Gold Bar

parks.state.wa.us, (360) 793-0420

DISCOVER PASS

4.4 miles round-trip, 700 feet elevation gain

⭐ *Waterfall form: tiered plunge*

Wallace Falls is the star attraction of this state park, also home to a nice campground with rustic cabins. The tiered falls have upper, middle, and lower sections—the first

NATURE NOTEBOOK

Location: _____   Date: _____

Co-naturers: _____

A haiku is a Japanese poem traditionally about nature, comprising three lines of specific syllables: five, seven, five. Write a haiku inspired by the waterfall on your hike.

_____

_____

_____

dramatically plunges 265 feet into a large amphitheater, then churns and tumbles two more times, sending a cool spray in every direction. The path starts under hissing powerlines, though on a clear day, views of Baring and Mount Index make up for it. At a junction, take a right through a fern-shrouded hemlock forest to an ascent up stairs and switchbacks to the lower falls. Climb higher to get a stunning view at the middle falls viewpoint, the turnaround spot.

PALOUSE FALLS, COLUMBIA PLATEAU

off SR-261 S from Washtucna

parks.state.wa.us, (509) 646-9218

DISCOVER PASS

1 mile round-trip, no elevation gain

⭐ *Waterfall form: cataract plunge*

The Palouse River roars as it drops nearly two hundred feet into a mammoth basalt basin scoured by water that once made itself known even more thunderously—an ice age flood. This breathtaking cataract draws visitors by the thousands each year to experience its power firsthand and photograph its beauty, which sits in stark contrast to the surrounding dry coulee country. Keep to the designated trail for your own safety. This official state waterfall is at peak magnificence in spring just after sunrise or before sunset.

WATERFALLS YOU CAN DRIVE TO

These waterfalls can be enjoyed just steps from their parking areas.

- **Nooksack Falls, Mount Baker.** From the viewing platform behind a fence, gawk at the top two-thirds of this segmented cataract plunge waterfall.
- **Christine Falls, Mount Rainier.** Stair steps lead to a view of this 40-foot plunge waterfall, beautifully framed by a stone masonry bridge.
- **Madison Falls, Olympic National Park.** The maple-shaded path to this horsetail falls is short, sweet, and paved, so the viewpoint is accessible for those who use wheelchairs and strollers.

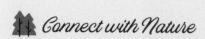 *Connect with Nature*

Learn to photograph a waterfall like a pro. Aim for morning or evening to avoid sunlight bouncing off the water. The blurred, silky appearance of waterfalls in many photos is the result of a long shutter speed. Use a steady tripod and experiment a bit, trying a two-, one-, or half-second shutter speed. When composing your shot, frame the waterfall with some of the surrounding forest or rocks to give a sense of scale and depth to the photograph.

PADDLE A CANOE

THE RHYTHM OF CANOEING SETTLES THE MIND AND ENLIVENS THE SPIRIT

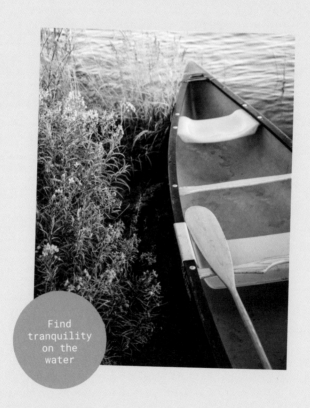

Find tranquility on the water

photo by Ian Keefe

HERE ARE SOME THINGS you might see in a wetland from a canoe: turtles sunning themselves on a log, the intricate construction of a beaver dam, Mallards nibbling at your fingers, a motionless Green Heron stalking her prey. Get up close and personal with aquatic wildlife from the unique perspective of being on the water.

Dip your paddle in the waters of Native history. The Coast Salish people were superb mariners and carved elegant dugout canoes, each from a single western red cedar tree. Their ornate boats, embellished with symbolic characters like the orca or raven, ranged in size from small watercraft to seaworthy vessels as long as 70 feet. They deftly navigated local waterways in pursuit of salmon runs, trade, war, and travel to potlatches. Pacific Northwest Coast peoples like the Salish and Haida favored canoes over the sea kayaks used by Arctic Indigenous peoples; what canoes lacked in cover from the elements, they made up for in their ease of loading both supplies and people.

A good rule of thumb for where to launch a canoe is to stick to calm freshwater. For the average paddler, the open saltwater of Puget Sound with its strong currents and tides is better suited to kayaks. Start with half-day paddles, then work your way up to overnight canoe camping trips.

THE BASICS OF PADDLING A CANOE

Canoeing is easy to learn, though sustained paddling requires some core strength and stamina. Start with short outings to master the basic techniques for efficient, comfortable paddling. Always wear a life jacket; you want a snug fit. Practice getting in and out of the canoe when you're on shore and it is in water, grasping the gunwale (the canoe's top edge) to stay steady and keep a low center of gravity. To paddle, hold the paddle with the grip in one hand and the shaft in the other, arms about shoulder-width apart. You're forming a box with your paddle, two arms, and chest; maintain this box while you paddle and keep your arms in your line of sight as they line up each stroke.

This is key, because the power for each stroke comes from your torso rotation, not your arms. For the basic forward stroke, reach out and place your paddle in the water well in front of you, then rotate your torso as you draw the paddle back, toward you, keeping the shaft vertical. Use short strokes, take the paddle out of the water just as it passes your hip, and feather the blade in the recovery phase so it slices the air instead of catching it. Meanwhile, your lower body helps to stabilize the canoe. Other fundamental strokes to learn are the draw stroke to move the boat sideways, and the J stroke for steering. When riding tandem, paddle on opposite sides and switch at the same time. The person in front provides most of the power, and the person in back steers.

WHERE TO GO

The first two destinations have a livery on-site for hourly canoe rentals, and the paddling is perfect for beginners. As you graduate to mountain lakes and canoe camping, you'll need your own boat, which can be securely tied upside-down to the roof rack on your car for transport. Canoes may be made of fiberglass, aluminum, plastic, or wood, and start around $700 new. Rent a canoe for a nightly rate at your local outdoor store.

WASHINGTON PARK ARBORETUM

University of Washington Waterfront Activities
Center, Seattle
Canoe rental May–September
3710 Montlake Blvd NE, recreation.uw.edu
(206) 543-9433

To the north is a sprawling wetland teeming with bird life, the Union Bay Natural Area. To the south is another wetland, the Washington Park Arboretum. Fit in both if you have time, otherwise paddle south around Marsh Island and under the 520 Bridge to explore the marshes on the arboretum's edge along Foster Island and into Duck Bay. Skirt alongside lawns of lily pads where Pied-billed Grebes build their floating nests, safely protected on the water from predators. Most paddlers traveling through the arboretum spot ducks, herons, and turtles, and Osprey and Bald Eagles overhead. If you're lucky, you might see a shy muskrat or a pair of fantastically beautiful Wood Ducks who use the nest boxes placed here for them. Note: Boat access to a small portion of the arboretum's wetlands is limited due to ongoing 520 Bridge construction through 2023; look for signage that directs boaters away from construction.

MERCER SLOUGH, ENATAI BEACH PARK

Canoe rental (weekends only) May–September
3519 108th Avenue SE, Bellevue
bellevuewa.gov, (425) 452-6885

Start at Enatai Beach Park's boathouse where REI rents canoes by the hour, or meet up with city naturalists here for a half-day guided canoe trip into Mercer Slough on weekend mornings, May–September. Paddle east hugging the shoreline, then under the concrete ribbons of I-90 into the mouth of Mercer Slough, a lush wetland totaling 320 acres and bisected vertically by a canal over 2 miles long. Poke your way up the marshy canal, serenaded

---

NATURE NOTEBOOK

Location: _____   Date: _____

Co-naturers: _____

The rhythm of paddling through still waters quiets your mind's chatter and syncs up with your breath. If you pay attention, you'll notice rhythm within and around you, especially in nature. What rhythms have you observed in nature?

_____

_____

_____

_____

_____

by the Marsh Wren's percussive trills. Herons, rails, and bitterns love this reedy habitat. Got your own canoe? There's a put-in at the Sweyolocken Boat Launch (3000 Bellevue Way SE) on the southern shore of the canal.

DIABLO LAKE, NORTH CASCADES NATIONAL PARK

SR 20 east of Marblemount
nps.gov/noca, (360) 854-7200

The brilliant water of Diablo Lake owes its surreal hue to glacial runoff full of pulverized rock that contains the mineral olivine, painting the lake a vibrant jade on sunny days. On a clear morning, backdropped by craggy Cascade peaks bejeweled with glaciers, this reservoir is probably the most scenic place you could paddle a canoe in the whole state. Head to Colonial Creek Campground, where you'll find a dock from which to launch your boat and a place to pitch your tent. The primo experience here is to park in the lot, then load all that camping gear into your canoe, and paddle up the lake for an hour or so to one of the national park's three scenic, private boat-in campgrounds. Each has a tent pad, privy, bear box, picnic table, and campfire ring. Swing by the ranger station in Marblemount to get a free backcountry camping permit. To paddle a multiday camping trip in this area, Ross Lake Resort provides portage service for small boats for a fee. North Cascades Institute leads outings in the lake in an eighteen-person Salish-style canoe.

MORE CANOE CAMPING TRIPS

- **Potholes State Park, Moses Lake.** Ice age floods carved depressions in the earth here, then a dam filled them up. What remains is a huge desert oasis—hundreds of small islands in a shallow sea with its own soundtrack, the

LEARN MORE

Washington Water Trails Association works to preserve safe and legal access to the state's waters as well as nice shores to land on and places to camp. The Center for Wooden Boats hosts workshops where you can build your own 14-foot canoe in a week. In Suquamish, the JayHawk Institute boasts a collection of traditionally carved and painted Northwest Coast canoes, available to view by appointment.

flapping wings of shorebirds and the rusty hinge call of Yellow-headed Blackbirds. Camp at the park or on any of the islands that have room to pitch a tent.

- **Cooper Lake, Okanogan-Wenatchee National Forest.** All twenty-two campsites at Owhi Campground are walk-in tent sites, just a stone's throw from this pristine Cascades lake. Carry your canoe to camp, or use the vehicle-accessible boat launch further up the road and paddle to the wildlife-rich western shore for sublime mountain paddling.

- **Lake Ozette, Olympic National Park.** Launch from the ranger station boat ramp and hug the western shoreline of the lake as you paddle south about 4 miles, around Shafers Point and into Ericksons Bay and the park's only boat-in campground.

- **Takhlakh Lake, Mount Adams.** Pronounced "TOCK-lock" and backdropped by glacier-flanked Mount Adams, this pristine mountain lake has its own Forest Service car campground with the same name where you can pitch your tent, then launch your canoe from a sandy beach for scenic paddling. Pack your trout fishing pole and a frying pan for the perfect weekend.

DETOUR TO THE DESERT

CANYON COUNTRY BLOOMS WITH WILDFLOWERS AND BIRDSONG

Hiking the Ancient Lakes Trail

photo by Jeff Parsons

CASCADIA IS A LAND of contrasts, none more stark than when you venture from the misty emerald forests of Western Washington to the state's arid eastern half. In spring the vast Columbia Plateau is warmer, drier, and, unlike most trails in the Cascades and Olympics, not under several inches of snow. Colorful in places and austere in others, this landscape of basalt canyons, dry coulees, and sagebrush is crisscrossed with lightly treaded trails that provide relief for spring fever in the form of warmth and sunshine.

If you hear "desert" and think barren, you're in for a nice surprise—our shrub-steppe habitat is full of life, though many plant and wildlife species here face threats of habitat fragmentation and degradation. About half the fragile shrub-steppe ecosystem that once carpeted Eastern Washington is gone. On that which remains you may encounter elk, bighorn sheep, coyotes, sagebrush lizards, jackrabbits, rattlesnakes, and an array of migratory songbirds and raptors. Some birds are strongly associated with sagebrush and you'll only find them in sage habitat, like sage-grouse (who only lay their eggs under sagebrush), Sagebrush Sparrow, Brewer's Sparrow, and Sage Thrasher. Wildflowers put on a vibrant show each spring. Look for desert specialties like the bright fuchsia blossoms atop spiky hedgehog cactus, arrowleaf balsamroot, sagebrush violets, clumps of phlox, and bluebells.

WHERE TO GO

The best desert hiking trails in Washington are concentrated around Ellensburg and Yakima within state wildlife recreation areas, with a few other superb hikes scattered throughout the Columbia Plateau. Go in late April, May, or early June for the brilliant but brief display of wildflowers and the most active migratory bird life.

L. T. MURRAY STATE WILDLIFE RECREATION AREA

Umtanum Canyon, SR 821, 13 miles south of Ellensburg, wdfw.wa.gov, (360) 902-2515

PARKING FEE

Step into a riparian oasis in the heart of Washington's dry sagebrush steppe country. The trail begins at the Yakima River and gently meanders up the lush basalt canyon alongside Umtanum Creek, crossing over it and back again in a few places.

Spring hikers are serenaded by a chorus of migratory birdsong, from bluebirds, orioles, and many species of warblers. Lewis's Woodpeckers nest here, their flapping crow-like flight notably different from the undulating flight of other woodpeckers. Bighorn sheep and deer roam the sloped canyon walls, and a Prairie Falcon pair often nests here. Watch for the sight or sound of a rattlesnake; hiking with a walking stick reduces the chances of surprising one. Desert wildflowers color the canyon bottom, and sapphire-blue sky stretches for miles overhead. The trail becomes overgrown at three miles, a good place to turn around. There are nice, flat campsites every mile or so along the trail.

COLUMBIA BASIN WILDLIFE AREA

Ancient Lakes, Ancient Lake Road, Quincy wdfw.wa.gov, (509) 765-6641

DISCOVER PASS

Welcome to the channeled scablands, where ancient lava flows met with ice age flooding, leaving behind the mighty Columbia River and a patchwork of soaring basalt benches, isolated mesas, and wide coulees across a vast portion of Eastern Washington. Venture into Potholes Coulee on an old jeep track to

The shrub-steppe country along the Yakima River

photo by Dave Hoefler

a trio of aptly named Ancient Lakes flanked by towering basalt (4.4 miles round-trip). The route to the lakes is easy and fairly flat, though once at the lakes, optional scrambles over talus to reach sweeping views are more challenging and require good hiking boots. A plunging waterfall pours from the coulee's rim into one of the lakes, splashing onto columnar basalt steps in its descent.

Tall sagebrush, rabbitbrush, and bunchgrass carpet the flat of the coulee. Plentiful wildflowers greet hikers in May, including yellow bells, hedgehog cactus, yarrow, balsamroot, and yellow paintbrush. Western Meadowlarks and Red-winged Blackbirds provide a continuous soundtrack for your rest stop by the lakes. Small game birds like Chukar and quail scurry across the trail. Rattlesnakes are common ground-dwellers here, so look before you step.

As you traverse along the base of the cliffs, look up and you'll see hungry Violet-green Swallows and White-throated Swifts darting

LEARN MORE

Desert Hikes of Washington, by Alan L. Bauer and Dan Nelson, is a wonderful source for detailed route descriptions.

89

NATURE NOTEBOOK

Location: _____ Date: _____

Co-naturers: _____

Observe the palette of canyon country, first from a distance and then up close. From afar you'll see muted earth tones: tan, rusty brown, dusty sage green. Up close, though, the desert in bloom holds every shade of the rainbow, from red to violet. Try to find each color in the desert's flora and fauna. Describe what you found.

_____

_____

_____

_____

_____

_____

_____

_____

_____

_____

_____

_____

_____

_____

_____

HIKE SAFELY IN DESERT COUNTRY

PACK YOUR OWN WATER.
In an arid climate you'll want 2 liters per person for a half-day hike, more for a full day.

EXPECT NO SHADE.
Apply strong sunblock and wear clothing that can protect against harsh sun and wind, including sunglasses and a wide-brimmed hat.

THIS IS TICK COUNTRY.
Wear light-colored clothing so you can spot ticks on yourself and your hiking partners. Check yourself and your dogs as soon as you return to the trailhead, before you get into the car. Feel around your scalp for bumps. Change into clean clothes, stuffing the hiking clothes into a garbage bag. When you get home, put the clothes into the dryer and run it on high for ten minutes—it kills the ticks.

WATCH FOR SNAKES.
Rattlesnakes may be on or just beside the trail. Carry a hiking stick to avoid surprising one—move brush or thump a rock before you step. Keep dogs leashed.

OBSERVE, DON'T DISTURB.
Observe elk or bighorn sheep from a distance, taking care not to disturb them. Do not dig up cacti and other desert plants to take home.

TEN ESSENTIALS.
Always pack the Ten Essentials in your backpack.

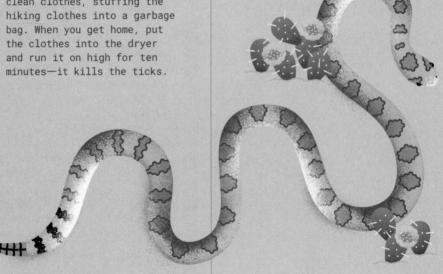

around for juicy bugs. They probably won't get to all the mosquitoes, so pack bug dope on this trail. Bring in all your drinking water, as the lake contains irrigation runoff and isn't safe to drink, even when filtered. Overnight campers will find lovely spots to pitch a tent on grassy patches near the lakes, some with shade. Enjoy sleeping under a giant sky full of stars that only the desert provides as you're lulled to sleep by a chorus of frogs and coyotes.

STEAMBOAT ROCK STATE PARK

Northrup Canyon, 51052 Highway 15, Electric City
parks.state.wa.us, (509) 633-1304
DISCOVER PASS

Walk and gawk through this steep-walled valley of eroded basalt cliffs among aromatic sagebrush, shady aspen, and willow trees to an old ranch homestead (3 miles round-trip). The Northrup family settled in this remote canyon in 1874, constructing an irrigation system and planting the area's very first orchard. Ruins of the homestead's cabins, barns, and even a chicken coop remain on-site. Turn around at the homestead for an easy outing, or continue on for a slightly more challenging outing as the trail climbs steeply up to Northrup Lake, a nice pond to bait a trout (6 miles round-trip).

Keen observers will note signs of the ecological transition zone this trail traverses, where sagebrush steppe mingles with open ponderosa pine and fir forest. The end result is a scenic landscape, especially when the meadow is in spring bloom of balsamroot and lupine, and low sunlight washes the cliffsides with color. Early morning hikers may be rewarded with the downward spiral tune of the Canyon Wren and spot the several species of owls or woodpeckers who call the canyon home. Quail, Ring-necked Pheasant, and Wild Turkeys may also be seen. Leash your dogs and bring hiking poles or a stick to tap as you go in case a rattlesnake is lurking in the grass beside the trail.

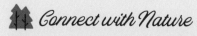

Connect with Nature

Advocate on behalf of your public lands and wildlife. Follow local conservation organizations on social media, such as the Nature Conservancy of Washington (@Conserve_WA on twitter) and Conservation Northwest (@ConservationNW), then respond to their calls to action by contacting your elected officials.

GATHER WILD EDIBLES

EDIBLE GREENS AND WILD BERRIES,
FROM PLANT TO PLATE

Tall
Oregon
grape

DOES THE PHRASE "gathering wild edibles" sound like something relegated to the hunter-gatherers of prehistory? Not anymore. If you're searching for deeper connections with Mother Nature in your everyday life, get in on the renaissance of foraging for wild food. There's something magical about tasting a black huckleberry straight from the bush, or snacking on a bit of chickweed as you walk through your neighborhood. Diverse habitats and lots of public land make the Pacific Northwest a hot spot for this delicious hobby. And spring is the perfect season for it.

Many tasty wild foods await spring foragers in our nearby forests, urban parks, and even backyards: tender miner's lettuce, fiddlehead ferns, chickweed, spicy nettles, juicy salmonberries, and tart thimbleberries. Modern foragers seek many of the same edibles that sustained Indigenous peoples along the Northwest Coast for thousands of years, though the latter gathered a wider variety than the average forager does today. The Coast Salish harvested the parts of more than one hundred edible species of plants—from the protein-rich roots of common camas reminiscent of sweet pumpkin when roasted, to the inner bark of red alder trees, which was dried, ground, then baked into breads or used to thicken soups.

You can gather berries and wild greens on most public lands for personal use— from national forests to state parks, and most county and city parks. Large urban parks are great spots for novice foragers to get acquainted with common edibles like salmonberry or nettles—try Discovery Park in Seattle or Point Defiance Park in Tacoma. Whether you set out to gather nettles for pesto or pop a few salal berries into your mouth on a hike, foraging food from the wild fuses a connection between you and the earth.

SAFE AND SUSTAINABLE FORAGING

Now that you've imagined the Pacific Northwest as your garden, learn how to gather wild greens, berries, and seaweed in ways that are both safe and sustainable.

Never eat anything you aren't sure is edible. If you wonder, toss it yonder—or better yet, don't pick it in the first place. Buy a good field guide to edible plants to make a positive identification before you put a leaf or berry into your mouth. Go slow, learning a few plants at a time. Get to know the toxic plants in the region so you can always avoid them, particularly poison hemlock. Take a class or join an edible plant walk with a trusted guide so you can gather wild edibles with confidence.

Forage on public lands, or get the landowner's permission to gather edibles on private property. Keep to healthy forests or beaches for edibles, and steer clear of roadsides and borders with conventionally farmed land that may have been sprayed with pesticides. Forage edibles with ecological stewardship in mind, such as when they're in abundance. Don't trample other vegetation to reach your edibles.

Gather only what you know you will use, and only for personal use. Leave plenty behind for the plant to reproduce itself and for wild animals like bears and birds who have to eat, too. Greens and berries are free of charge to forage on public land, though some lands require an access pass to park.

WHAT TO FORAGE

WILD GREENS

Dandelion. This common garden foe was brought by early explorers and has been foraged by Indigenous peoples ever since.

Toothed, oblong leaves cluster into a circular pattern called a rosette. Fresh young leaves from shady spots with moist soil are the tastiest, especially before the flower head starts to open, after which they'll lean bitter. Look for dandelion in your neighborhood and city parks but avoid lawns that may have been treated with pesticides.

Fiddleheads. The tightly coiled shoots of the lady fern emerge from the soil in spring and soon unfurl into an inedible fern frond, so nab them quick, cutting off a few inches of soft stem with the coiled top. Fiddleheads from the delicate lady fern have woodsy licorice notes and are a delicious side dish to fish or a simple pasta. Blanch them, then sauté or roast them with a little butter and salt. Lady ferns flourish in damp woods around boggy areas. If you're on a spring hike and smell skunk cabbage, look for lady fern nearby.

Douglas-fir. Snip the fresh green tips and steep in boiling water for a subtle minty tea. Medicinal uses include anti-inflammatory properties and vitamin C.

Stinging nettles. Wear your garden gloves when harvesting this nutritious, prickly herb that looks like mint until you get closer and examine the leaves. Nettles prefer moist meadows, wetlands, and woodlands. Harvest when young, February–April. The stem and

LEARN MORE

Northwest Foraging: The Classic Guide to Edible Plants of the Pacific Northwest, by Doug Benoliel, is the premier guide to edible plants in the region, with detailed illustrations to assist in identifying important characteristics of plants. Alderleaf Wilderness College in Monroe and Earthwalk Northwest in Issaquah offer in-depth courses on foraging for wild edibles.

leaves have tiny hairs that sting. Hold the stalk with your gloved hand as you snip off the top five inches of the plant with scissors. Then take your haul of bold, spicy greens home and make a pot of nettle soup or tea. To remove the sting, nettle stalks should be blanched for a few minutes before going into your recipe. Transfer them to an ice bath then remove the tough stalks and they're ready for pesto or soup.

BERRIES

Salmonberry. The earliest of the native brambleberries to ripen, these golden-orange beauties emerge as chinook salmon

 Connect with Nature

Eat your weeds! Here's a simple, elegant nettle soup: Gather a half pound of nettle leaves (about half a paper grocery bag of nettle tops, or 5 cups of loosely packed leaves). Start by blanching the nettles in boiling water for two minutes, then plunge them into an ice bath. In a pot, combine 3 cups of broth and about 1/3 pound of cubed gold potatoes. Once these are tender, add the blanched nettles and simmer gently for a few more minutes. Purée with an immersion blender and finish with salt and pepper to taste and a few splashes of cream. Bon appétit!

return to our rivers each spring. Find them along streams or in sun-spotted forests. Salmonberries are soft, juicy, and usually sweet, though there's a lot of variation in color and taste from one patch to the next, so sample until you find a bush that suits you.

Thimbleberry. These velvety red berries evoke a tart raspberry with small, crunchy seeds. Pick and eat them along the trail as you hike because they're soft and don't store well, though you can also make jam with them if you do it right away. This fuzzy-leafed shrub likes damp areas in lowland woods with some sun, like forest edges or streambanks.

Oregon grape. Make a batch of jam from foraged berries that tastes like a Northwest forest. This sharp-leafed green shrub grows under Douglas-fir, with clusters of dainty yellow flowers that yield to small, dusty purple berries in early summer. Some palates find the fresh berries too tannic or spicy, but in jam married with a generous amount of sugar, they taste like a complex, earthy grape.

NATURE NOTEBOOK

Location: _____   Date: _____

Co-naturers: _____

How does a wild berry look, smell, and taste different from a store-bought berry? List some of your favorite recipes that could incorporate foraged wild foods.

_____

_____

_____

_____

_____

_____

_____

SPRING TO A WILDFLOWER TRAIL

FIND EARLY BLOOMS THAT BID WINTER FAREWELL

Balsamroot bloom at Dalles Mountain Ranch

WHAT'S YOUR FAVORITE harbinger of spring? Northwest nature announces winter's departure in delightful ways, like the sweet song of a migrant warbler just back from the tropics or apple blossoms adorning a tree like ornaments. A particularly large, solitary three-petaled white bloom that festoons the floor of our Northwest woods shouts the loudest: spring has arrived! Look for the emergence of western white trillium in early April, dotting the moist forest understory.

Trillium, a sign of spring in the Northwest

But spring wildflowers begin their bloom even before the first trillium. In March, musky-smelling skunk cabbage pokes through the cold soil in swampy patches of forest, cracking open a neon yellow bract to reveal a knobby flower spike. East of the Cascades, the shrub-steppe debuts its stunning flower show in early April. In the Columbia Gorge, sunny hillsides transform into carpets of balsamroot and lupine by late April. The forested trails around Hood Canal explode with the fireworks of native rhododendrons in May.

WHERE TO GO

These locales are sure to enthrall visitors, but take care to stay on paths and not trample the wildflowers.

DALLES MOUNTAIN RANCH LOOP, COLUMBIA HILLS STATE PARK

SR 14 east of Dallesport, Columbia Gorge
parks.state.wa.us, (360) 902-8500
DISCOVER PASS
6.9 miles round-trip, 1060 feet elevation gain
⭐ *Arrowleaf balsamroot, lupine, cushion fleabane*
A few hikes in the Columbia Gorge are renowned as "most Instagrammable places" during the epic balsamroot-lupine bloom from mid-April through May. This one tops the list, as the perfect selfie-with-blossoms

photo op is mere steps from the car. Park at the upper trailhead at Crawford Ranch and head south into fields upon fields of gorgeous blooms. If you've come for photography, get here early for the best light and fewest hikers.

ESMERALDA BASIN, TEANAWAY

SR 970 east of Cle Elum
fs.usda.gov/okawen, (509) 852-1100
NORTHWEST FOREST PASS
7 miles round-trip, 1750 feet elevation gain
⭐ *Elephant's head lousewort, yellow arnica, scarlet gilia*
In late spring this hike through flower-filled Esmeralda Basin gives you an early taste of summer wildflower hikes to come. The trail climbs alongside the north fork of the Teanaway River through boggy meadows and around rock gardens brimming with a wide variety of wildflowers to Fortune Creek Pass with views of Hawkins Mountain, Ingalls Peak, Lake Ann, and more stunners. Look for a plethora of purple Jeffrey's shooting stars along streams and the showy scarlet gilia in clumps among rocks.

MOUNT WALKER, OLYMPIC NATIONAL FOREST

US 101, MP 300 on Hood Canal
fs.usda.gov/olympic, (360) 765-2200

SPRING WILDFLOWERS TO SPOT

There's no need to wait for the July snowmelt on alpine meadows to ramble through colorful fields abloom. Get a good field guide to wildflowers and hit an early wildflower trail. Go slow—many wildflowers are showy and obvious alongside the trail, but just as many are small, elegant, inconspicuous beauties. You'll be glad to have a magnifying glass in one hand to examine the dainty varieties. Take care to not pick or damage wildflowers while admiring their untamed beauty.

Pacific bleeding heart. These elegant, heart-shaped pink flowers gracefully dangle from long stems in shady areas at low to mid-elevations.

Common camas. These spiky blue-to-purple flowers often carpet meadows at low to mid-elevations; the edible bulbs were a staple food for Northwest Native tribes.

False Solomon's seal. In shady lowland forests and streamsides, this elliptical-leaved beauty's stalk bears clusters of tiny, perfumed cream-colored flowers, breathtaking under a magnifying lens.

Arrowleaf balsamroot. On dry, sunny slopes in the shrub-steppe and Columbia Gorge, this bright yellow star in the sunflower family grows in clumps with fuzzy leaves shaped like arrowheads, peaking in May.

Spreading phlox. Look for phlox in different hues (blue, pink, or white) growing in loose mats like a carpet at sunny, rocky mid-elevations in May (higher in summer).

Bitterroot. This gorgeous blossom has many rosy-pink petals and grows in arid rocky areas, even sunny, windswept places where few other plants could survive.

NORTHWEST FOREST PASS

4 miles round-trip, 2000 feet elevation gain

⭐ *Pacific rhododendron*

Hike here in late May or early June for a spring blossom spectacle featuring the state's official flower, the native Pacific rhododendron. It grows west of the Cascades and is particularly abundant on trails surrounding Hood Canal. Ranging from pastel pink to deep fuchsia, the blooms pop brightly in the green forest understory. Other blooms you might spy up to the mountain summit are salal and the official flower of our southern neighbor, the yellow blossoms of Oregon grape. The summit rewards you with a sweet view to the west of the Olympic peaks.

ICICLE RIDGE, OKANOGAN-WENATCHEE NATIONAL FOREST

Icicle Road south of US 2, Leavenworth fs.usda. gov/okawen, (509) 548-2550

NORTHWEST FOREST PASS

6 miles round-trip, 1800 feet elevation gain

Lupine and balsamroot at Dalles Mountain Ranch

⭐ *Glacier lilies, paintbrush, arrowleaf balsamroot*

Just outside Leavenworth, the switchback trail up to sunny Icicle Ridge sheds its snow early, with peak wildflowers in April and May. Expect a steady climb, though bountiful blooms like glacier lilies, lupine, and paintbrush provide lots of excuses for rest stops. The fire-scarred ponderosa pines along the trail are a magnet for hungry woodpeckers. When you reach the saddle, there's a stretch of easy ridge wandering through balsamroot to views of Tumwater Canyon.

SNOW MOUNTAIN RANCH, COWICHE CANYON CONSERVANCY

2648 Cowiche Mill Road, Cowiche

cowichecanyon.org

6.2 miles round-trip, 1250 feet elevation gain

⭐ *Bitterroot, yellow bells, phlox*

Snow Mountain Ranch is a spring delight to the senses; the aroma of sage fills the air, sunshine warms your skin, and the color blue paints the open sky. This former cattle

LEARN MORE

The Washington Native Plant Society leads guided native plant walks and hikes. *Best Wildflower Hikes Washington*, by Art Kruckeberg, Karen Sykes, and Craig Romano, highlights trails from sea to summit that are great for native blooms. Another great resource is *Washington Wildflower Hikes: 50 Destinations*, by Nathan Barnes and Jeremy Barnes.

ranch explodes with wildflowers, birdsong, and dragonflies in April and May. Pick up a map at the trailhead to guide yourself on the 13 miles of interconnected trails; a nice loop route is the Wildflower Trail to Bench Loop. Expect to see blooms of phlox, balsamroot, bitterroot, buttercups, daisies, yellow bells, lupine, and some of the other two hundred species of plants.

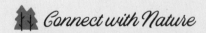 *Connect with Nature*

When you return from your hike, write and file a trip report for the Washington Trails Association (see Resources). Hikers around the state help each other get outdoors more by sharing reports. What flowers are in bloom? How are trail conditions? Your report can be short or long, basic or lyrical. Upload photos from your hike if possible.

NATURE NOTEBOOK

Location: _____ Date: _____

Co-naturers: _____

Spring blooms usher in a season of change and renewal. How has an experience in nature changed your life?

_____

_____

_____

_____

_____

_____

_____

Extra credit: Sketch your favorite flower.

FLY
A KITE

TAKE A MINDFUL STROLL ON THE BEACH TO NEW HEIGHTS

Flying a kite at Pacific Beach

WANT TO FEEL like a kid again? All you need is some wind and a kite.

People around the world have sent kites into the sky for centuries as signals or to learn about wind and weather. Benjamin Franklin hoisted a wired kite into a thunderstorm to prove his theory on the electricity in lightning. The Wright brothers observed kites to study aerodynamics before building their first airplane. These days kites are used for recreational fun, but flying them can still teach us a lot about the earth, wind, and sky—and about ourselves.

When it comes to choosing your first kite, think basic. Buy a single-line kite—try a classic two-stick diamond kite or a triangular delta kite, both crafted to fly in light wind (a steady breeze of 8 to 15 miles an hour). You'll also need kite line on a spool. Newer kites are lightweight, portable, colorful, fast, and have cool aerodynamics for performing tricks and stunts in the air. Once you master flying in a gentle breeze at your favorite beach, take your new hobby to new heights; toss your kite in your backpack and try it out at the subalpine summit of your next hike. Sharpen your skills on a dual-line sport or stunt kite capable of graceful aerobatics.

The best days for kite flying have a light breeze and no rain or lightning. Choose an open area away from kite-eating trees, powerlines, or other pesky obstructions. An uncrowded beach is a great choice, either on the ocean coast or on public beaches in Puget Sound, especially those with points. Large grassy fields and bluffs work, too. The more obstruction-free space, the more line you can let out and the higher you can fly your kite.

Now it's time to fly! Attach the line to the kite, and let out a few feet. Standing with your back to the wind, hold the kite in one hand while firmly grasping the spool in the other, then raise the kite high with the nose pointed up and loosen your grip. The kite should catch enough wind to go aloft. Slowly let out line from the spool and the kite will ascend. Reel it in a little if the wind slacks off. Expect the kite to sway a bit as it's tethered, but as you let more line out, it will steady itself. To reel your kite back in, simply do a hand-over-hand winding of your spool.

WHERE TO GO

The feeling of being one with the wind, the mindfulness required to keep your kite steady in the breeze, and the skills you build to help your kite twist, dance, and dive all add up to a new way to connect with nature and a fun hobby that gets you more time outside. For the best breezes, fly at these kiting hot spots around Puget Sound and on the Washington Coast.

GAS WORKS PARK
2101 N Northlake Way, Seattle
The flat top of "Kite Hill" is one of the best places to catch some wind in the city. Note to newbies: you won't find much free space to practice here on a clear, breezy Saturday, but you will enjoy the spectacle of colorful stunt kites in the air and have a chance to learn from the experts.

DISCOVERY PARK
3801 W Government Way, Seattle
Head to the wide, grassy parade grounds to catch the breeze coming off the water and across the bluff.

MAGNUSON PARK
7400 Sand Point Way NE, Seattle
Sand Point Head (also called "Kite Hill") is a grassy knoll overlooking Lake Washington with scenic views, consistent winds, and no trees to trap your kite.

MARINA BEACH PARK

470 Admiral Way, Edmonds

Just south of the Edmonds Marina, this beachfront park is the perfect place to watch the sun set over the Olympics with a kite spool in hand. When the tide is high, head to the large grassy knoll to fly your kites.

FORT CASEY STATE PARK

1280 Engle Road, Whidbey Island

DISCOVER PASS

The breeze beckons you to this local kiting mecca on the west shore of Whidbey Island, with panoramic views and lots of room—nearly 11,000 feet of shoreline plus an expansive green parade field.

LEARN MORE

Washington Kitefliers Association has inspired local kite enthusiasts since the 1970s. They host festivals, kite-building workshops, and kite-flying meetups. A free app called Weather Underground is a hit with kite flyers for its hyperlocal forecasts that give you real-time wind speed and direction. Attend a local kite festival to learn and mingle. The Westport Windriders Kite Festival happens each July, and the world-famous International Kite Festival in Long Beach takes place in August.

NATURE NOTEBOOK

Location: _____   Date: _____

Co-naturers: _____

Think back to your earliest memory of being in the outdoors. How old were you? What did you do? What memories can you recall?

_____

_____

_____

_____

_____

_____

_____

WHERE TO BUY A KITE

Specialty retail kite shops are hard to find these days, though a few still dot the Washington Coast, including Ocean Shores Kites in Ocean Shores and Hi Flyers Kites & Things in Pacific Beach. In the Seattle area, Prism Kites in Magnolia has a warehouse storefront that sells their own kites, which are lightweight, durable, and come in bright neon hues; chat with the owner for tips on how and where to launch your new kite. Sporting goods and toy stores may stock a few models of diamond or delta kites, but for a unique or stunt model, look online. Try thekiteshoppe.com, based in Vancouver, Washington, for a mammoth selection.

MARYMOOR PARK
6046 W Lake Sammamish Parkway NE, Redmond
Pick any one of the large grassy areas with nice exposure to southerly winds. The most popular kiting spot sits on the park's east side, a stone's throw from the rock climbing wall. You may be joined by colorful paragliders if the wind is truly spectacular.

CHAMBERS CREEK REGIONAL PARK
9850 64th Street W, University Place
This bluff-top park's central meadow was surely created with kite-flying in mind. The Pierce County Kitefliers Association hosts a weekend kite festival here each August with kite demonstrations, food trucks, and face painting.

LONG BEACH
Washington Coast
This beach town is the kite-flying capital of America; it is home to the World Kite Museum and the annual Washington State International Kite Festival. Colorful kites of all shapes and sizes dance in the sky here year-round.

GRIFFITHS-PRIDAY OCEAN STATE PARK
SR 109 N, Copalis Beach
DISCOVER PASS
Steady winds blast inland off the Pacific Ocean here, making it a prime spot for kite-flying on the North Beach area of Washington's coast. Just a few miles north is Pacific Beach State Park, another good stretch of sand for getting a kite in the air.

DIG FOR YOUR DINNER

FORAGE FOR BIVALVES ON SALISH SEA SHORES

Littleneck clams from Dosewallips on Hood Canal

THE COAST SALISH people have a saying: "When the tide goes out, the table is set." Standing in gumboots in the middle of a mudflat with an empty bucket and shovel in hand, you may wonder just what they meant. Littleneck clams are not sitting idle atop the sand waiting to be scooped up and tossed in a pot with a bit of garlic, chopped parsley, and a splash of wine. You have to dig for them.

Bivalves are picky about their home. Each species dwells in their favorite part of the intertidal zone, burrowed at different depths. Steamer clams like Manila are higher on the beach in mixed gravel and mud, burrowed just two to three inches below the surface and easily harvested at higher tide heights. Look for small holes in the ground, called "clam shows," then start scratching at the substrate with a small rake to unearth them. A bit lower on the beach, native littleneck clams show up with the Manilas. Oysters lie right on the beach attached to rocks or to each other. Down at the sandy low tide zone, burrowed deep, are the big guys that require a shovel. Butter and horse clams can dwell a foot or more below the surface; if you spot a clam show, dig a hole with your shovel alongside it, allowing the clam to fall into your hole without nicking its shell. Cockles live just inches deep in sandy areas of large estuaries and are easiest to locate with a long-handled rake, gently pulled through the sand.

To become a clam digger, obtain a shellfish license, some sort of bucket to hold your clams, and a hand shovel or hand rake (garden tools can do double duty here). The daily or annual shellfish/seaweed license is sold at marinas, sporting goods stores, or at wdfw.wa.gov. Tall rain boots keep your feet dry, and comfortable clothes are a must. Sturdy gardening gloves protect your hands from sharp substrate while you're digging or handling oysters. You'll need a pocket knife to collect oysters, as they must be shucked right on the beach so their shells are left behind. (They often have baby oysters attached to them—babies that will grow up to be adult oysters.) Load shucked oysters in a zip bag, and put them on ice immediately. A ruler or shellfish gauge will help you determine your keepers; clams must be at least 1.5 inches along the longest part of the shell, and oysters must be 2.5 inches (if they're small, put them back). Fill in the holes you dig, and mind the per-person limits posted at the beach, usually up to forty clams or no more than ten pounds, whichever is less.

Pollution has permanently closed beaches near the most urban parts of Puget Sound, yet there remain hundreds of miles of public beaches where you can safely collect clams and oysters. Some are open year-round, others have seasons to maintain healthy shellfish populations. Clamming beaches are routinely tested for marine toxins by the state Department of Health and will close if levels are concerning. A minus tide of −0.5 and lower is the most ideal for collecting clams and oysters. Start clamming an hour before low tide.

Eating your clams with good company is the delicious reward of all that digging. Keep your harvest in some seawater on ice until you get to a stove or campfire for your own clambake. Soak clams in cold saltwater for a few hours to purge the sand, then scrub the outsides of your catch under running water and they're ready to steam open. Garlic, wine, and butter are the secret to a delicious pot of steamed Manila or littleneck clams. Cockles are wonderful in chowder. Meaty butter and horse clams make the best fried clam fritters. Any foraged clams will shine in a seafood chowder and bouillabaisse, and you can also put them on a BBQ grill until they pop open, then top with a dab of melted butter and squeeze of lemon. Sauté oysters in butter with a touch of garlic and be amazed.

WHERE TO GO

Scenic clamming beaches dot the Salish Sea coastline from Birch Bay to Penrose Point. Visit doh.wa.gov/shellfishsafety (or call the Shellfish Safety Hotline at 800-562-5632) for an interactive map and the latest detailed information on beach locations open to clamming, harvest seasons, and marine toxin safety. Here are some clamming hot spots for first-timers.

WHIDBEY ISLAND

This long, sinewy island in Puget Sound boasts sheltered coves between its rocky bluffs and windswept spits, and several good clamming beaches on the island are open for harvesting in spring. On the island's south end, Double Bluff County Park on Useless Bay

LEARN MORE

Pacific Feast: A Cook's Guide to West Coast Foraging and Cuisine, by Jennifer Hahn, will inspire and guide you through clam digging and teach you how to whip up some forager's favorites like bouillabaisse with mussels and clams. Learn to harvest wild shellfish on a guided field trip with Human Nature Hunting.

is just 8 miles from the Clinton ferry dock, making it one of the easiest clamming day trips from the Seattle area. From the parking area, head to the right along the water to get some solitude and find some butter clams and native littlenecks.

The tidelands of Twin Lagoons on the cove's west end are home to Manila and native littleneck clams, butter clams, cockles, and even horse clams, reachable in the lowest

NATURE NOTEBOOK

Location: _____   Date: _____

Co-naturers: _____

How does nature fit in to your life? List three ways that your beach foraging trip for food you harvested, prepared, and ate yourself made you feel more connected to the natural world.

_____

_____

_____

_____

tides. This is also an excellent beach for harvesting Penn Cove mussels. Long Point, east of Penn Cove, is also good for mussels, cockles, and butter clams. For a camping trip, try Fort Ebey State Park, where fifty wooded campsites on a bluff are just a short hike up a beach full of clams at minus tide; to the east are beds of oysters and clams at West Penn Cove beach.

HOOD CANAL

A glacially carved fjord that forms the western lobe of Puget Sound, Hood Canal is famed for productive tidelands. The crown jewel for bivalve seekers is Dosewallips State Park—a shallow, pristine estuary that transforms into a giant clam bed at low tide, barely concealing a feast of littlenecks, Manilas, gapers, butter clams, oysters, and cockles. Pitch a tent at one of the park's 120 campsites, or rent a rustic cabin or platform tent. On the canal's south end sits Potlatch State Park, where a bounty of bivalves is just steps from a wooded campground with 70 sites. The mile of tidelands is home to Manila, butter, and varnish clams, and a plethora of oysters. The park is named in honor of the potlatch, a gift-giving ceremony the Skokomish Indian Tribe celebrated here.

HARVEST SEAWEED

Assemble a salad from an aquatic veggie garden, where lime green sea lettuce sprouts from rock pools and shadowy fronds of eelgrass tangle in the current. All Pacific Northwest seaweeds growing near shore are edible, and they also happen to be chock-full of vitamins and minerals. Use them in your everyday cooking—from purple laver for nori rolls to dried strips of bull kelp for a salty snack.

Harvest seaweed at low tide from where it's growing, attached to a rock or the ocean floor in the tide zone, or strands of bull kelp from a kayak. You can also find kelp washed up on the beach right after a big storm; test its freshness by bending it to see if it wilts (not fresh) or snaps (fresh!). Don't rip seaweed out of the sand; use scissors to clip it, leaving plenty behind so it can regenerate. Seaweed can be eaten raw when it's supple and sweet, pickled (bull kelp is wonderful sliced crosswise and made into dill pickles), or dried and stored.

Don't harvest your seaweed just anywhere—avoid beaches near sewage or industrial outflows that may be polluted, including all beaches on the east side of Puget Sound from Everett south to Tacoma. State park beaches are closed to seaweed foraging except for a monthlong springtime window at Fort Worden, Fort Flagler, and Fort Ebey State Parks. Great beaches for seaweed gathering include Iceberg Point on Lopez Island, Libbey Beach on Whidbey Island, and Freshwater Bay west of Port Angeles. Obtain a shellfish/seaweed license from wdfw.wa.gov, and you may harvest ten pounds per day.

SPRING

WATCH WILDLIFE

CLOSE ENCOUNTERS OF THE CRITTER KIND

Mountain goats in the Enchantment Lakes Basin

photo by Bruce McGlenn

IT'S A THRILL to encounter an animal in its natural, wild habitat. If exotic wildlife encounters are on your bucket list, how about watching elk graze in a hidden green valley or spotting a mama black bear and her cub noshing on trailside huckleberries in the Cascades? In Washington we share the mountains and forests with some pretty phenomenal wild creatures, and seeing them in the wild feels like a once-in-a-lifetime experience.

Spring is a season of migration, mating, and mothering, and the prime season to observe many species of animals, big and small, in their natural habitats as they wake from hibernation, find food, and raise their young. To increase your chances of spotting an animal, go when they're most active (for example, dawn or dusk). Know which animals to expect in the habitat you're in. Walk quietly and blend in so wildlife don't run off when they see, hear, or smell you. Wear neutral-colored clothing, eschew scented products, and speak in soft voices or not at all. Be patient—a sighting is not guaranteed, and sometimes you need to sit still in the same place for a long time until a nearby animal becomes active.

You may see some wildlife on any nature outing, but to spot a particular species that's not commonly encountered at random, choose the destination they're known to be in, in the right season, at the right time of day. Then, be thrilled.

WILDLIFE TO WATCH

BIGHORN SHEEP

On the lower eastern slopes of the Cascades, look for these beautiful mountain sheep on rocky terrain. For most of the year, the adult rams gather in herds, fighting out their dominance hierarchy by sparring and charging one another with their large curved horns. The ewes have much smaller spiked horns.

Where to see them. Look for herds or small groups of sheep on the Whistler Canyon trail in the Okanogan Highlands, Umtanum Ridge and Canyon, and Selah Butte.

BLACK BEARS

They usually hear or smell you before you spot them, so surprise close encounters are fortunately rare. Instead, keep an eye out for fresh bear scat (this tells you one is nearby), then keep your eyes peeled for movement, especially in open meadows or berry patches. Bears inhabit much of our wildlands from coastal beaches up to high alpine slopes. Nearly all bears in Washington are black bears; grizzlies are found only in the North Cascades up by the border with Canada.

Where to see them. According to hikers, you're most likely to see a bear in Olympic National Park on the Enchanted Valley trail (east fork of the Quinault River).

MOUNTAIN GOATS

These high-country icons are adapted to steep, craggy terrain, evading predators while taking in the view. Look for a white fluffy blob perched on a narrow rock ledge or

LEARN MORE

The Field Guide to the Cascades and Olympics, by Stephen Whitney and Rob Sandelin, is a handy, full-color guide to animals and plants in our region. Find wildlife viewing tips and locations on the Washington Department of Fish & Wildlife website (see Resources).

nearly sheer cliff face high in the Cascades. If you find yourself too close to one, back off—males can occasionally be aggressive (though more so in autumn when they're mating). Mountain goats are native to the Cascades and were introduced to the Olympics a century ago. Olympic National Park has recently relocated hundreds of the goats by helicopter to their volcanic native stomping grounds, however, so you won't see them at former haunts like Hurricane Ridge or Mount Ellinor.

Where to see them. Chances are high you'll see goats at Lake Ingalls in the Teanaway, the Boundary Trail at Mount St. Helens, the Enchantments near Leavenworth, and even near the top of Mount Si in the Issaquah Alps.

ELK

Two subspecies of elk make their home in Washington: Roosevelt elk on the Olympic Peninsula and Rocky Mountain elk east of the Cascade crest. We owe elk a great deal— Teddy Roosevelt protected what is now

Seeing an elk in the wild gets your heart thumping.

NATURE NOTEBOOK

Location: _____   Date: _____

Co-naturers: _____

Describe an encounter you've had with a wild animal in its natural habitat.

_____

_____

_____

_____

_____

_____

_____

_____

_____

_____

_____

_____

_____

Olympic National Park for Roosevelt elk, which were named for him. In spring and summer you'll see solitary elk or loose bachelor herds. Fall is the elk rut, where males show off their gorgeous large antlers and bugling skills, filling the valleys with music to compete for a harem.

Where to see them. Roosevelt elk are regularly spotted, heard, and even smelled around the Hoh and Quinault River valleys. Try the Hall of Mosses trail near the Hoh ranger station and the Kestner Homestead trail by Lake Quinault. Rocky Mountain Elk can be spotted at Oak Creek Wildlife Area and Turnbull National Wildlife Refuge.

WILD IN THE CITY

Find wildlife at an urban park near you. Dragonflies come in amazingly bright hues with big eyes and cool markings. Their four wings can propel them in any direction as well as hover. Spot one of the state's eighty species on a sunny day in late spring or

TIPS FOR SAFE AND RESPECTFUL ENCOUNTERS

When it comes to being near wildlife, follow these guidelines for your safety and theirs.

1. **Keep your distance.** If you spot an animal, stop or retreat; don't move toward them or follow them. Use a blind if there is one (a large boulder, your car) and use binoculars to get a closer look.

2. **Don't feed wild animals.** Our human food is unhealthy for them, and they have skills to find their own food. Critters used to humans feeding them may lose their fear of us, becoming habituated and perhaps aggressive. This may result in them ultimately being put down.

3. **Don't bring your dog.** If your goal is to see wildlife, leave dogs at home.

4. **Avoid eye contact and back away slowly.** If you have a surprise encounter with a black bear and it shows signs of aggression (throwing its head around, vocalizing, pawing at the ground), avoid direct eye contact. Don't turn your back on the bear; instead back away slowly and use a calm voice to tell the bear you're leaving. Don't scream, run, or throw things at the bear.

 Connect with Nature

Become a volunteer with Conservation Northwest (see Resources), which leads the Citizen Wildlife Monitoring Project, one of the largest citizen-science wildlife monitoring efforts of its kind in North America. Volunteers document wildlife using remote cameras where state and federal agencies don't have the resources to go, and track wildlife in the I-90 corridor.

photo by Alexandra MacKenzie

An eight-spotted skimmer at Union Bay Natural Area

summer in a pond or marsh, like the reconstructed wetlands at Seattle's Magnuson Park or Tacoma's Snake Lake. Pearrygin Lake just outside Winthrop is a dragonfly bonanza on sunny days.

Beavers in the city? Yep—biologists say there are dozens of active beaver colonies in Seattle and other urban areas, and the large furry rodents are most active at dawn and early morning. Look for them at Seattle's Meadowbrook Pond or Golden Gardens, McClane Creek Pond in Olympia's Capital State Forest, or the Hazel Wolf Wetlands in Sammamish.

Salamanders are amphibians and need water to survive. Washington has twenty-five species of salamanders and frogs. The large Northwest salamander inhabits our urban ponds surrounded by moist forest. It's dark brown and has deep vertical grooves on the sides of its body, which is shaped like a lizard but has skin like a frog. They can be spotted at Camp Long's "Pollywog Pond" in West Seattle.

CREATE A HAVEN FOR WILDLIFE

INVITE NATURE INTO YOUR YARD AND INTO YOUR LIFE

Painted lady
butterfly in
the garden

CLOSE ENCOUNTERS WITH nature enrich our lives in many ways, from boosting our curiosity to reducing stress. Our days are too busy to carve out time for a quick walk through the park, yet our hectic lives leave us needing those experiences even more. Why not entice local wildlife to come your way? In a few simple steps, welcome wildlife into your yard by creating a refuge for songbirds, butterflies, and other native critters.

A typical yard has a well-kept lawn, sheared shrubs, and manicured flowerbeds that are of little use to native wildlife. It likely requires watering, fertilizer, perhaps some pesticides, and time to maintain. When you convert some or all of your yard to a wildlife-friendly habitat, you'll swap hours of weeding and watering for joyful connections to nature. And when you landscape with nature in mind, even if it's just a small plot or container garden, you help counter the cumulative loss of wild places to urban development.

LEARN MORE

Audubon's Nature Shops (various locations throughout the state) sell bird feeders, wildlife guide-books, bird baths, nest boxes, and more. Washington Native Plant Society hosts plant sales and gardening classes. The awesome *Landscaping for Wildlife in the Pacific Northwest*, by Russell Link, dives deep into the wildlife ben-efits of native plants and offers various how-to instructions, such as creating a dragonfly pond in your yard and building a bat house.

You might start with a modest plot or raised bed in your front yard that you plant with a native ground cover, some laven-der or sunflowers, and a few tall flowering shrubs such as oceanspray or serviceberry that are favored by pollinators like native bees and butterflies. These horizontal lay-ers of plant foliage will give songbirds and other creatures a safe refuge from predators as they forage for food and raise their young. Maintaining your garden without pesti-cides will help keep wildlife healthy. If you have only a small patio or balcony, plant a container with a native rhododendron or red-flowering currant that provides nectar for passing hummingbirds.

SIMPLE STEPS TO CREATE A SMALL WILDLIFE SANCTUARY IN YOUR YARD

Pick a size and location. Consider a corner of your front yard or a wide border along a fence. Areas near windows, patios, and porches are the best wildlife viewing areas. Sketch a rough design plan for your space on paper and update as you go.

Remove existing grass. Smother it using an easy sheet mulching method. Cover the grass with overlapping pieces of cardboard. Wet the area down with a hose, then top it with five inches of compost and mulch. Wait a month or two, and you're ready for plant-ing. The cardboard will decompose along with the dead grass and roots and get recy-cled back into the soil by garden-friendly earthworms.

Choose plants suited for conditions of your plot. Opt for shade-tolerant plants for shady areas, plants that thrive in moist soil for wet areas, and erosion-control plants for steep slopes.

NATURE NOTEBOOK

Location: _____   Date: _____

Co-naturers: _____

Record wildlife species over time in your wildlife haven, and share observations about how their presence and behavior changes through the seasons.

_____

_____

_____

Select plants for wildlife, from food to shelter. Hummingbirds, bees, and butterflies need nectar; finches like seeds; and robins and waxwings eat berries. Wildlife species have preferred layers of vegetation, so include some groundcover plants and native wildflowers, low shrubs, high shrubs, and if you have a larger space, a tree for the canopy. Vertical and horizontal connectivity allows wildlife to travel up and down and in and out through the different layers of vegetation.

Buy your plants. Check local nurseries for natives, and search out spring native plant sales. Your county's conservation district is a good resource.

Plant your plants. Space them with room to grow. Dig a hole twice as wide and deep as the plant's root ball, filling around it with organic soil. Water new plantings generously until autumn rains start.

Don't kill things. Pesticide-free yards benefit bees, birds, and even salmon, as surface water drains to streams. Most insects (98 percent!) are beneficial to a healthy ecosystem, and birds and bats depend on bugs for food. If your plants and soil are healthy, they'll be more resistant to pests. Remove large pests like snails by hand. Prune out tent caterpillar infestations. Wash aphids off plants with the spray of a hose. Set out a shallow dish of beer to drown slugs.

Don't clean up. A clean and tidy garden doesn't support much life. Leave leaf litter as organic mulch, and seed pods to feed sparrows and finches. Dead wood and snag

---

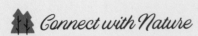 *Connect with Nature*

Make your wildlife haven official as a Certified Wildlife Habitat—check out the National Wildlife Federation website (see Resources) for tips on how to get started.

NATIVE PLANT LIST

Entice pollinators and hungry wildlife with these ten Pacific Northwest native plants that evolved alongside native wildlife to provide shelter and food. Once established in your garden, they'll seldom need to be watered, and are naturally resistant to most pests.

Kinnikinnick: groundcover, prefers sun. Wildlife benefit: nectar and pollen, larval host for butterflies/moths.

Fireweed: wildflower, prefers sun. Wildlife benefit: nectar and pollen, attracts hummingbirds.

Salal: low shrub, grows anywhere. Wildlife benefit: nectar and pollen, fruit, larval host for butterflies.

Cascade Oregon grape: low shrub, prefers shade. Wildlife benefit: nectar and pollen, fruit.

Pacific rhododendron: tall shrub, prefers part shade. Wildlife benefit: nectar and pollen, larval host for butterflies/moths.

Serviceberry: tall shrub, prefers sun. Wildlife benefit: nectar and pollen, fruit, larval host for butterflies/moths.

Red-flowering currant: tall shrub, prefers dry soil. Wildlife benefit: nectar and pollen, fruit, attracts hummingbirds.

Indian plum: tall shrub, prefers shade. Wildlife benefit: nectar and pollen, fruit.

Vine maple: tree, prefers moist soil. Wildlife benefit: nectar and pollen, seeds.

Douglas-fir: tree, prefers sun. Wildlife benefit: seeds, nesting site, larval host for butterflies/moths.

---

trees provide food and shelter for birds and critters.

Birds love fresh water. Add a water feature to your wildlife haven, like a shallow bird bath with gently sloped sides.

Keep cats inside. Especially at dawn and dusk, and during the spring/summer breeding season.

Add bird feeders. Anna's Hummingbirds overwinter here and appreciate sugar water. Flickers and other woodpeckers, Bushtits, and chickadees love suet cakes, and black-oil sunflower seeds are a hit with finches.

Install a nest box. Find DIY plans for building species-specific boxes at NestWatch (nestwatch.org), or buy them locally. Nest boxes should be made of real wood (western red cedar is a top choice) and free of paint or varnish. Watch from your window as a brood of baby wrens or chickadees hatches and then fledges. Consider installing a leafcutter or mason bee box if you have a veggie garden—these mellow bees are hardworking pollinators. Masons knock off work in May or June, so for late summer veggies it's the unsung leafcutter bee that you want to encourage.

CYCLE AROUND AN ISLAND

TWO-WHEELED ROAD TRIPS IN THE MIDDLE OF THE SALISH SEA

Cruiser bike on a Washington beach

PATCHWORKED WITH small farms, grass prairie, green forest, and rugged shoreline, islands of the Salish Sea are Washington's cherished jewels. An island escape may be a ferry ride away, then you're driving off the boat and into a landscape where the pace is slower and the pasture is greener. But next time don't drive. Leave your car on the mainland, and take your bike.

The best way to experience a Northwest island is from the saddle of a bicycle in spring, pedaling the country roads over gentle hills, around lavender fields and llama farms, and under the shade of madrona trees. There's always a lookout up around the corner to spot passing whales, or a beach down the way to take a stroll. Some of the islands, like Lopez, are flat (and in the off-season, lightly visited), seemingly tailor-made for a starter cycling tour. Others, like Orcas, are more hilly, curvy, and challenging. Ride for a day or make it a weekend—most islands have campgrounds so you can haul some gear and sleep under the stars (make reservations, they fill fast!). All of them have inns and seaside eateries for a more plushy overnight getaway.

Island cycling is primarily on paved roads, so bring your commuter road bike or a touring bike, made of durable steel for longer road trips and heavier loads (like camping gear), and with wider tires that can handle the occasional dirt path. A touring bike is constructed to support front and rear racks to hold up to four panniers for stowing your gear. Fit your bike at home (adjust saddle height, handlebars) but bring along a basic bike tool kit for maintenance and repairs. Make sure you have a mounted bike pump with valves that fit your bike, a tire jack or levers, an extra tube, and patch kit. Learn to repair or change an innertube before you head out on your first cycling trip, and brush up on cycling hand signals and rules of the road. Front and back lights help with visibility in traffic, as does a brightly colored shirt or jacket. It goes without saying: a helmet is a must.

WHERE TO GO

If this is your first cycling road trip, choose an island with flat terrain good for easy pedaling—and pace yourself. Plan your route in advance using a paper map or an app like Google Maps that lets you plot your route and expected pitstops; you might include a bike shop to chat with a local about good routes, a grocery store for picnic supplies, and a beach for eating lunch and exploring a tide pool. Pack small bills of cash for spontaneous stops at honor-system farmstands.

LOPEZ ISLAND

The flattest of the larger San Juan Islands, Lopez consists of quiet country roads that crisscross family farms and peaceful pastures. Tiny Lopez Village is the only town, just a few short streets with cafes and a grocery store. Berry farms, public beaches, and restaurants are scattered throughout the island. Rent bikes and pick up a cycling map that details the recommended 30-mile loop. Agate Beach is a perfect spot for a picnic lunch before you explore tide pools at Shark Reef Sanctuary.

Camping. You'll find both forested and waterfront campsites at Spencer Spit State Park (parks.state.wa.us)—reservations are essential. Odlin County Park (sanjuanco.com), only 1 mile south of the ferry terminal, has waterfront campsites.

GUEMES ISLAND

Haven't heard of Guemes Island? Most travelers ferry-bound for the San Juans haven't, and that's precisely why this smaller, quieter island is perfect for cyclists who like the road (mostly) to themselves. Load your bike onto the Guemes Island Ferry (operated by Skagit County) in Anacortes for a five-minute sail. Just off the ferry dock, swing by the Guemes Island General Store for supplies—it's your only opportunity. The main road that follows the island's perimeter totals about 10 miles. On the island's east end, park your bike and hike up the 1-mile trail to the top of Guemes Mountain for incredible views of nearby islands, ocean straits, the Skagit River delta, and jagged peaks of the North Cascades.

LEARN MORE

Get cycling routes and maps, cycling safety tips, and learn bicycle laws in Washington at wsdot.wa.gov. *Cycling the Pacific Coast* by Bill Thorness as well as his *Bicycling Puget Sound* are indispensable tools for planning cycling road trips. The Cascade Bicycle Club, which advocates on behalf of cycling rights and routes, teaches cycling safety and bike maintenance, and hosts beginner cycling lessons.

NATURE NOTEBOOK

Location: _____   Date: _____

Co-naturers: _____

Ancient peoples built cultural rituals around the change of seasons. Our modern indoor lives soften our senses of change in nature, but with a little practice you'll find yourself tuning in. Describe five things you noticed on your ride that are signs of spring.

_____

_____

_____

_____

_____

_____

_____

CYCLING TRIP CHECKLIST

Here's a list of things you don't want to forget on a cycling road trip.

- ☐ Good-fitting bike helmet
- ☐ Bike lock
- ☐ Mounted tire pump
- ☐ Tire jack or levers
- ☐ Patch kit and spare tube
- ☐ Emergency kit (bike tools, first aid)
- ☐ Bike lights (front, back) with extra batteries
- ☐ Bike storage bags (panniers)
- ☐ Mounted water bottle
- ☐ Cycling clothes (no cotton) and gloves
- ☐ Sunglasses or goggles
- ☐ Raingear
- ☐ Food and energy snacks
- ☐ Map, route, and compass

VASHON ISLAND

You'll break a sweat cycling on hilly Vashon Island, a stone's throw southwest of Seattle and north of Tacoma and reachable from both by ferry. Start at the island's northern ferry dock from West Seattle and start pedaling hard—the ride begins with a slog up the Vashon Island Highway into town. On Saturdays, make your first stop the Vashon Farmers Market for yummy picnic bites. The Vashon Island Loop is a 32-mile ride around the island's perimeter (add 10 miles to that if you loop in a side trip around Maury Island), and climbs about 3800 feet in total elevation. Picnic at Point Robinson on the eastern tip of Maury, or at Lisabuela Park beach on Colvos Passage. For less traffic, create your own route using country roads—bring cash and empty panniers to fill from the abundant roadside farmstands.

RAFT DOWN A RIVER

NATURE, WITH A SIDE OF ADRENALINE

Rafting on the Sauk River

EVERY RIVER HAS a story to tell. Its currents carry reflections of the fish and wildlife that depend on it, the people who made passage through it, the orchards and fields that drink from it, and the forces of nature that shaped it. When you're running a river—dipping and splashing your paddle as you pull a raft through the current, punching through its rowdy rapids, and gliding into its calm eddies—you become part of its ever-changing story.

Rivers transform dramatically through the seasons. Low water in summer can't be rafted, but water levels rise after autumn rain. In the Cascades and Olympics, many rivers run full and fast during the spring snowmelt, creating the rapids that draw whitewater lovers. On a year with heavy snowpack and mild spring temps, the melt is nice and slow, extending the whitewater rafting season for months, sometimes into August. Occasionally, when spring temps run high, the snow melts too quickly, swelling rivers to highwater; if this creates dangerous conditions for river rafting, trips are rescheduled.

You experience a river differently in a boat than from its shore. Rafting on swift water requires you to pay attention to flow, velocity, rapids, holes, boulders, large woody debris, and other obstacles. It gives you the opportunity to observe and imagine how rivers flow within the landscape and over time, powerfully altering it. Witness wildlife, like river otters, Osprey, mergansers, and American Dippers, up close.

River runners learn to read the river in front of them as they go. What's below the surface up ahead? How to best navigate the raft around that boulder or hole? Is it possible to assess the current by how it moves around logs? Before running a big rapid, a rafting guide will often stop the boat to scout the best route from shore—ask if you can join them.

Not all rafting trips in Washington are on whitewater. Rivers and rapids are rated on a scale by "class" that relays how technical the water is—from Class I (mostly smooth with some small waves) to Class V (turbulent water and gushing rapids that require complex maneuvers). There is a Class VI, so extreme it's unrunnable by raft. The class of a river or rapid usually changes with the flow.

RIVERS TO RUN

NOOKSACK RIVER, NORTH CASCADES WEST
Class III+, 6 miles, May–August
Churning through steep-walled canyons, the first few miles of the upper gorge of the Nooksack are pure adrenaline—intense and relentless Class III+ rapids that will knock your neoprene socks off. Then, this river of cold glacial water off Shuksan and Baker spills into a serene valley of mossy old-growth woods nestled in between glistening peaks.

UPPER SKAGIT RIVER, NORTH CASCADES WEST
Class II/III, 9 miles, March–September
After putting in at Goodell Creek, you'll run the Upper Skagit as it pushes through a lush old-growth valley flanked by granite peaks

LEARN MORE

Check river conditions and water levels at the Northwest River Forecast Center (see Resources).

of North Cascades National Park. The run's thrilling highlight is Dolly Parton Rapids, where the river churns through two massive boulders.

WENATCHEE RIVER, CENTRAL CASCADES EAST

Class II/III, 15 miles, April–July

It's the most popular rafting river in the state for its succession of thrilling whitewater through shelves of sandstone with names like Bad Boy Rapids, Rock and Roll, Drunkard's Drop, and Grannie's Panties—all dependent on the pace of Cascade snowmelt. The put-in is in Leavenworth, the take-out is Huck's Landing in Cashmere. When you have some experience under your PFD, a wilder trip on the Wenatchee starts higher and tumbles along some Class V rapids through Tumwater Canyon.

NATURE NOTEBOOK

Location: _____   Date: _____

Co-naturers: _____

Is this your first time traversing a wild, scenic river from a raft? Describe what you saw and experienced from inside the river that is unique and distinctly different from observing it from the shore.

_____

_____

_____

_____

_____

_____

_____

_____

_____

_____

_____

WHAT TO EXPECT ON A GUIDED RAFTING TRIP

Ready to run a river? You won't need prior rafting experience, but you should know how to swim. Pick a local, reputable rafting outfitter who runs a river on the mellow side for first-timers with a few Class III whitewater rapids for thrills. Guided rafting is well regulated in Washington, with many safety protocols, and guides must put in fifty hours of whitewater training. Your outfitter will provide wetsuits and neoprene booties (you will get wet, and that glacial water is cold!), personal flotation devices (PFDs), and helmets, and likely shuttle you from a meet spot to the launch site.

Expect a safety talk and paddling tutorial before you hit the river, including what to do if you get tipped out into the water and how to avoid hypothermia.

SKYKOMISH RIVER, CENTRAL CASCADES EAST

Class III, 5 miles, May–August

Run the Sky's spinning and rolling rapids as you tumble along a valley cut through snow-capped granite peaks. Or, when you're up for it and don't mind the chance your raft will flip, why not give the more adventurous run on the Main Skykomish (9 miles) a shot? It includes the notorious Class V Boulder Drop.

WHITE SALMON RIVER, SOUTH CASCADES

Class III/IV, 8 miles, April–September

Fed by glaciers atop Mount Adams, the azure water of the White Salmon rushes toward the Columbia River, slipping through narrow basalt rock canyons and plummeting over Husum Falls, known as one of the world's tallest waterfalls you can run a raft over. This run is as stunning as it is technical and challenging.

WORK ON A FARM

GO COUNTRY ON A HAYCATION

Goats on a Skagit Valley farm

ARE YOU A LOCAVORE? That's someone who eats locally—foods that are organically and sustainably grown and produced close to home, from seed to plate. When you choose to eat locally, you're not only deepening your own roots in the soil that feeds you; you're investing in a more sustainable economy. Connect with the food on your plate and get a taste of country life on a getaway to a real working farm.

During a typical farm stay, expect to help with hands-on chores and commune with barn animals. Spend the night in on-site accommodations that range from rustic yurts to bed-and-breakfast rooms. As a guest on the farm, there's a good chance you can cook up your own farm-fresh meal, with eggs you gathered in the chicken coop and produce you picked yourself. Depending on the farm, chores might range from harvesting veggies to leading a herd of llamas to pasture.

Smell earth in the air (probably manure, too), cake your boots with mud, and maybe even get some hay stuck in your hair—if you want to. There's no pressure; farm-stay hosts are eager to share their knowledge with curious guests, and chores are both educational and optional. No one will mind if you skip feeding scraps to the pigs to steal an afternoon nap atop a bale of hay.

WHERE TO GO

For small-scale farmers, welcoming visitors and sharing their knowledge of rotational grazing or goat-milking techniques is not only fun, it provides some extra cash.

NETTLES FARM

4300 Matia View Drive, Lummi Island
nettlesfarm.com, (360) 758-7616
The farm is owned by Riley Stark, a connoisseur of heirloom-bred chickens that produce beautifully hued eggs and flavorful meat, including his small flocks of red, white, and blue Poulet de Bresse chickens. Your farm stay at Nettles must include a chat with Stark on how he forages the island's woods with his truffle hound and fishes for salmon off the island's beaches using an ancient reef net technique. There are two farmhouse rooms that sleep up to four and have fully equipped gourmet kitchens for you to cook your own locavore dinner.

Farm chores. Feed the goats and chickens, and gather eggs in the morning. During harvest times you can pick berries, pears and other tree fruits, veggies and herbs, and even help forage for wild edibles. In summer months the farm offers a hen butchering class, de-feathering and all.

CHELAN VALLEY FARMS

2393 Green Avenue, Manson
chelanvalleyfarms.com, (509) 435-1815
Set in rolling hills above Lake Chelan on the shores of Roses Lake, your agritourism experience here starts with a friendly greeting from a trio of farm dogs and a tour of the orchards, vineyard, and fields of flowers. This working farm runs a flower CSA (community-supported agriculture) for residents of the Chelan Valley, and you'll enjoy meandering through colorful fields of daffodils in early spring, followed by dahlias, sunflowers, and more. The estate vineyard supplies grapes for the farm's newly launched wine brand. Farmers Chad and Jeana built the guest digs—a gleaming white modern farmhouse that sleeps four—in 2019 to share their passion for local agriculture and viticulture with travelers. You'll find everything you need to relax and unwind: a full kitchen with farm-fresh eggs, fireplace, and wide-open views to watch the sun set behind the snow-capped Cascades. If you can only come for a

🌲 Connect with Nature

Be a locavore for a whole day! This takes some planning, so sit down and craft your recipes for each meal (include beverages!) and figure out how to source all the ingredients within 150 miles of your home. Notice the effort that goes into it, and also the number of local farmers and producers you are supporting with just one day of eating 100 percent local.

NATURE NOTEBOOK

Location: _____   Date: _____

Co-naturers: _____

Sustainable farming focuses on land and water practices that promote conservation and feed the community. There's another key ethical element, though: giving animals a good life—and that starts with empathy. If you were a farm animal, which would you be and why?

_____

_____

_____

_____

_____

_____

_____

_____

_____

_____

_____

day visit, time it for one of their fun spring events, like building bird houses or DIY bouquet making.

Farm chores. Pet the goats and gather eggs from the chickens. Guests can pick flowers in summer, and apples and pumpkins later in the year.

PACA PRIDE GUEST RANCH

28311 Mountain Loop Highway, Granite Falls
pacaprideguestranch.com, (360) 691-3395

This 17-acre homestead sits in the foothills off the Mountain Loop Highway. A herd of quirky Huacaya alpacas dots the hillside pasture, with fir forest framing their view of Mount Pilchuck—nice work if you can get it! The "work" of these long-necked, doe-eyed beauties is to grow dense fleece coats all year long in preparation for shearing. This popular event is open to the public in late June and yields highly coveted hypo-allergenic fiber in rich tones like chocolate, chestnut, and ivory, which is handspun into limited-edition Pendleton wool blankets, hats, and socks (sold on-site at the ranch store). Your stay includes a guided tour of the alpaca ranch and the principles of permaculture, a sustainable agriculture model that centers on working with nature rather than against it; their rotational grazing system reduces impact on the meadows, and microgreens sustain the alpaca herd all winter long. Sleep in one of the cozy and furnished yurts; heated showers are a short stroll away.

Farm chores. Alpacas are gentle animals, and you can hand-feed them along with

A curious sheep at pasture

LEARN MORE

Check out Farm Stay USA, a non-profit project that connects travelers with the local farms and ranches that love to host them.

offering them chin scratches and soft hugs. Help move the herd from one meadow to another. Guests can also collect eggs from the ranch's free-range chickens.

SUMMER

- ○ Explore a Tide Pool
- ○ Sail a Boat
- ○ Backpack Overnight
- ○ Watch Whales
- ○ Hike in the High Country
- ○ Go Sea Kayaking
- ○ Catch a Trout
- ○ Splash in a Mountain Lake
- ○ Pitch a Tent
- ○ Sleep in a Fire Lookout
- ○ Hike to a Glacier
- ○ Go Stargazing
- ○ Drop a Crab Pot

What's your cue that summer has arrived? One day it's spring, and the next, you've got windows rolled down and sleeves rolled up. Some declare the official start of summer with the first lick of an ice cream cone or nap in a hammock. Mid-day tides get low then lower still, while night skies clear to reveal an ocean of stars. Hikers cheer for the annual openings of the North Cascades Highway and Chinook Pass, both harbingers of summer adventures to wildflower meadows. Whatever your summer prompt is, you know it's time to get outside.

Live in the sunshine, swim the sea, drink the wild air.
—Ralph Waldo Emerson, "Merlin's Song"

Some years, Western Washington holds on to cool, cloudy weather until early July, which can be frustrating for those on the wet side of the state; the season can feel too short at just eight weeks or so. Summer starts in May and June where the sun reliably shines east of the Cascades and in the Columbia River Gorge. Come August, snow has melted in the high country, and blooming wildflowers carpet alpine meadows of nearly every peak in the Cascades and Olympics, if only for a short while. This is the month for sub-alpine hikes and shooting stars.

Carefree summer days are the best, especially when they draw you outside on a lark. Be ready for safe adventuring on a whim by keeping gear like your bike helmet or life jacket handy right by the door. Purchase fresh sunblock at the start of each summer. Cool Northwest mornings often give way to full sun on summer afternoons, so pack sunscreen and shades on all your outings.

EXPLORE A TIDE POOL

LIFE ABOUNDS BETWEEN THE TIDES

Purple sea star at Seahurst Park

THERE ARE CERTAINTIES in nature, like a full moon every 29.5 days, or the bloom of your rhododendron each spring. Another is the rhythm of the sea. Twice a day, every day, the ocean tide comes in (high tide), and twice a day the tide goes out (low tide). When the low tide is really low, called a minus tide, fascinating underwater micro-cosms are revealed in small saltwater pools in the alcoves and crevices of rocks and sand.

"Tidepooling" is when you head out to a beach during a low tide and poke around the rocks, nooks, and crannies to spot exposed aquatic life. Look for vibrant sea stars, chitons attached to a patch of rock, tickling sea anem-ones poking out of a pool, scurrying shore crabs, rough barnacles, patterned sea slugs, purple urchins on the substrate among the holdfasts of bull kelp, moon snails, jellyfish, colorful sea cucumbers, limpets, and more.

The best tidepooling in Puget Sound and along the Washington Coast is in summer, usually during the months of May, June, and July when we periodically get low minus tides at midday. A minus tide is any tide below zero, with zero defined as the local mean lower low tide. The lower the tide, the more intertidal habitat is revealed. This pat-tern continues for several days and returns every few weeks during summer months. Find upcoming minus tide times for your favorite beach at tides.net or on a smart-phone app like Tide Alert. Most hardware stores sell annual tide tables.

Put on your tall rubber boots, grab a field guide, and get to a local beach to explore the rocky shores and mudflats of the intertidal zone and the cool critters that live there.

WHERE TO GO

During a minus tide any public beach will have depressions in the sand or small pools that host a variety of marine life. Some public beaches are particularly great for tidepooling because they have large rocks that create siz-able tide pools with lots of crevices and nooks for animals to hide in.

SEAHURST PARK
1600 SW Seahurst Park Road, Burien

With nearly a mile of beach end to end, a low tide visit to this Puget Sound waterfront park offers plenty of sand to explore, and a few clusters of large boulders harbor delicate rocky tide pools. Look for the lump of a moon jelly on the sand, and red sea cucumbers at the base of rocks at the low tide line.

CONSTELLATION PARK
3521 Beach Drive SW, Seattle

Just south of the Alki Point Lighthouse is a stretch of rocky beach with some of the best tide pools in the city. Squat down to check the undersides of boulders for ochre sea stars and painted anemones.

CARKEEK PARK
950 NW Carkeek Park Road, Seattle

Low tide unveils about 20 acres of rocky tide-lands. To find tiny creatures that hide under-neath big rocks, gently turn one over. Look for mossy or lined chitons attached to the rock's underside, as well as hermit crabs, periwin-kle snails, barnacles, and limpets. Remember to carefully place the rock back just as you found it.

RICHMOND BEACH SALTWATER PARK
NW 190th Street, Shoreline

This rocky beach at low tide is a haven for dozens of invertebrates, from decorator crabs to leather stars. Watch for red rock crabs scurrying sideways through the eel-grass beds.

CATTLE POINT
Southeastern tip of San Juan Island

Part of the San Juan Island National Historical Park, the point is chock-full of tide pools that compete for your attention with spectacular views of the Strait of Juan de Fuca and possible orca sightings. Interpretive signs about tide pool ecology guide you along.

SALT CREEK RECREATION AREA
3506 Camp Hayden Road, Port Angeles

The Tongue Point Marine Sanctuary here on the Strait of Juan de Fuca features the kind of rocky intertidal habitat you'd find further west on the wild Olympic Coast. Look for purple sea urchins, many types of sea stars, chitons clinging to everything, and the tapestry of barnacles stuck to rocks like pave diamonds.

RIALTO BEACH
End of Mora Road, west of Forks

This stunningly picturesque beach is dotted with rocks, driftwood, tons of tide pools, and massive spires and sea stacks that magically come onshore at low tide. The tidelands are famous for ochre sea stars in many colors (orange, brown, and purple) and giant green anemones, favorites of photographers. For fewer tourists and more tide pools, hike north to Hole in the Wall (3 miles round-trip).

NATURE NOTEBOOK

Location: _____ Date: _____

Co-naturers: _____

What is the oddest, most surprising critter you found in a tide pool? Were you able to identify it? Describe the creature in vivid detail.

_____

_____

_____

_____

_____

_____

_____

TIDEPOOLING TIPS

CHOOSE A DAY WITH A MINUS TIDE.
Wear shoes that can get wet, like water sandals or rainboots. Bring a basic field guide to marine wildlife and seaweed.

STICK TO PUBLIC BEACHES.
In Washington, public access to tidelands adjacent to private property is not protected by law.

ARRIVE EARLY.
Arrive on the beach about an hour before the low tide time. Follow the water's edge as it recedes, exploring tide pools as they are revealed. After the low tide time has passed, move toward shore as incoming tides can be swift and unpredictable.

STEP WITH CARE.
The intertidal zone is fragile habitat. While the critters here are adapted to pounding surf and frigid temps, they aren't used to stomping boots and prodding fingers. Avoid crushing anemones and tiny crabs by stepping instead on bare rock or sand. Beware of slippery seaweed.

BE GENTLE.
If you wish to touch a sea star or feel the fringe on an anemone, a soft touch with a wet finger is the least disturbing to them. Don't pry sea stars off of rocks or overhandle crabs.

TIDEPOOL WITH EXPERTS.
At many beaches throughout Puget Sound, experienced marine naturalists are on hand during the lowest tides to help you discover intertidal treasures. Naturalists take great care when handling critters, and they've been trained how to do this with minimal impact to the animals. Watch and learn.

BEWARE OF THINGS THAT HURT.
The bite of a red octopus, pinch of a crab, or sting of a jelly-fish really hurt, so look but don't touch.

LEARN MORE

Carry a good guidebook in your pack, like *The New Beachcomber's Guide to the Pacific Northwest*, by J. Duane Sept, with full-color photos and detailed descriptions of marine life in the intertidal zone.

SAIL A BOAT

TAKE THE HELM IN THE SALISH SEA

Sailing off Blake Island

SPARKLING SEAS surround many of our cities and neighborhoods—Puget Sound, Hood Canal, Lake Washington, Lake Chelan, the Columbia River—all beautiful to look at and even more fun to play in. Add a light wind and the gumption to take on a new challenge, and you're sailing.

Sailing is freedom. As the sail unfurls and catches a breeze, you're moving. Feel the hull lift beneath you and the boat pick up speed as your stomach does a flip and you find your sea legs. Soon salty air kisses your cheeks and wind whips your hair as the boat slices a path through the water. This sensory, tactile experience engages both physical and strategic mental skills. Though the sport carries a bit of an elitist rep, community sailing programs with lessons and boat rentals make it more affordable and accessible. For attire, skip the stripes and khakis—Pacific Northwest sailors favor flannel and cozy fleece.

Think sailing is too complicated? It's a challenging hobby, but you could be ready to skipper a small sailboat after a few lessons on the water. Prep before a class with books and videos to teach yourself basic sailing knowledge—the parts of a sailboat (bow, stern, mainsail, keel, helm, mast), types of sailboats (sloop, ketch, schooner), useful knots, how to raise the sails, how to trim the sails, and maneuvers like tacking and jibing—that way your lessons on the water will be well spent putting this knowledge into practice. The essential skills to master on the water are how to read wind direction, steer the boat in a straight line so you can trim the sails, and determine when a sail is trimmed accurately.

Get ready for some close encounters with nature on a sailboat. Watch for the spouts and splashes of whales and dolphins (the latter may approach boats with interest). Gulls, herons, and cormorants skim the water in search of food, and may even perch on a boat rail.

LEARN TO SAIL

On a budget? Look to nonprofit community sailing centers for both lessons and rentals. For a splurge, book an immersion experience on a live-aboard sailboat. Basic swimming skills are usually required for any sailing program. Below are a handful of (the many) sailing schools and learning opportunities around Puget Sound. The best way to gauge if a school is a good fit is to call and chat with an instructor.

SAIL SAND POINT

7861 62nd Avenue NE, Seattle
sailsandpoint.org, (206) 525-8782
On the shore of Lake Washington, this community boating center offers beginner and advanced sailing classes for kids and adults with lessons on the water and on shore. Learn essential boating safety and all the skills to rig and sail a variety of boats. Need-based scholarships are available.

MOUNT BAKER ROWING AND SAILING CENTER

3800 Lake Washington Boulevard S, Seattle
seattle.gov/parks, (206) 386-1913
Sign up for the eighteen-hour Learn to Sail class for sailing theory, water safety, rigging, boat handling, tack, jibe, and recovering from a capsize. Learn on small dinghy sailboats on Lake Washington. Women-only classes are offered. After completing the course, you'll be eligible for Sunday afternoon open sailing—check out a boat from their fleet of windsurfers, Vanguard 15s, Lasers, and Optis.

SEATTLE YACHT CLUB

1807 E Hamlin Street, Seattle
seattleyachtclub.org, (206) 325-1000
Learn your way around a sailboat plus steering, tacking, jibing, tying knots, and more.

Master sailing basics on Seattle's Portage Bay in six in-depth lessons, taught on the water with Laser and V15s.

THE MOUNTAINEERS

7700 Sand Point Way NE, Seattle
2302 N 30th Street, Tacoma
www.mountaineers.org

Offered in spring through the Seattle and Tacoma branches, The Mountaineers course teaches you how to crew a sailboat, including rigging, docking, sail trimming, and maneuvering. Learn sailboat safety as well as how to use charts and navigational aids.

PUGET SOUND SAILING INSTITUTE

3501 Harborview Drive, Gig Harbor
pugetsoundsailing.com, (253) 383-1774

This is the premier sailing school in Puget Sound, with class locations in Gig Harbor, Tacoma, Des Moines, and Seattle. Take the Basic Keelboat course if you're a novice—a deep dive into sailing terms, trimming the sails, tacking/jibing, knots, docking,

NATURE NOTEBOOK

Location: _____   Date: _____

Co-naturers: _____

If you could sail away in your own sailboat, where would you go? What would you take with you, and what would you leave behind?

_____

_____

_____

_____

_____

_____

_____

_____

_____

navigation, and more. There is no class-room—instead, learn much of the basics with a textbook and online videos prior to two full days of on-the-water instruction, ending with an American Sailing Association certification.

CHARIOT ADVENTURES

Squalicum Harbor, Bellingham

chariotadventures.com, (360) 961-6657

Chariot is an Annapolis 44 fiberglass sloop made in 1963. In the Cruise n' Learn class, you'll depart Bellingham for a mini-cruise around the San Juan Islands over six days and nights. This live-aboard immersion course is hands-on learning in the field—you'll finish with the skills needed to be certified to charter a boat or cruise your own.

JOIN A PUBLIC SAIL

Immerse yourself in sailing culture on one of these public sails, learning the ropes with a pro skipper and crew.

CENTER FOR WOODEN BOATS

1010 Valley Street, Seattle

cwb.org, (206) 382-2628

DONATIONS ENCOURAGED

Join volunteer skippers and their crew on a public sail on Lake Union, every Sunday year-round (sign-up begins at 10 A.M., first-come, first-served). They sail a schooner, ketch, yawl, and sprit sail.

SCHOONER ZODIAC

355 Harris Avenue Suite 104, Bellingham

schoonerzodiac.com, (206) 719-7622

PER-PERSON FEE

LEARN MORE

Each September, the Wooden Boat Festival in Port Townsend at Point Hudson showcases the beauty of wooden boats and the richness of our maritime culture. Jumpstart your nautical knowledge with how-to videos from the American Sailing Association; topics range from tying knots to docking tips. Stay safe on water with the American Red Cross; find a local provider for swimming lessons, read about small boat safety, and get water safety tips. Interested in buying your own? Gig Harbor Boat Works builds beautiful, handcrafted small sailboats at reasonable base prices.

Help the crew raise the *Zodiac*'s four sails; her mainsail is the largest on the West Coast. As the schooner cruises the Salish Sea for three hours, lend a hand to maneuvering the 160-foot windjammer trimmed in shiny brass and polished mahogany. Public sails are usually on Sundays, spring–fall.

SOUND EXPERIENCE

Departs from ports across Puget Sound

soundexp.org, (360) 379-0438

PER-PERSON FEE

Take a turn at the wheel and help raise the sails on *Adventuress*, a century-old National Historic Landmark tall ship. This gaff-rigged schooner first launched in 1913 and has been completely restored in recent years. Public sails are offered Sundays, April–October.

BACKPACK OVERNIGHT

MAKE CAMP IN THE WILD

Backpacking on Mount Rainier

WASHINGTON'S backcountry has wild and remote places you have to see to believe. There are hanging valleys paved with wildflowers, deep cirques with glistening tarns, and spots you can pitch your tent at the toe of a glacier—all beyond the reach of day hikers. To get there, grab some hiking boots and pack your backpack.

Backpacking is an overnight or multiday hike where everything you need to camp in the woods comes with you in a large pack. That includes your tent, sleeping bag and pad, food, water filter, cooking supplies, and personal items. The gear is lightweight, compressible, and packable. A good backpack will comfortably distribute most of its weight onto your hips, and some to the front of your shoulders. When fully loaded, your pack should weigh no more than 20 percent of your body weight.

Backpacking opens the door to deep wilderness you wouldn't get to otherwise. But be warned—falling asleep under a starry sky to the *hoo-hoo-hoo* of a screech owl and taking your morning coffee beside a pristine mountain lake might be addictive. Fortunately, you'll never run out of gorgeous places to backpack.

BACKPACK LIKE A PRO

Heed this expert advice before you hit the trail.

Keep it easy. Choose a well-maintained trail sans rough terrain or difficult stream crossings. Try for less than 1200-feet elevation gain and less than 6 miles of hiking to the spot you plan to set up camp.

Research your hike. Check trail conditions, read trip reports, look up any passes or permits you need, and keep up on the weather forecast. Locate where established backcountry campsites are from guidebooks or topo maps so you'll know where to camp. The local ranger station will also have recommendations on where to set up camp.

Train for your hike. A few short day hikes wearing a full pack and your hiking boots will help prepare your legs and lungs for the real thing.

Follow a packing list. And check it twice. Be discerning about any extras like books or camera equipment—you'll feel each additional pound (see "Backpack Checklist" in this chapter).

Hike with others to share the load. When you backpack solo, that pack is heavy. Go with a friend (ideally an experienced backpacker), and you carry the tent while they pack the food and campstove. Plus, you'll have someone to play cards with at camp.

Practice "leave no trace" ethics. Don't hike off-trail, pack out your trash, respect wildlife from a distance. Bury or pack out your waste.

Pack lightweight, tasty meals with loads of calories. You'll need them. Pre-packaged meals made for backpackers (freeze-dried or dehydrated—just add boiling water) have upped their gourmet game, from risotto to pad thai, and make planning a cinch. Breakfast might be instant oatmeal with a handful of raisins and walnuts, lunch might be crackers with sliced cheddar and summer sausage. Pack lots of snacks, from energy bars to gorp.

Protect your food from rodents and bears. Don't eat food in the tent or store it in your backpack overnight. Instead, bring food in a bearproof canister or bag that fits into your backpack. Before bed, put all your food and scented toiletries in the container and place it on the ground at least 100 feet from your camp (downwind is preferred, and remember where you put it!) or hang the bag 12 feet high and 10 feet from the nearest tree trunk.

Follow a topo map. Green Trails maps are particularly great for backpacking—all hiking trails are shown in green, and everything you need to know is labeled, from the names of rivers to the campsites. Don't forget your compass.

Pack your pack properly. Start with your compressed sleeping bag in the bottom, followed by heavy things like the tent, food container, stove, and fuel, balancing the weight on both sides of the pack. At the very top goes lightweight, easy-to-access stuff: a fleece, raingear, topo map, day snacks, and water filter. Water bottles usually go into two made-to-fit side pockets. The sleeping pad and chair kit can be strapped to the outside of the pack. A front fanny pack or hip belt pouch is a nice place to stash your camera, sunglasses, bug dope, Swiss Army knife, bandanna, and sunblock.

Safety first. Ideally, backpack with a friend, but always tell someone where you're going and when you plan to return. Know the basics of wilderness first aid. Bring moleskin for blisters and treat them the minute you notice them. Hike with sure footing.

WHERE TO GO

These beginner backpacking hikes can be overnights (hike in one day, camp, hike out the next day) or three-day trips, where you keep the same camp for two nights and use the middle day to relax or explore further on a day hike.

BAKER RIVER, MOUNT BAKER-SNOQUALMIE NATIONAL FOREST

SR 20 at Milepost 82
fs.usda.gov/mbs, (360) 856-5700
NORTHWEST FOREST PASS
5 miles round-trip, 300 feet elevation gain

The path starts on the busy trail to East Bank Baker Lake; once that peels off, enjoy the solitude in this ancient cedar forest with moss-clad boulders and a small cave. Hug the riverbank for a while then pull away for some crossings and a beaver pond before entering North Cascades National Park. Just over half a mile more, the trail ends at the confluence of Sulphide Creek and Baker River, and your campsite. On a clear day, don't miss the view of Seahpo Peak and Jagged Ridge while standing at Sulphide Creek—there are a dozen or so distant waterfalls plunging from the glaciers above. Baker River's water is a beautiful turquoise blue, draining the glaciers on many surrounding peaks, including Shuksan and Blum. In midsummer keep an eye out for tasty huckleberries along the trail. Stop at the North Cascades Park headquarters in Sedro-Woolley for a required free backcountry camping permit.

INGALLS CREEK, ALPINE LAKES WILDERNESS

US 97, 13 miles north of Blewett Pass
fs.usda.gov/okawen, (509) 548-2550
NORTHWEST FOREST PASS
11 miles round-trip, 1450 feet elevation gain
One of the earliest backpacking hikes to melt out, this trail rambles through ponderosa

pine and around huge boulders alongside Ingalls Creek, roaring and turbulent with rapids in late spring. Spectacular early season wildflowers peek out of the forest floor—bright paintbrush, balsamroot, calypso orchids, and lupine among them. Hike in a little or a lot—the periodic creekside campsites start about 1 mile in and continue to the confluence with Falls Creek at 5.5 miles in.

HOH RIVER TRAIL, OLYMPIC NATIONAL PARK
US 101, south of Forks
nps.gov/olym, (360) 374-6925
NATIONAL PARK PASS

10.6 miles round-trip, 300 feet elevation gain
If you want the easiest hike in the most beautiful setting, this should be your first backpack. On the west side of the Olympic Mountains, 140 inches of rainfall a year mingle with massive snowmelt to produce one of the world's rarest ecosystems—a temperate rain forest. Right from the start at the Hoh Visitor Center (pick up your free backcountry camping permit here—it's required), you pass through a vibrant cathedral of ancient trees, cloaked in moss and lichen. Keep an eye out for the majestic Roosevelt elk who live here. Continue to Five Mile Island and its scenic campsites.

Olympic National Park's Hoh Rain Forest

BACKPACKING CHECKLIST

Your gear list for backpacking will vary depending on the time of year, number of nights, and whether you're solo or sharing the load with a friend. This checklist covers the basics; you may find a few items (like an inflatable pillow or a chair kit that converts your sleeping pad into a seat) to be unnecessary. Or, you might add a few comforts that aren't listed here, like a flask of bourbon, a book, or small lantern. Get creative to lighten your load: for example, copy— or tear out—the relevant page of your hiking guidebook and leave the rest of the book at home, and portion out medications and toiletries to bring only what you'll use. Choose lightweight gear and dehydrated food. Your full backpack should weigh about 20 percent of your body weight.

- ☐ Backpack
- ☐ Tent
- ☐ Sleeping pad and chair kit
- ☐ Sleeping bag
- ☐ Camping pillow
- ☐ Backpacking stove
- ☐ Stove fuel
- ☐ Matches or lighter
- ☐ Lightweight cookset (pots, spatula)
- ☐ Bowl, cup, and spork
- ☐ Gallon zip bag for pack-out garbage
- ☐ Biodegradable soap, sponge
- ☐ Handkerchief or bandanna
- ☐ Food: meals and snacks
- ☐ Coffee, tea, cocoa
- ☐ Bear canister or a cord and bag to hang food

- ☐ Pocketknife or multitool
- ☐ First-aid kit (customized with your meds)
- ☐ Water filter
- ☐ Whistle (a signal for help)
- ☐ Headlamp and extra batteries
- ☐ Cell phone for camera (optional solar charger)
- ☐ Toothbrush and paste
- ☐ Toilet paper and trowel
- ☐ Wet wipes
- ☐ Hand sanitizer
- ☐ Insect repellant
- ☐ Raingear
- ☐ Long underwear (top and bottom)
- ☐ Fleece or wool sweater
- ☐ Puffy coat

- ☐ Hiking boots or trail runners
- ☐ Camp shoes or sandals
- ☐ Gaiters
- ☐ Sock liners
- ☐ Hiking socks
- ☐ Shorts, pants, shirts (light layers)
- ☐ Warm hat and gloves
- ☐ Sun hat or visor
- ☐ Water bottle
- ☐ Trailhead parking pass
- ☐ Backcountry camping permits
- ☐ License or ID
- ☐ Topo maps for your trail
- ☐ The Ten Essentials (see introduction)
- ☐ Car keys

NATURE NOTEBOOK

Location: _____ Date: _____

Co-naturers: _____

Memories can be linked to our sense of smell. The scent of the sea, a summer rain shower, or pine needles in the sun may evoke a memory from a past experience in nature, sometimes all the way to childhood. What are some smells in the natural world that are connected to memories for you?

_____

_____

_____

_____

_____

_____

_____

_____

_____

_____

_____

_____

_____

_____

_____

_____

WATCH WHALES

ORCAS AND HUMPBACKS AND GRAY WHALES, OH MY!

Look for orcas in the Salish Sea.

photo by Tim Coleh

THE WATERS OF Puget Sound see lots of hustle and bustle—sailboats and ferries crisscross from island to mainland, while cargo and cruise ships fill the shipping lane. It's easy to forget that under all that human activity lies a world of incredible sea life—porpoises, dolphins, harbor seals, river otters, and even a few massive humpback whales. Washington's waters are rich aquatic habitat for around thirty species of marine mammals, not least the beloved icon of the Pacific Northwest: the orca. Seeing a pod of orcas in the wild is a thrill.

You might know orcas as "killer whales" though they're not technically whales (rather, the largest species of dolphins), nor do they kill humans (seals and sea lions aren't so lucky). These distinctive black-and-white creatures live in all oceans, but the three Southern Resident orca pods of the Salish Sea (the J, K, and L pods) are quite special—they stay in their family group for life and eat chinook salmon. They're also endangered; recent counts find fewer than seventy-five orcas among the three pods. Transient orcas (called Bigg's killer whales) swim through Puget Sound in smaller pods in search of food like marine mammals and even other whales.

Want to see a dancing, breaching, spouting pod of orcas? How about a massive gray or humpback whale? You might get lucky with a chance whale sighting from the deck of a ferry (especially the Edmonds/Kingston and Mukilteo/Clinton runs in fall and winter), so keep an eye out. But if you really want to see whales, head to the right lookout in the right season—summer. Pack binoculars and a picnic, spread out a blanket, and wait. Scan the water, looking for spouts (they look like a big puff of mist) or a moving ball of large splashes, and focus your binoculars on that spot. If you see a whale-watching boat out there and it stops, look at the boat through your binoculars to see which way the boaters are gazing—and follow their sightline, perhaps to a breaching pod of killer whales!

WHERE TO SPOT WHALES

LIME KILN POINT STATE PARK
San Juan Island
DISCOVER PASS

On the island's west shore, Lime Kiln State Park is known as the best spot in the Northwest to watch wild orcas from land, especially in summer. This is also a good spot to spy gray whales, humpbacks, and minkes.

ICEBERG POINT
Lopez Island

Hike just over a mile to the stunning rocky point through madrona trees from Agate Beach County Park on the southern tip of Lopez Island. Points that poke out into the sea tend to be good perches for spotting whales. Pods of Southern Resident orcas pass right by this point in summer and early fall.

ALKI BEACH
West Seattle

Transient orcas might pop up any time of year here looking for a seal to snack on, and the Southern Resident orcas venture this far south in the Sound occasionally to find salmon. From the beach, look north to Discovery Point, then northwest to Bainbridge Island. Orcas tend to travel in the middle of the channel.

POINT DEFIANCE PARK
Tacoma

This forested peninsula juts into the Sound at the confluence of three narrow straits (Dalco and Colvos Passages and the Narrows), so whales moving from one end of the Sound

NATURE NOTEBOOK

Location: _____ Date: _____

Co-naturers: _____

Which marine mammals did you see on your outing, and what field marks or behaviors helped you identify them?

_____

_____

_____

_____

_____

_____

LEARN MORE

Find new whale-watching spots with The Whale Trail, which identifies viewing sites through the Salish Sea and along the Pacific Coast. The Whale Museum in Friday Harbor on San Juan Island (62 First Street, Friday Harbor) is loaded with fascinating, engaging exhibits for learning all about orcas and other marine mammals of the Salish Sea. The Orca Network connects whales to people in the Pacific Northwest, and one way they do so is to congregate marine mammal sightings into an updated list and map—once you get started, submit your own sightings.

to the other pass through. Head to the north shore near the ferry dock—walk the beach and look for harbor seals as well as gray, humpback, and minke whales. See Southern Resident orcas as they sometimes come this far south in search of fish to eat. Five Mile Drive circles the park with pull-out vistas in every direction—great for stopping in any season and scanning for whales with binoculars.

FIRST BEACH
La Push, Washington Coast

There are many fantastic lookouts and beaches to spot migrating gray whales on the coast, though this one has special significance. The majestic whale appears in many folktales of the Quileute Nation here in La Push, and in spring a whale song and dance is performed during the Welcoming of the Whales ceremony, honoring the gray whales as they begin to return from the south to their summer feeding grounds in Alaska.

WHALES OF WASHINGTON

Humpback whale. The Salish Sea has had a humpback comeback after commercial whaling drove the population to freefall a century ago. They're here, and they're huge—around 50 feet in length (similar to the gray whale). Look for a pointed head shape and long front flippers (fins). Humpbacks are baleen whales—they filter water through their mouth to trap krill and plankton for food.

Gray whale. Look for these ginormous creatures off the Pacific Coast during their 13,000-mile annual journey. The best months for spotting are December–January as the whales swim south to Baja, and late March–April as they return north to the Bering Sea. A few hundred grays stick around all year and come inland—keep an eye on Saratoga Passage in spring when the "Saratoga Grays" come to feed on ghost shrimp. Lobtailing (slapping the tail loudly on the water) and breaching are common behaviors to watch for.

Orca (killer whale). These inquisitive, heavy-bodied dolphins are cetaceans, the same taxonomic order as whales and porpoises. Notice their pattern—jet black on top with a white eyebrow, and white underneath. Behind the very large dorsal fin (tall and straight in males, curved in females) is the unique-as-a-fingerprint gray saddle patch. Whale researchers can quickly identify individuals by this patch. Orcas do a lot of spyhopping (the head pops up vertically and looks around) to search for prey.

HIKE IN THE HIGH COUNTRY

THE HILLS ARE ALIVE WITH THE WHISTLING OF MARMOTS

Indian paintbrush at Marmot Pass

SOME OF THE most phenomenal trails in the Northwest lead you to the upper reaches of the Cascades and the Olympics, but to access their snow-free paths and subalpine meadows, one must have patience. Then, come midsummer as lingering snowfields melt out, a fleeting alpine nirvana is revealed where avalanche lilies adorn the slopes and stark scenery takes your breath away. By mid-September, the snow starts falling all over again. The window to hike in the high country is short, so don't dawdle!

As you hike up a mountain, the habitat changes from montane forest to subalpine meadow with scattered clusters of conifers. Finally, from timberline to the highest peaks is alpine tundra. The elevation of timberline (above which trees don't grow) varies depending which side of the Cascades you're on, ranging from 5200 feet in the Olympics to 6000 feet east of the Cascade crest.

Plants and wildlife evolved clever adaptations to survive in the harsh alpine biome, where the soil is poor in nutrients and wind is near constant. Flowering plants like purple mountain saxifrage, spreading phlox, and smooth douglasia form dense mats that spring right out of rock crevices, their low stature helping them dodge ruthless wind in summer and stay well insulated by snow in winter. Small, hairy leaves preserve moisture, while deep taproots anchor them in unstable soils.

Mountain goats evade predators in the alpine tundra with their impressive ability to navigate steep, rocky slopes. The furry pika, a relative of rabbits, evolved short ears to hold in heat. Marmots hibernate over half the year in burrows under the large boulders of alpine talus slopes, bulking up under their thick coats in summer on alpine sedge, mosses, and lichens. White-tailed Ptarmigan are a small grouse that live above 7000 feet in the Cascades, molting into a cryptic snow-white plumage in winter and a speckled gray granite-like plumage in summer to evade predators.

WHERE TO GO

These epic hikes lead you through subalpine meadows and into alpine tundra. Unless you know how to use an ice axe, wait until the trail is free of lingering snowfields that pose a problem for nontechnical hikers. Pack a windbreaker—you'll need it above tree line. Alpine plants are fragile and take years to regenerate, so watch your step.

MARMOT PASS, BUCKHORN WILDERNESS, OLYMPIC NATIONAL FOREST

US 101 south of Quilcene

fs.usda.gov/olympic, (360) 765-2200

NORTHWEST FOREST PASS

10.5 miles round-trip, 3500 feet elevation gain, high point 6000 feet

This trail rolls a whole mountain's worth of habitats into one consistently uphill hike. Enter the Buckhorn Wilderness and its lush old-growth cedar and hemlock forest cloaked in moss and ferns as you climb along the Upper Big Quilcene River. Midway to the pass (2.6 miles) is Shelter Rock Camp, beyond which the trail leaves the river and climbs out of the montane forest. Beautiful subalpine meadows burst with colorful blooms here in late July, often shrouded in wisps of fog. Look for orange and magenta paintbrush, lupine, phlox, blue delphiniums, fireweed, and more. After passing Camp Mystery, cross the tree line to dry and rocky alpine fields at the pass and stunning panoramic views of the eastern face of the Olympic peaks—so close you can almost reach out to touch them.

SKYLINE DIVIDE, MOUNT BAKER

SR 542 east of Glacier

fs.usda.gov/mbs, (360) 599-2714

NORTHWEST FOREST PASS

9 miles round-trip, 2500 feet elevation gain, high point 6560 feet

Ascend gently through the woods with just a few switchbacks, gaining 1500 feet in 2 miles to the ridgeline. Here begin the blooming meadows, grassy knolls, and open views. Amble up and down the ridge toward Kulshan (the Native name for Baker) as the vistas stretch further. On a clear day you'll have a sweeping view of Cascade peaks to the east, and a good topo map will help you tell Mount Ruth from Mount Shuksan. Turn

NATURE NOTEBOOK

Location: _____   Date: _____

Co-naturers: _____

Plants and animals astound with their capacity to thrive in harsh habitats. Write down a few wildlife or plant adaptations you observed in the alpine or subalpine biomes.

_____

_____

_____

_____

_____

_____

_____

_____

_____

_____

_____

_____

around when you've had your fill of flowers and views, or hike all the way to the base of Hadley Peak; continuing farther is for climbers only. Pack plenty of water on this trail, as fresh sources aren't easy to find.

SPRAY PARK, MOUNT RAINIER

SR 165 to Mowich Lake
nps.gov/mora, (360) 829-9639
NATIONAL PARK PASS
8 miles round-trip, 1700 feet elevation gain, high point 6500 feet

Spray Park on the mountain's northwest side puts on one of the biggest and best wildflower displays with a fraction of the crowds seen at Sunrise or Paradise. The first two miles or so take you gently up and down through open forest, followed by a series of switchbacks to a park-like meadow. Look for lovely blooms like bistort, lupine, avalanche lilies, magenta paintbrush, and heather, all to the accompaniment of the music of whistling marmots. Hike as far as you like, then turn around and hike back out. If you want a longer hike, continue on to Seattle Park, another huge mosaic of meadows and cool rock gardens.

SNOWGRASS FLAT—GOAT LAKE LOOP, SOUTH CASCADES

FR-2150, 22 miles south of Packwood
fs.usda.gov/giffordpinchot, (360) 497-1100
NORTHWEST FOREST PASS
8.2 miles round-trip, 1600 feet elevation gain, high point 5830 feet

Beauty and grandeur follow you throughout this hike into the Goat Rocks Wilderness, the remains of an ancient stratovolcano that's eroded and weathered so it forms a divide of sorts between Mount Rainier and Mount Adams. Plenty of craggy ridges and peaks are accessible to scramblers. Hike this out-and-back from the Berry Patch trailhead to the flower-filled flat, or carry a full backpack and extend the hike to Goat Lake for a 13-mile loop back along Goat Ridge—there are lots of nice backcountry campsites before and after the lake. The "flat" is one of the prettiest subalpine wildflower meadows in the South Cascades, with expanses of colorful lupine punctuated by bright paintbrush and the whimsical white pasqueflower. Fuchsia Lewis's monkeyflower bloom in clumps along pristine streams.

photo by Vera Gorbunova

 Connect with Nature

Sketch and paint the subalpine landscape *en plein air*. Pack some pencils and a sketchpad, and a small watercolor palette and brush if you like. Find a view and a nice rock to sit on while you sketch the landscape. For inspiration, check out *Colors of the West*, by Molly Hashimoto, a Seattle artist who teaches how to connect with nature by observing, sketching, or painting it.

GO SEA KAYAKING

SEE THE SEA, FROM THE WATER

Time in a kayak is downright magical.

photo by Jennifer Poole

WHEN YOU ARE nestled in an enclosed sea kayak, you sit low in the hull. You're not on *top* of the water as much as you're *in* it. Dipping your paddle in and propelling yourself forward, the boat is an extension of your body—this is the magic of sea kayaking. Steer around a bed of bull kelp or get into position to take the wake off a passing boat with only gentle rocking. You're in control of your boat, just as you're in control of your own body. And you're smiling, because you're paddling through saltwater in the Salish Sea.

With experience and practice, a seaworthy kayak gives you access to tidal waters that a small canoe can't, from exploring the San Juan Islands to Seattle's Elliott Bay. Come eye to eye with curious river otters, watch seabirds plunge for prey, and glide around dancing jellyfish. Wild islands and remote corners of Puget Sound are suddenly within reach along the 150-mile Cascade Marine Trail, dotted with public shorelines and more than sixty kayak-in campsites.

If you're new to sea kayaking, stick to sheltered bays and inlets for your first few outings. The open waters of Puget Sound can challenge you later with light wind, strong currents, and big boat wakes once you've got some solid experience and know-how under your PFD (that's personal flotation device—always wear one on the water). Pay for a guided paddle your first time out for expert instruction on water safety, basic paddle strokes, how to steer with the rudder, tides, and currents, and how to do a wet exit and self-rescue if the kayak capsizes.

WHERE TO GO

Rent a kayak by the hour or for a full day at on-the-water outfitters throughout Puget Sound—this gives you a taste of paddling without buying or transporting your own boat. While sit-on-top kayaks are fun on hot summer days in very sheltered water, opt for a closed-top sea kayak in Puget Sound. A rented kayak should come with a double-bladed paddle, spray skirt, PFD, and accessories like a paddle float and bilge hand pump. Although you'll likely be comfortable in a T-shirt and shorts during the summer, if you get hooked and want to kayak year-round, consider renting a wet suit or paddling jacket.

DEER HARBOR

Shearwater Kayak Tours
138 N Beach Road, in Eastsound, Orcas Island
shearwaterkayaks.com, (360) 376-4699
The San Juan Islands are a paddler's paradise, offering everything from jaw-dropping scenery to the chance of spotting a pod of orcas. Orcas Island is patchworked with swatches of farmland, pockets of forest, and small villages. Rocky headlands shelter glassy coves, and smaller islands dot the sea. Start with a guided paddle trip here to learn how to safely cross a small passage with semiopen water.

Guided kayak trip. A pro guide will start your day with a talk on kayaking basics. Learn about the gear, how to sit in your kayak, and how to hold your paddle. Then get into a stable two-person kayak and paddle off to a small, undeveloped island and enjoy a picnic lunch and beach exploration before paddling back.

LAKE UNION

Northwest Outdoor Center
2100 Westlake Avenue N, Seattle
nwoc.com, (206) 281-9694
In the middle of Seattle is a big, beautiful lake ringed with funky houseboats and city parks, including the emerald hilly jewel, Gas Works Park. From your sea kayak, paddle

around and give yourself a tour. Watch out for the float planes! For less bustle and more nature, head through the Montlake Cut and duck into the wildlife-rich wetlands of the Washington Park Arboretum.

Rent a kayak. Experienced staff at the local rental spot will present a quick lesson on how to paddle, steer, and stay safe on the water. They'll likely offer sea kayaking classes, too.

ELLIOTT BAY

Alki Kayak Tours
1660 Harbor Avenue SW, Seattle
(206) 953-0237

Explore the Seattle waterfront and the industrial mouth of the Duwamish River with views of Mount Rainier and the Olympic Mountains. You might be surprised how much wildlife successfully dodge huge cargo ships in these waters, from cormorants to sea lions.

NATURE NOTEBOOK

Location: _____   Date: _____

Co-naturers: _____

The Salish Sea is home to many birds who live much of their lives on or right by saltwater—cormorants, loons, diving ducks, herons, and more. Count and list all the different species of birds and other marine animals you see on your kayak trip.

_____

_____

_____

_____

_____

_____

_____

_____

_____

LEARN MORE

Washington Water Trails Association protects and promotes public access to shorelines and marine trails for human-powered watercraft. They're your go-to resource for planning paddles on the Cascade Marine Trail. The indispensable *Sea Kayaking: Basic Skills, Paddling Techniques and Trip Planning*, by Dan Henderson, is outstanding for teaching safety and techniques, paddle strokes, and gear. Plan your trips with the tides and currents from NOAA.

Rent a kayak. Reserve ahead and rent a kayak by the hour, then take a guided paddle around Elliott Bay or an overnight kayak camp trip to Blake Island. An introduction to sea kayaking class will teach you safety and basic strokes.

LIBERTY BAY

Olympic Outdoor Center

18743 Front Street NE, Poulsbo, (360) 297-4659

Poulsbo's Scandinavian roots are the real deal, reflected in the town's picturesque setting, a fjord-like inlet backdropped by jagged peaks. Liberty Bay is small and sheltered, perfect for a beginner kayak paddle. When the tide is high, paddle up the inlet for wetlands and wildlife around Fish Park.

Rent a kayak. Choose from single or double sea kayaks, rentable by the hour at the dock on the Poulsbo waterfront. Start with a basic instruction and safety talk and get some guidance on interesting places to paddle in the bay.

HOOD CANAL, BRINNON

Hood Canal Adventures

251 Hjelvicks Road/US 101 at Yelvik's Beach, Brinnon, kayakbrinnon.com, (360) 301-6310

This 1.5 mile-wide channel of saltwater is not a canal at all, but a long, glacially-carved fjord. Most of the shoreline is private property, though a handful of state parks make good paddling destinations, like the Dosewallips Estuary, Potlatch State Park, and Twanoh State Park.

Rent a kayak. Rent a single or double kayak by the hour or by the day. Guides will take you out if you want some expert instruction; trips may include Bald Eagle watching and estuary exploration.

SOUTH PUGET SOUND

Boston Harbor Marina

312 73rd Avenue NE, Olympia

bostonharbormarina.com, (360) 357-5670

Paddling the south end of Puget Sound is quieter than its northern counterpart, with fewer sailboats and cargo ships to dodge, and no big wakes from cruise liners or car ferries. The "South Sound" is everything below the Narrows, and includes several uncrowded inlets and islands. For paddlers, one of the highlights is a wild oasis only reachable by boat: Hope Island Marine State Park, with beautiful beaches, primitive campsites, and more than 2 miles of hiking trails. A crossing of Budd Inlet is required to get there, so don't attempt this on your first paddling trip; instead, skirt the shoreline of Budd Inlet to the south toward downtown Olympia and back.

Rent a kayak. Rent a single or double kayak for some of the best per-hour and per-day prices in all of Puget Sound.

CATCH A TROUT

FIND A LAKE, BRING A ROD, REEL IN YOUR DINNER

Fishing for rainbow trout in Fish Lake

photo by Lindsay O'Connell

ANGLING IS FISHING with a rod and line. It's a sport for some, and a way to put dinner on the table for others. At the edge of a still lake on a quiet afternoon, fishing is a communion with nature.

If you're new to angling, everything about it might seem complicated. Head down the fishing aisle at any sporting goods store and you'll see jigs, flies, spinners, and lures in every color, size, and shape imaginable. How do you choose? The rod and reel aisle is even more confounding—fly-fishing or spin fishing? Cast from a bank or a boat? Head to salt-water or freshwater? Fish for salmon, perch, or trout? Catch-and-release, or catch-and-cook? Option overload sets in and suddenly you don't feel much like fishing anymore.

Here's the thing—you probably already know how to fish. As a child, did you bait a rod with worms to pull bluegill from a local pond? Recall the thrill of feeling a tug on your line, or the focus on the task at hand—reel and pull, reel and pull to quickly bring the writhing little fish close to the shore. With one hand you'd gently fold down the fish's fins front to back so they didn't poke you, and with the other, you'd carefully remove the bait hook from its mouth. You'd return the fish to its pond, or put it in a bucket of water to take home to your family for a buttery, pan-fried dinner. That's fishing!

You'll need a rod-and-reel combo (spinning rods are the most common; a spincast rod with a push-button release is even easier for novices), fishing line, some tackle (lures, bobber, sinker), needle-nosed pliers for removing tricky hooks, a state fishing license, and a lake or pond that has fish in it. You can learn to tie on a lure, cast your fishing rod, and how to safely remove a hook from YouTube tutorials, but you'll learn faster and feel more confident doing all those things if you take a one-day class or workshop on fishing for beginners. Pick up new techniques and tricks by chatting up fellow anglers at a local dock.

Once you master the rhythmic cast-and-reel of spin fishing in a lake, take a collapsible rod with you to pull trout and bass on your outdoor adventures, from canoeing to mountain backpacking. Before long, branch out to fly-fishing, stream fishing, surf fishing, or even ice fishing!

Experiment with your bait—part of the fun is figuring out which lures attract which fish. If you cast a spoon lure for trout and you don't get a bite after ten casts, switch to a spinner. A lure's color can make a difference—a general rule is natural hues work best in clear water, and brighter colors in murky water. Try live bait on a hook (it's fun to dig your own earthworms after a rain), but skip this for catch-and-release as the fish might gulp the whole hook and not survive; for this reason live bait is banned in national parks.

WHERE TO FISH

The Washington Department of Fish and Wildlife stocks more than five hundred lakes and streams annually with over fifteen million trout and kokanee (land-locked sockeye salmon) for fishing opportunities—find a stocked lake near you at wdfw.wa.gov. Cast your fishing rod from public docks, piers, banks, shorelines, row boats, or canoes. Stay safe around water by wearing a personal flotation device (PFD). Here are some favorite fishing holes.

LAKE WASHINGTON
Seattle
⭐ *Rainbow trout, cutthroat trout, yellow perch, bluegill, and smallmouth bass*
There are twenty-nine public fishing piers around the perimeter of Lake Washington

(see a guide to all of them at wdfw.wa.gov). Try David E. Brink Park (555 Lake Street S, Kirkland) for catching a bucket-full of yellow perch (worms bait them especially well). Drop a rubber worm lure at Luther Burbank Park (2040 84th Avenue SE, Mercer Island) to bait bass.

FISH LAKE
Chiwawa River Road, Leavenworth north of Lake Wenatchee State Park
⭐ *Yellow perch, rainbow trout, and German brown trout*

For public fishing, access the lake through Cove Resort, the Forest Service–approved concessionaire, on the lake's south shore. Expect to pull rainbow and brown trout here, though you may want to rent a boat from the resort to move around the lake and find them. In winter, when conditions are right, ice fishermen descend here with their huts and cookstoves to pull yellow perch.

LEADER LAKE
Off SR 20 between Twisp and Okanogan
⭐ *Rainbow trout, bluegill, yellow perch, largemouth bass, and crappie*

Try casting off the fishing dock or from shore to get a feel for what's biting. Fish in early summer for the best chance at large, tasty rainbow trout. This scenic lake also has a campground run by the Department of Natural Resources for a nice weekend of camping and fishing.

Fishing for trout in a mountain lake

photo by Luke Mattson

FISH HANDLING TIPS

- Keep the fish in water as much as you can. A fish out of water is like a human under water—they can't breathe.

- Wet your hands before handling fish so you don't damage their protective mucus layer.

- Hold a small fish with one hand; grip from the top, first smoothing down the spiky dorsal fins then securing gently behind the gills. Grasp a larger fish with two hands from underneath (behind the gills and under its belly).

- You can remove a hook from the mouth of a small fish by hand. In larger fish or those with sharp teeth, use needle-nosed pliers to grip the hook and pull it out.

- If a fish has ingested the hook (more likely with live bait), leave it there and cut the line. These fish aren't likely to survive so if you're keeping some fish to cook, make it these (and promptly put them in a cooler with ice).

- If you are releasing it, return the fish to water right away by gently placing it horizontally in the lake and letting go.

CATCH & COOK

If you hook enough fish for dinner, it's time to prep it for the campfire. Watch the "How to clean trout" tutorial at youtube.com/theWDFW. Leave skin on the butterflied trout and season the inside generously with salt, pepper, and garlic powder. Insert several slabs of butter, close the fish, then wrap it in foil, making a tight packet. Place the packet on the cooking grate over the fire until the foil packet puffs up, about ten minutes, moving the packet as needed to cook evenly, flipping it once. Alternatively, roll the seasoned fish fillets in cornmeal and pan-fry it in lots of butter over a campstove or fire.

NATURE NOTEBOOK

Location: Date:

Co-naturers:

Yellow perch are marked with broad vertical stripes, rainbow trout are speck-led and have a beautiful horizontal iridescent band that displays a rainbow of color, and crappie are greenish and mottled black all over. Notice the subtle beauty of the fish you see, and sketch them here:

LEARN MORE

For fishing regulations, catch limits, seasons, and to get a license, contact the Washington Department of Fish & Wildlife at (360) 902-2464. The Fish Washington mobile app provides up-to-date fishing regulations, locations of fishing access points, instructional videos, and more. Every June, WDFW holds a Free Fishing Weekend along with Fishing 101 workshops throughout the state. Great fishing tutorials from WDFW are on their YouTube channel. Get involved in activism for fish habitat and preserving wild fish populations with the Wild Fish Conservancy or Washington's Trout Unlimited.

HORSETHIEF LAKE

Columbia Hills Historical State Park, Lyle, off SR-14

⭐ *Rainbow trout, largemouth bass, and bluegill*

Stocked with trout since the 1960s, this "lake" is a diked-off cove on the Columbia River. Cast in spring or early summer for trout, and all summer for bass and smaller fish like crappie or bluegill.

NEWMAN LAKE

NE Newman Lake Drive, Spokane

⭐ *Tiger muskies, largemouth bass, bluegill, yellow perch, and catfish*

East of Spokane on the border with Idaho is Newman Lake. Launch a canoe from the Washington Department of Fish and Wildlife boat launch or cast from the nearby fishing pier, which has benches for your comfort. Unique here are tiger muskies, with a limit of one, at least 50 inches long.

LELAND LAKE

165 Leland Valley Road, Quilcene, off US 101 on Hood Canal

⭐ *Largemouth bass, bluegill, yellow perch, rainbow trout, and brown bullhead catfish*

Cast from the public dock or walk along the shore casting in the shadows of overhanging trees. Make it a camping weekend at the adjacent Jefferson County Leland Lake Campground.

SPLASH IN A MOUNTAIN LAKE

GLACIAL WATER FEELS GOOD

Colchuck Lake in the Alpine Lakes Wilderness

IMAGINE HIKING in the mountains when the trail leads you over a rise, revealing a shimmering lake cradled in an ice-polished granite punchbowl. Its milky waters are a bold hue somewhere between sapphire and cerulean. You wonder, *How did this lake get here, and why is it such a spectacular color of blue?*

The Olympic and Cascade mountain ranges are dotted with lakes, from the woodsy lowlands to high alpine flanks of the tallest peaks. If a trail can be engineered through the landscape to reach one of these mountain pools, it probably has been—lakes are among the most popular destinations for hikers, especially on a hot summer day. Dip a toe in to test the waters, wade in a little, or go all in for a cold plunge. *Brrrrr!* Mountain lakes are fed by snowmelt and glaciers so expect very cold water if you wade in. Lake bottoms may be sandy or rocky, jagged or smooth, so pack water sandals to protect your feet.

When you come to a mountain lake, look for clues to its origin in the surrounding landscape. Are there streams draining in or flowing out? Did glacial debris or a rock slide form a natural dam? One clue is elevation—many of the subalpine and alpine lakes in both the Olympics and Cascades are nestled in cirque bowls scooped out long ago by glaciers. These cirque basin lakes are called tarns, and often appear a milky turquoise or emerald color from all the reflective glacial silt in the water. Lakes lower on mountain slopes may sit in valleys or U-shaped basins once scoured by ice and now fed by snowmelt.

WHERE TO GO

There is no lifeguard on duty in the wilderness, so you're swimming at your own risk. Here are some spectacular mountain lakes.

BAGLEY LAKES LOOP, MOUNT BAKER

Mount Baker Highway (SR 542)
fs.usda.gov/mbs, (360) 599-2714
NORTHWEST FOREST PASS
2 miles round-trip, 150 feet elevation gain

This lake hike is atop an active volcano, with magma inside and ice on top. The trail skirts around beautiful glacial tarns ringed with granite outcrops and huckleberry bushes—go in late summer for ripe berries and early fall for fiery foliage. Loop clockwise around Lower Bagley Lake and alongside the alpine stream that flows down Upper Bagley Lake with open views to a looming peak with a very flat top, the aptly named Table Mountain. A twin arch stone bridge spans the outlet stream from Upper Bagley Lake (photo op!)—after you cross it, the trail to the right leads back to your car. Before you head back, head left and meander along the upper lake's shore until you find a great spot to lunch and maybe dip your feet in the ice-cold water. A longer loop extends the hike from Bagley Lakes up to include the half dozen or so Chain Lakes (8 miles round-trip, 1600 feet elevation gain).

ASHLAND LAKES, MOUNTAIN LOOP HIGHWAY

Mountain Loop Highway east of Granite Falls
dnr.wa.gov/MorningStar, (360) 854-2882
DISCOVER PASS
5.5 miles round-trip, 800 feet elevation gain

It's one of the wettest spots on the Cascade Range's western slope, and this rain forest has spongy moss, slimy slugs, and stinky skunk cabbage to prove it. Get close to beaver dams, lily pads, and frogs on the puncheon (wooden plank boardwalk) that comprises much of the trail. The path skirts around three tranquil lakes fringed with pristine

NATURE NOTEBOOK

Location: _____ Date: _____

Co-naturers: _____

Describe the lake using all your senses. What color is the water? Is it warmed by the sun or cold from snowmelt? How does it move? What signs of wildlife do you see by the lake? What sounds do you hear?

_____

_____

_____

_____

_____

_____

_____

_____

_____

_____

sphagnum peat bogs—first a wetland home to dragonflies (especially in summer) called Beaver Plant Lake, then Upper Ashland Lake, and finally to the largest, prettiest, and most remote of all, Lower Ashland Lake.

LAKE DOROTHY, STEVENS PASS

US 2 Milepost 46
fs.usda.gov/mbs, (425) 888-1421
NORTHWEST FOREST PASS
3.5 miles round-trip, 800 feet elevation gain

The perfect lake hike has two essentials: irresistible water for swimming and an access trail just hard enough to work up a sweat along the way. This sparkling mountain gem in the Alpine Lakes Wilderness offers both. What it doesn't deliver is solitude, although the 2-mile long lakeshore offers room to spread out. A spur trail to the lake's outlet takes you to a giant log jam, the best photo op of the lake, and access for wading in. The main trail continues on a high path along the lake's eastern shore, interspersed with short side trails down to campsites, picnic spots, and access points for taking a dip. Extend your hike for 2 more miles along the shore of Lake Dorothy and up over a saddle to smaller, uncrowded Bear and Deer Lakes. About 1 mile from the trailhead, the trail crosses Camp Robber Creek, which falls into a perfect swimming hole—just in time for a refreshing plunge.

SHEEP LAKE, MOUNT RAINIER

SR 410 east of Chinook Pass
fs.usda.gov/mbs, (360) 825-6585
NORTHWEST FOREST PASS
5 miles round-trip, 400 feet elevation gain
The gentle, scenic trail to Sheep Lake is actually a small portion of the Pacific Crest Trail, the 2600-mile route from the Mexican border to the Canadian border that backpackers complete over the course of several months. This route travels through open mountain hemlock forest punctuated with clearings of wildflowers (in midsummer) and loaded huckleberry bushes (ready for picking in late summer). The turnaround point is placid Sheep Lake, fringed with meadows and the perfect spot for a midday picnic and a refreshing swim.

LEARN MORE

See Washington Trails Association's hiking guide to search for more trails to lakes.

COLCHUCK LAKE, LEAVENWORTH

Icicle Road to FS Road 7601
fs.usda.gov/mbs, (509) 548-2550
NORTHWEST FOREST PASS
8.4 miles round-trip, 2200 feet elevation gain
When it comes to mountain lakes you can reach on a day hike, Colchuck Lake is the crème de la crème—a gorgeous azure pool of silty glacier runoff tucked into a bowl scooped out of exposed granite. From the Lake Stuart trailhead, the hiking is easy along Mountaineer Creek, its snowmelt waters tumbling over granite boulders, with glimpses of craggy peaks of the Stuart Range through clearings in the lodgepole and ponderosa pine. After crossing the creek on a sturdy bridge, the real work begins up switchbacks, across a boulder field, and up more switchbacks until suddenly the prettiest blue water sprawls before you and spectacular Dragontail Peak looms above. Your (very) cold plunge awaits.

 *Connect with Nature*

Placid mountain lakes are the perfect surface for skipping stones. Look for a flat rock that's of uniform thickness, 2 to 3 inches diameter, not too heavy. Hold it between your thumb and middle finger, your pointer finger hooked around the edge. Facing the water, throw the rock with a low sidearm pitch, cocking your wrist and giving it a quick flick for spin as you release the stone so it'll skip across the water.

PITCH A TENT

WAKE UP IN THE WOODS

A secluded campsite in the North Cascades

CAMPING IS FIR NEEDLES in your hair and stars in the sky. It's bats zooming overhead at dusk, and the hoot of an owl at midnight. Camping is toasty, gooey marshmallows singed to perfection over a crackling fire. Camping is no Wi-Fi, and sleeping on the ground. Camping is fun.

If you didn't grow up in a camping family, the idea of pitching your own tent in the woods might make you sweat a little. First, there's ample planning involved, like ironing out where to go and procuring all the gear you need. Then there's figuring out how to do all the camping things once you get out there—pitching the tent, fiddling with the campstove, or dealing with unexpected rain. If you don't have all this mastered already, it might seem far too much work for a few woodsy nights under the Milky Way.

Power through the effort to go camping the first time, and future trips will be a cinch. Break down the prep into four bite-sized pieces: follow a good gear list, plan out meals, reserve your campsite in advance, and try out your gear at home first.

GET IN GEAR

The up-front investment in camping gear will give you sticker shock, but there are ways to cut corners, and you'll enjoy years of use if you take care of your gear. Short a few things? Borrow from friends or rent some items to fill in the gaps.

The most important and expensive purchase is the tent. You'll pay more for a lightweight one, but then you can also use it for backpacking or bike camping. How much space do you want? A two-person tent is actually tight for two people, with room only for sleeping bags and nothing else; a four-person tent adds space but also weight. Is the rain fly going to keep you dry in a downpour? Is the tent assembly simple and easy? Choose your sleeping bag thoughtfully, too. Do you want ultralight down fill or synthetic? A mummy shape for warmth or rectangular for freedom of movement? How warm does it need to be? For warm-season camping, aim for one rated 30–50° F. If you can, go to a gear store and actually get into some bags to try them out. Then decide what you'll sleep on—a cot, air mattress, or basic sleeping pad. The rest of the gear—from camp chairs to stoves—is fairly straightforward.

Master your meals. Gather the exact portions of ingredients for each meal into a large ziplock (with a recipe card if needed)—this saves room and prep time at camp. Portion things for the cooler, too—if you use cream in your coffee, pour only what you'll use into a small, leak-proof capped bottle (Nalgene makes great ones). What makes great campground food? Think yummy but simple—hot dogs on a stick roasted over a fire with mustard and kraut is classic, a pot of chili with fixins, oatmeal with lots of fruit toppings, fancy grilled cheese sandwiches with bacon and apple slices toasted to perfection in a pie iron. Cook on a stove, over the campfire, or a little of both—bring a campstove and fuel along in case of a burn ban.

Reserve your campsite. Skip the last-minute scramble to hunt down a vacant campsite by reserving it ahead of time. Most state park campgrounds take reservations, just a handful of national park campgrounds do, and national forest campgrounds are somewhere in the middle. State park campgrounds can be reserved up to nine months in advance at washington.goingtocamp .com or (888) CAMPOUT. National park and national forest campgrounds can be reserved up to six months in advance at recreation.gov or (877) 444-6777.

Test gear at home. Assemble your tent in the backyard or a city park first so you're familiar with how it's put together. Test-run your campstove somewhere outdoors—attach the fuel canister, learn how to prime it, and make sure it lights. If taking an air mattress, confirm your air pump fits the valve and fix any leaks.

WHERE TO GO

First-timers will want a car-camping campground that can be reserved in advance, has bathrooms with plumbing, and has recreational opportunities on-site. The campsite should have a flat place to pitch a tent, a picnic table, and a campfire ring. A campground host will sell firewood by the bundle, so bring cash. Here are five wonderful campgrounds that fit the bill.

MORA, OLYMPIC NATIONAL PARK
Off SR 110 east of Forks
nps.gov/onp, (360) 374-5460
NATIONAL PARK PASS

Spacious campsites are nestled in the privacy of old-growth woods along the Quillayute River, ancestral lands of the Quileute Tribe. One of the few national park campgrounds on the wild Olympic coast, Mora stands out for its proximity to stunning Rialto Beach, and its massive drift logs, rocky tide pools, pounding surf, and offshore sea stacks. From Mora, take a nearly 2-mile hike along the River Trail and try to spot wildlife.

Setting up your tent is easy with a bit of practice.

photo by Kike Arnaiz

COLONIAL CREEK CAMPGROUND, NORTH CASCADES NATIONAL PARK

SR 20 at Diablo, nps.gov/noca, (877) 444-6777

CAMPGROUND FEE

Camp along the shores of turquoise Diablo Lake under glaciated crags of nearby peaks. A few trails depart from the campground, including a climb to the top of Thunder Knob and a stroll along beautiful Thunder Creek. Park rangers give nature talks at the amphitheater on summer evenings. No boat rentals at the lake, but there's a launch if you bring a canoe. Each campsite provides a bear-proof cabinet for food storage.

MORAN STATE PARK

3572 Olga Road, Orcas Island
parks.state.wa.us, (360) 376-2326

CAMPGROUND FEE

Pitch a tent at your lakeside campsite, then decide what to do first! There are four freshwater lakes with swimming beaches and boats to rent, many miles of trails through old-growth forest, and the park has its own mountain (Mount Constitution—hike to the top and tour the old CCC-era fire lookout). Cascade Lake is stocked with kokanee, cutthroat, and rainbow trout. Ferry lines can be a bear in summer, but walk on with your camping gear and take the Orcas Island Shuttle to the park.

OHANAPECOSH, MOUNT RAINIER NATIONAL PARK

Off SR 123, nps.gov/mora, (360) 569-2211

NATIONAL PARK PASS

Tucked in the southeast corner of the park, Ohanapecosh is well away from the hustle and bustle of the summer crowds at Paradise and Sunrise, but still within an hour's drive of each, making it the perfect base camp. Campsites are strewn about the magical old-growth forest, and a wild river runs right through the middle of the campground. Hike the half-mile nature loop trail through enormous Doug firs and hemlocks to the bubbling waters of the Ohanapecosh Hot Springs. Up the road a bit is the famed Grove of the Patriarchs trail—an easy, flat loop to some of the biggest trees on earth. This campground has a small park visitor center and natural history museum.

CURLEW LAKE STATE PARK

62 State Park Road, Republic
parks.state.wa.us, (509) 775-3592

CAMPGROUND FEE

Set in open and dry lodgepole pine, the lower-loop tent sites on a berm have great views of the lake—reserve one of those. Curlew Lake is known for wildlife watching and fishing for rainbow trout (the lake is amply stocked, so bring a pole and frying pan). Bring a bathing suit for the sandy swimming beach on hot days. They used to pan for gold here—maybe it's worth a try! Stretch your legs on the 1.6-mile Curlew Lake Nature Trail along the shoreline.

LEARN MORE

The indispensable car camper's bible is *Camping Washington: The Best Public Campgrounds for Tents & RVs*, by Ron Judd. It offers loads of detail on every public campground, punctuated with the author's signature humor.

Want to rent some gear? Choose a tent, sleeping bag, campstove, or a full car camping set at your local outdoor store. Washington State Parks partners with Arrive Outdoors to rent camping gear on a budget, and it gets shipped to your house ([213] 559-2482).

NATURE NOTEBOOK

Location: _____   Date: _____

Co-naturers: _____

Be still, watch and listen to the sounds of the night. Describe each sound
you hear. Is there rustling in nearby brush? It could be a raccoon, coyote,
opossum, or skunk. A hoot from a tree? Toads or bullfrogs singing in a nearby
pond? Are bats circling overhead?

_____

_____

_____

_____

_____

_____

_____

_____

_____

_____

_____

_____

_____

_____

_____

_____

CAR CAMPING CHECKLIST

The key to a great car camping checklist is to trim it down to the basic necessities with a handful of comforts tossed in. This checklist gets you started—add a few items unique to your needs.

SHELTER

- ☐ Tent (poles, rain fly, ground cloth)
- ☐ Extra tarp and rope
- ☐ Camp chairs

SLEEPING

- ☐ Sleeping pad, cot, or air mattress
- ☐ Sleeping bag
- ☐ Pillow (or pillow case to stuff clothes in)
- ☐ Extra blanket

COOKING

- ☐ Campstove
- ☐ Fuel
- ☐ Matches or lighter
- ☐ Cookset (pots, spatula)
- ☐ Eating utensils (plates, cups, forks)
- ☐ Garbage bag
- ☐ Ziplock bags, various sizes
- ☐ Biodegradable dish soap and sponge
- ☐ Bucket for washing dishes
- ☐ Napkins, dish towels
- ☐ Paper towel roll
- ☐ Can and bottle opener, knife
- ☐ Cooler and ice
- ☐ Tablecloth
- ☐ Jugs of drinking water
- ☐ Empty jug for transporting water
- ☐ Foil and plastic wrap

FOOD

- ☐ Ingredients for each meal
- ☐ Fruit and snacks (high on variety)
- ☐ Salt, pepper, cooking oil
- ☐ Coffee or tea, cream and sugar
- ☐ Hot cocoa mix (and insulated mugs)
- ☐ Drinks (pop, milk, juice)
- ☐ Popcorn and campfire popper
- ☐ Makings for s'mores

SAFETY

- ☐ First-aid kit
- ☐ Insect repellent
- ☐ Citronella candle
- ☐ Sunblock
- ☐ Duct tape (for quick repairs)
- ☐ Moleskin (for blisters)
- ☐ Aloe vera gel
- ☐ Calamine lotion
- ☐ Hydrocortisone
- ☐ Allergy medication
- ☐ Over-the-counter pain reliever
- ☐ Water filter
- ☐ Whistle (a signal for help)
- ☐ Headlamp or flashlight and batteries
- ☐ Directions to nearest ER
- ☐ Cell phone (optional solar charger)

PERSONAL ITEMS

- ☐ Towel and washcloth
- ☐ Biodegradable soap and sponge
- ☐ Toothbrush and paste
- ☐ Toilet paper
- ☐ Wet wipes
- ☐ Hand sanitizer
- ☐ Deodorant

CLOTHING

- ☐ Raingear
- ☐ Fleece jacket
- ☐ Down vest or jacket
- ☐ Hiking shoes or boots
- ☐ Camp clogs
- ☐ Warm socks
- ☐ Base layer (long underwear)
- ☐ Shorts and pants
- ☐ Shirts (think layers)
- ☐ Pajamas
- ☐ Swimsuit
- ☐ Warm hat and gloves
- ☐ Sunglasses and hat

MISCELLANEOUS

- ☐ Small broom
- ☐ Quarters for shower
- ☐ Hiking guidebook
- ☐ Road atlas
- ☐ Water bottle
- ☐ Campground reservations info
- ☐ Directions to campground
- ☐ Emergency contact numbers
- ☐ Camera
- ☐ Daypack with the Ten Essentials (see the introduction)
- ☐ Books and games
- ☐ Pocketknife

SLEEP IN A FIRE LOOKOUT

HIKE UP AND LOOK OUT OVER THE WORLD

Miner's Ridge
fire lookout
in the fog

photo by Kim Brown

I went out in my alpine yard and there it was . . .
hundreds of miles of pure snow-covered rocks and
virgin lakes and high timber. Below, instead of
the world, I saw a sea of marshmallow clouds.
—Jack Kerouac, *The Dharma Bums*

IN AUGUST 1910, wildfires engulfed three million acres of forest in the West in just a few days. Known as "the Big Burn," the devastation was a wake-up call; wildfires can be enormously destructive. "Put it out" became the Forest Service battle cry, ushering in a century of wildfire suppression. It's a mixed legacy still standing today in more than ninety backcountry fire lookouts in Washington, perched atop remote peaks with panoramic views.

National parks and forests relied on volunteers called fire spotters to scan the scenery for a sign of smoke. Then, from inside their fire lookout, a circular mapping tool called the Osborne Fire Finder pinpointed a rough location of the fire. The spotter might radio a nearby fire lookout to corroborate the location using triangulation. Fire fighters were called in to reach the wildfire before it grew too big or destructive.

For the lookout volunteers back then (and a few still today), the stint meant lonely weeks on end high in the mountains, watching and waiting for smoke or flame that may never come—it's an outdoorsy introvert's dream vacation. When there's no fire to spot, there are books to read, landscapes to sketch, and, for some, prose to write. In 1956, twelve years before the land under his boots would become North Cascades National Park, Jack Kerouac was stationed for sixty-three days as a fire scout in a cabin atop Desolation Peak. His experiences that summer, and the pull he felt between his urban bohemian lifestyle and his odyssey into the wilderness, were chronicled in his soulful novel *The Dharma Bums*. Kerouac's friend and fellow beat poet Gary Snyder had a stint in the nearby Sourdough Mountain lookout a few years prior.

These days, drones, satellites, and remote cameras have replaced most lookout towers, which once numbered nine thousand across the US. Those that remain are fiercely protected and regularly maintained by preservation organizations. A few hundred lookouts are still staffed with fire spotters throughout the West, including thirty in Washington. Many inactive towers still stand as relics from a waning era for hikers to visit and appreciate, and some are repurposed as lofty rental cabins for a unique getaway.

WHERE TO GO

These three fire lookouts can be reserved in advance as rentals. Washington has six additional fire lookouts that you can stay in, but they're first-come, first-served—find them at firelookout.org.

HEYBROOK LOOKOUT

Mount Baker-Snoqualmie National Forest,
Skykomish District, US 2 east of Index
recreation.gov (for reservations)
Rentable May 1–October 31, sleeps 4
2.6 miles round-trip, 850 feet elevation gain
Start with a hike that goes up, up, up through second-growth woods just over 1 mile to the lookout tower (1700 feet)—and wow, what a tower! Climb the stairs up 67 feet to the fire lookout cabin, where you'll feel like you're suspended in midair above the ridgeline as you sip your morning coffee and enjoy views through wraparound windows of Mount Index, Bridal Veil Falls, Mount Baring, and

Mount Persis. The Everett Mountaineers has restored this cabin, which dates back to 1965. Amenities include a bed, table and chairs, propane stove, pots and dishes, coffee pot, and lanterns. A vault toilet is down the stairs and down the ridge a bit.

EVERGREEN MOUNTAIN LOOKOUT

Mount Baker–Snoqualmie National Forest,
Skykomish District, off US Highway 2 at
Skykomish, north on Beckler Road
recreation.gov (for reservations)
Rentable July–October, sleeps 4
2.8 miles round-trip, 1425 feet elevation gain

Oh, the views. You'll wonder if it's all worth it driving up about 22 miles of mostly gravel Forest Service road to reach the trailhead. You'll sweat a little on the semirugged ascent through wildflower meadows and berry fields into the Wild Sky Wilderness. But when you reach the ridge and the cute lookout cabin (5585 feet), you'll know it was worth it and then some. Views from Glacier Peak to the north, Mount Rainier to the south, and everything in between can be enjoyed from inside the lookout thanks to large windows on all four sides. Backpack in with all your gear, including water—there's none available at the lookout or on the trail. The cabin has beds and mattresses, table and chairs, a propane stove, lanterns, cooking and coffee pots, and dishes. A vault toilet is located a short hike away down the ridge.

LEARN MORE

The Forest Fire Lookout Association promotes the protection, enjoyment, understanding, and restoration of fire lookouts. The Washington lookouts mentioned here are profiled on their website.

Hiking Washington's Fire Lookouts, by Amber Casali, highlights forty-four memorable lookouts in the Olympics and Cascades. Connect with other fire lookout enthusiasts on the private Facebook group, Fire Lookouts of Washington.

QUARTZ MOUNTAIN LOOKOUT

Mount Spokane State Park, Spokane, off US 2 at
Skykomish, north on Beckler Road
parks.state.wa.us, (888) CAMP-OUT (for
reservations)
Rentable June 15–September 30, sleeps 4
5 miles round-trip, 750 feet elevation gain

This wood-frame cabin dates back to 1979, when Washington's Department of Natural Resources built it atop a 40-foot tower on Mount Spokane so spotters could scan for signs of flame and smoke. When technology replaced its utility, Washington State Parks rescued it from demolition, moved it to a 10-foot tower on the rocky summit of Quartz Mountain to the south, and restored

 **Connect with Nature**

Want to visit all of Washington's ninety fire lookouts? A handful of peak-baggers have completed the challenge, affectionately called the SLOW list (Standing Lookouts of Washington). Learn more and view photos of all of them at peakbagger.com.

its original beauty. The 14-by-14-foot lookout (5129 feet) has wraparound windows and deck so you can enjoy views across to other summits like Mount Spokane and Mount Kit Carson—south into the Spokane Valley, and east into the peaks and lakes of the north Idaho panhandle. To get there, set off from Selkirk Lodge for the 2.5-mile hike up to the lookout, bringing all your gear in a backpack. There's no electricity, but a propane cooking stove is provided as well as other amenities— campfire ring with wood, table and chairs, drinking water, beds and mattresses, cutting board, a nearby vault toilet, and more.

NATURE NOTEBOOK

Location: _____   Date: _____

Co-naturers: _____

To the Beat poets, a stint as fire lookout was a paid writing retreat with a view. Try writing a poem from a fire lookout or from the peak of a mountain, taking inspiration from the surrounding landscape.

_____

_____

_____

_____

_____

_____

_____

_____

_____

_____

_____

_____

_____

HIKE TO A GLACIER

RIVERS OF ICE CARVE OUR CRAGGY PEAKS

Observing
Big Four
Ice Caves

photo by Kim Brown

DO YOU KNOW WHERE your drinking water comes from? There's a good chance some of it started in a glacier. In the Pacific Northwest, glaciers give us life—they feed streams for drinking water, crops, and salmon, and their meltwater spins the turbines of hydroelectric dams for the region's power. Unfortunately, they're shrinking.

Alpine glaciers are massive bodies of ice that move down a mountain, formed over very long periods of time from snowfall. They're not fixed in time or space—glaciers are always moving from the force of gravity (albeit slowly, from a few feet to 100 feet per year). They've sculpted our beloved North Cascades into a jagged alpine wonderland, and tinted our mountain tarns an exquisite shade of blue. As a glacier scrapes against the earth, it grinds up the surface rock into a fine silt, which gets incorporated into the ice— this is why glacial lakes appear cloudy and reflect light as shades of aqua or emerald. The part of a glacier that touches the surface moves a tad more slowly than the rest of it; these varying speeds can rip open the glacier's surface to form a crevasse.

Washington has 186 named glaciers, making it the second most glaciated state after Alaska. Glaciers top all of the state's high peaks. Mount Rainier's twenty-five glaciers cover about five times as much ice as the glaciers on all of the other Cascade volcanoes combined, and it has both the largest glacier (Emmons) and the lowest terminus elevation glacier (Carbon) in the contiguous United States. Mount St. Helens had eleven named glaciers before its 1980 eruption; now just two remain. The Olympic Mountains have glaciers as well, with seven on Mount Olympus and eight more cloaking nearby peaks. Over the past century, glaciers in the North Cascades have shrunk by half. A warming climate foretells more years of insufficient snowpack and rapid receding of glacier ice.

WHERE TO GO

When you hike to a glacier, you'll reach its toe or snout—that's the terminus of a glacier. It'll likely be a massive, dirty hunk of ice. Glacial melt, milky with fine silt, pours out into small streams, which combine into bigger streams, then rivers. When hiking around glacier snouts and ice caves, stay back! It's tempting to want a closer look at the glacier face, but ice chunks and boulders can melt off and come tumbling down. Unless you're an experienced mountaineer, use binoculars and behold the glacier's wonder from afar.

PARK BUTTE–RAILROAD GRADE
SR 20 Milepost 82, Mount Baker
fs.usda.gov/mbs, (360) 856-5700
NORTHWEST FOREST PASS
7 miles round-trip, 2250 feet elevation gain
Start your hike on the Park Butte Trail and allow time to be slowed down by the wildflower bloom as you pass Schriebers Meadow in midsummer. Around 2.5 miles is the signed junction—head right to walk a small slope up to the Railroad Grade, an open ridge with smatterings of small boulders. You're essentially hiking on a glacial moraine, which is till smashed into existence by the massive Easton Glacier that soon comes into view. The later in summer you hike this trail, the farther you're able to get before hitting snow and the more you'll be able to gawk at the glacier's fissured ice and treacherous crevasses. Take care to not hike too close to the right edge of the moraine, as it's starting to crumble. Over the past three decades, the Easton Glacier has dropped about a quarter of its ice volume.

CASCADE PASS TO SAHALE ARM, NORTH CASCADES NATIONAL PARK

Cascade River Road off SR 20
nps.gov/noca, (206) 386-4495
11.8 miles round-trip, 3940 feet elevation gain

The hike starts with countless shaded switchbacks. Hang in there! After those first 2 miles, the exertion eases and trees part like a curtain to reveal the reason you came. Wildlife sightings are common—black bear, marmots, pikas, mountain goats, and the elusive White-tailed Ptarmigan. Wildflowers carpet rolling meadows, peep from rock crevices, and frame glistening mountain streams. The scenery is unrivaled—glorious crags, deep green valleys, and glaciers so close

NATURE NOTEBOOK

Location: _____   Date: _____

Co-naturers: _____

What is your role in minimizing climate change? List a few things you pledge
to do to help curb the pace of global warming and save the glaciers.

_____

_____

_____

_____

_____

_____

_____

_____

_____

_____

_____

_____

_____

_____

you can feel the cool breeze blow off them. Hanging glaciers on the 8200-foot Mount Johannesburg (and other nearby peaks) let loose small avalanches in an intensifying rumble. Cascade Pass makes a fine turn-around for a shorter hike, but it's worth pushing on up the flowery ridge and over rock scree to the awesome beauty of Sahale Arm, the top of a glacier-carved cirque. The hike ends at the toe of the Sahale Glacier and the Sahale Glacier Camp (permit required), one of the most scenic campsites in the Cascades, with flat spots ringed with rocks to protect against the wind.

CARBON GLACIER, MOUNT RAINIER NATIONAL PARK

Off SR 165 south of Carbonado
nps.gov/mora
NATIONAL PARK PASS
18.4 miles round-trip, 1800 feet elevation gain
This massive river of ice has the lowest terminus altitude of any active glacier in the lower forty-eight states; it flows for 5 miles down nearly the whole length of Mount Rainier to about 3500 feet in elevation. It's also the thickest glacier—its ice is 700 feet in places. The glacier's snout is now out of day hiking range due to a major washout of the Carbon River Road near the park entrance several years ago. Make the trip an overnight backpack, or mountain bike the 5 miles of old road, then hike past Ipsut Falls and up the Wonderland Trail to the Carbon River Suspension Bridge—the safe vantage point of the massive glacier's toe, a thick blob of dark ice (hence its name) out of which flows a stream of milky water that becomes the Carbon River. The glacier owes its sooty hue

to the rock debris falling off the sheer cliff called Willis Wall.

BIG FOUR ICE CAVES, NORTH CASCADES

Mountain Loop Highway east of Verlot
fs.usda.gov/mbs, (360) 691-7791
NORTHWEST FOREST PASS
2.2 miles round-trip, 200 feet elevation gain
Warning: once you reach this frozen wonder, do not venture near, inside, or on top of the ice caves. Many people have died doing so. There's a huge hunk of snowy ice that looks like a giant snow drift at the base of some 4000-foot cliff walls that prop up the north face of Big Four Mountain. Is it a glacier? Scientists aren't sure—some years it has melted down to show very little snowpack, then the size of the ice pack increases after a few winters of robust snowfall and it appears to be a glacier again—Big Four Glacier. Each winter, snow and avalanches fall down the sheer cliff walls and add to the pile. It starts to melt as the weather warms, and by midsummer the ice caves appear at the glacier's base. The trail in through the conifer forest is easy and short.

GO STARGAZING

BEHOLD THE NIGHT SKY

The Milky Way from Lake Wenatchee State Park

photo by Benjamin Massello

ON A CLEAR summer night, go outside at dusk and look up. Even in the city, a few of the brightest stars and planets will peer back at you like tiny lanterns. As the sky darkens, twinkling stars appear faster than you can count them. Your eyes might piece together familiar constellations—formations named for gods and mythical creatures by the ancient Greeks, each accompanied by a story. The stars don't move, but we do; as Earth spins and rotates around the sun, our Pacific Northwest view of the stars shifts.

Gazing at the vast night sky can be grounding, particularly in uncertain times. Take notice as the moon changes over the month from full to a waning gibbous to a new moon to a waxing crescent. The phases are so predictable they can be forecast fifty million years into the future. Some watch the stars and planets for existential pondering—the universe reveals its deepest mysteries to us if we are curious and courageous enough to explore it.

With some basic stargazing know-how, you've got a new after-dark pastime on your camping trips, and even in your backyard. Stars, planets, the moon, and meteors are visible from almost anywhere, but you'll see far more of them away from the light pollution of urban areas. Choose a night distant from a full moon—you've got a twelve-day window that's ideal. Here's how to get started.

FIND CONSTELLATIONS

Constellations organize the sky into a celestial map. Head out on a moonless night and use a stargazing app like SkyMap that displays stars, planets, and constellations as you point your smartphone around the night sky (use the dimmest setting so your eyes adjust well to the dark). Find the most recognizable shape in the northern night sky—the Big Dipper. It looks like a soup ladle and is not a constellation itself but is part of Ursa Major, the great bear. With your eyes, draw a straight line through the two outer stars of the ladle (they're called Merak and Dubhe) and extend that imaginary line beyond the ladle's lid—it points to Polaris, the North Star, and the last star of the Little Dipper's handle. From here, make out other constellations like Cassiopeia, Cepheus, and Draco.

VIEW THE MOON

You need only binoculars and a full moon (or close to it) to view its whole surface up close—a tapestry of mountains, craters, and vast, dark seas called mares, ancient lava beds that early astronomers mistook for seas. The lightest areas are lunar highlands, or mountains. Do you see a prominent crater near the moon's south pole with radiating rays? This is Tycho. The moon's craters, formed when asteroids and meteorites crashed into its surface, lend it that Swiss cheese appearance.

LEARN MORE

Get a night sky app for your smartphone or tablet. Sky Map and Sky Guide are excellent options. The Seattle Astronomical Society holds several "star party" field trips a month around the city and nearby suburbs, led by expert astronomers. Connect with Dark Skies Northwest, the local chapter of the International Dark Sky Association. They work to solve the problem of light pollution to preserve the beautiful night sky. Listen to NPR's daily audio segment *Stardate* for cool space facts and current astronomical events.

WHERE TO FIND DARK SKIES

Washington's darkest skies are found in large swaths of public land, such as national parks and forests. High meadows and ridges at tree line in the Olympics and Cascades are prime stargazing locales. Darksitefinder.com can help you find other areas free of light pollution. Here are some top spots.

THE OLYMPIC COAST.
Pitch a tent on an Olympic National Park beach and gaze the night away. The darkest skies in the state are wide open over the Pacific Ocean, so there's no better place to watch a meteor shower.

ARTIST POINT.
On a clear night with little to no moon, drive to this stellar vista of the cosmos at 5000 feet elevation tucked between Mount Shuksan and Mount Baker.

SUNRISE.
This spot on the eastern slope of Mount Rainier has zero light pollution and sits above tree line, so you have a wide open sky—perfect for spying meteors or gawking at the Milky Way.

OBSERVATORIES

THEODOR JACOBSEN OBSERVATORY, UNIVERSITY OF WASHINGTON, SEATTLE.
Built in 1895 with a refracting telescope from the same era, this campus observatory in the UW Astronomy Department frequently opens its doors to nonstudents for free open houses and astronomy talks.

EDWIN E. RICHIE OBSERVATORY, BAINBRIDGE ISLAND.
See the night sky through the largest publicly accessible telescope in the region, and stay for cosmic talks with the Battle Point Astronomical Association in their planetarium.

GOLDENDALE OBSERVATORY STATE PARK HERITAGE SITE, GOLDENDALE.
DISCOVER PASS
The wide-open skies of Eastern Washington look pretty amazing through this giant hilltop telescope. See the northern lights during geomagnetic storms.

Unlike Earth, the moon has no atmosphere to burn them up before they collide. Notice how its surface appears static, night after night? From Earth we always see the same side of it, and rely on satellite images to know what's on the other side. At moonrise, you'll see the most detail and relief on the moon's surface—find the moon phase calendar at stardate.org.

SEE THE MILKY WAY

Nearly everything you see in the night sky without a telescope is part of the Milky Way galaxy. But unless you're in the right place at the right time, you've perhaps never seen the Milky Way in all its glory—a stunning, nebulous band of glowing light in the night sky comprising billions of stars. Earth sits on the outer edge of the densest part, so we have a

Nighttime at Third Beach, Olympic National Park

NATURE NOTEBOOK

Location: Date:

Co-naturers:

Gazing at the night sky reminds us that although we are small compared to the universe, we are a part of it; the brightest, farthest stars are made up of the same thing we are—stardust. In what ways do you feel connected to the cosmos?

stellar view. You need very dark, clear, summer skies to see the Milky Way—search for the darkest skies during a new moon to experience this astral wonder.

WATCH THE PERSEID METEOR SHOWER

What are you doing at night the second week of August? Look up! A meteor shower occurs when Earth passes through a stream of cosmic debris (meteoroids) that hit Earth's atmosphere at high speeds, burning up on entry and giving off a shooting stream of bright light (hence their nickname, shooting stars). The Perseids are remnants of the comet Swift–Tuttle. This shower typically peaks August 11–13. If this coincides with a full moon, set your alarm and look for meteors in the dark hour before dawn. To see dozens of meteors, flee the city's lights and spread out a blanket, lie down, and gaze up.

Once your eyes adjust, you'll see meteors in various places in the sky.

SPOT THE NORTHERN LIGHTS

The Aurora Borealis is the sky's natural light show—a glowing display of reds, greens, and blues caused by solar storms on the sun. These storms eject charged particles into space. Earth's magnetosphere repels most of them, but this protection is weakest at the North and South Poles. When the charged particles interact with nitrogen and oxygen, they expel photons; the result is a wash of color in the night sky, with different hues tied to various levels of the atmosphere. To see this celestial phenomenon for yourself, you have to be in the right place at the right time, with an open view to the north along the horizon. Aurora chasers check with NOAA's Space Weather Prediction Center for the nightly Aurora forecast.

DROP A CRAB POT

TRAP DINNER IN YOUR LOCAL BAY

Fresh catch
of Dungeness
crab

FEW CULINARY ADVENTURES are more quintessentially Northwest than tossing a crab pot off a dock and eating whatever crawls inside, hoping for male Dungeness crab large enough to be a keeper. Our most famous and delicious crustacean is known for tender, sweet meat and can be caught with minimal gear and just a little know-how.

Most active at slack current (just before high or low tides), Dungeness crab live in shallow sand-bottomed bays and sheltered coves of eelgrass beds of Puget Sound, Hood Canal, and the Strait of Juan de Fuca, as well as coastal bays and nearshore habitat. To catch some, you'll need a crab trap (pot or ring), some bait, a gauge to measure them, and the proper fishing license. Crab pots are hefty wire cages with one-way entry doors. You can leave them in place for hours. Ring nets are open, and crabs crawl onto them to feast on the bait, getting trapped as you pull the ring up. Check them often—it's an active and fun experience.

Rent crabbing gear at docks and marinas throughout Puget Sound and the coastal estuaries. You don't need a big boat—walk out on a dock and drop a pot, or paddle a kayak offshore a bit and toss a crab ring or two. Some intrepid crabbers forego the trap altogether, pull on waders, and head out into the water on a minus tide, picking them up out of the eelgrass one at a time by dip net.

WHERE TO GO

Crabbing is open for a summer and fall season in Hood Canal and most of Puget Sound north of Seattle, and nearly year-round on the coast. Unlike clamming, crabbing isn't restricted to specific beach tidelands—if a region is open, you can crab anywhere.

LEARN MORE

You'll find detailed crabbing tutorials from Washington Department of Fish & Wildlife on their YouTube channel. At the department's website you'll see crabbing regulations and license info, crabbing regions, seasons, and catch days. Buy crab traps and gear at your local fishing shop.

GRAYS HARBOR, WASHINGTON COAST

Crabbing hubs line the coast from the mouth of the mighty Columbia River and Willapa Bay up to Westport and Ocean Shores. Set on a snug cove, the fishing village of Westport is the top spot for dropping a crab trap from a dock, no boat required. Stop at one of the bait shops or fishing charters on the waterfront to rent a crab ring, obtain a license, and pick up other supplies, then walk out on Float 20, at the end of Neddie Rose Drive. Drop your pot or toss your ring, then wait (bring a good book and lawn chair to pass the time). Pull up your ring every fifteen minutes or so to check your haul.

HOOD CANAL, EAST OLYMPIC PENINSULA

Shallow and protected, Hood Canal is perfect for crabbing by kayak. Rent one or bring your own and try a crab pot specifically designed for kayaks. Pick up some bait and a shellfish license at the Brinnon General Store.

DUNGENESS BAY, NORTH OLYMPIC PENINSULA

All the bays in this part of the Strait of Juan de Fuca are great for crabbing (Dungeness,

NATURE NOTEBOOK

Location: _____ Date: _____

Co-naturers: _____

What was your favorite part of your crabbing experience? Would you do it again?

_____

_____

_____

_____

_____

_____

_____

_____

_____

_____

Sequim, and Discovery Bays), though there's something extra special about pulling a big Dungie out of its namesake waters. Get the full experience by walking into the water in waders with a dip net a few hours before a minus tide. With your back to the sun to reduce glare, look for the purplish-brown shell of a crab making its way on sand through the tangled eelgrass. If you've got a boat, launch it from Landing Park and crab out on the water.

EDMONDS FISHING PIER, CENTRAL PUGET SOUND
The public fishing pier south of the ferry landing in Edmonds is a top spot for urban crabbing. Pair it with watching the summer sun set behind the Olympics.

CRABBING 101

HOW TO CATCH A CRAB

Bait your crab trap and drop it in the water with a crab float tightly attached so you know where it is. The trap sits on the bottom, anywhere from 5 to 50 feet below; bring plenty of crab throw line for each trap. Wait at least fifteen minutes for rings, an hour or overnight for pots. When it's time to retrieve the trap, pull in the buoy and give a hard tug on the rope of the submerged crab ring, pulling hand over hand all the way up. Do it fast! If you pull slowly, the spunky crabs may escape the trap.

Now comes the fun part: figuring out who to eat! To avoid getting pinched, hold a crab by its hind legs like a purse, or scoop it up from behind with your thumb on top of its shell and your fingers underneath, well away from the pincers. Measure at the widest portion of the shell and identify gender (males have a distinct, rather phallic-looking abdomen patch). Keep the crab if it measures at least 6.25 inches and is male; others should be gently returned to the water. The daily catch limit for Dungeness is five in Puget Sound, six elsewhere. You can keep up to six Red Rock crabs too—they're smaller and less meaty but so tasty. Place your live catch in a cooler topped with a saltwater-soaked towel, and cook them as soon as possible.

Crabbing is random. Test an area and be ready to move if you're not getting keepers. Some years yield more than others. Weather can impact crabbing—recent rain sends a torrent of freshwater into estuaries, and crab much prefer saltwater. Conversely, high tide brings more saltwater into estuaries, improving your chances. The quality of bait matters too—some crabbers swear by raw chicken, while others say you need fresh, smelly stuff like a salmon carcass to get a cast of crabs on every pull.

HOW TO COOK AND EAT A CRAB

Toss the live, whole crabs into a big pot of well-salted boiling water and cook for fifteen to twenty minutes, then plunge them into ice water for several minutes. Fresh crab is so tasty with a dip in melted butter or a squeeze of lemon, but have a can of Old Bay seasoning on the table, too. For easy cleanup, spread newspaper over a picnic table, pass out the nutcrackers, bibs, and butter, and get cracking. Save leftover meat for cheesy crab melt sandwiches. Don't cook crab in a hotel room or vacation rental if there are rules against it; instead, if the service is available, have your crab cooked and cleaned at the local dock where you rented your crab rings, or cook outdoors over a campfire or propane stove.

FALL

- ○ Find Weird Geology
- ○ Hike to Fall Color
- ○ Hunt for Beach Treasure
- ○ Ride a Mountain Bike
- ○ Forage for Fungi
- ○ Saddle Up on a Horse
- ○ Pick Your Own Apples
- ○ Try Geocaching
- ○ Hike in the Rain
- ○ Be a Lighthouse Keeper
- ○ Soak in a Hot Spring
- ○ Bike to Wineries
- ○ See Salmon Run

Our senses compete for the delights of fall—the brilliant hues of fall foliage, the tart crunch of a fresh-picked apple, the woodsy warmth of a crackling campfire. This is why we must save some vacation days. When we're lucky, the mild Pacific Northwest climate bestows on us a second summer of sorts in September and early October, suspending the late autumn drizzle that becomes persistent if not daily west of the Cascades come November. Marry this with post-tourist season solitude and fall is a strong contender for the best season.

Every leaf speaks bliss to me, fluttering from the autumn tree.
    —Emily Brontë, "Fall, leaves, fall"

Autumn is harvest season, when all those tended orchards, fields, and vineyards bear the fruits of diligent labor and love. The crispest pears and brightest pumpkins are poised for picking, and grapes are piled up ready to be crushed so their juices may someday become wine. Head to a small orchard and vineyard for some hands-on harvesting (and tasting).

Exploring outdoors in fall calls for extra preparation and caution, especially in the backcountry. The days grow shorter as the season unfolds, and weather can change on a dime. Keep an eye on the time, as it gets dark by late afternoon, earlier under a dense canopy of trees. Pack plenty of extra clothes and raingear, energy snacks, and batteries for your headlamp or flashlight, and consider bringing along emergency shelter in case of an unexpected night in the woods. Consult the weather forecast. Many trails are snow-free into early October, but an early storm can change that—check the current conditions of your chosen trail by calling the ranger station before a hike. Hunting season starts in August, and it might surprise you to see bear hunters at Forest Service trailheads or hear a rifle shot while hiking. Stay visible by wearing a blaze orange vest over your jacket.

FIND WEIRD GEOLOGY

ECCENTRIC LANDSCAPES AWAIT THE CURIOUS

Sea stacks at Ruby Beach

WE LIVE IN one of the most geologically active regions on Earth. On a clear day, five active volcanoes dominate Washington's skyline. Snow-topped and beautiful, these peaks give no hint of the destruction they could unleash. Our seismic past keeps us on our toes. Then there's Puget Sound—its seafloor scooped out like ice cream when a gargantuan ice sheet retreated seventeen thousand years ago. Many iconic Northwest landmarks are real-life evidence of our geologic story—from strange rock forms carved by mega floods in the Grand Coulee to quirky offshore sea stacks of basalt sculpted by centuries of pounding waves.

WHERE TO GO

Curious about the geologic events that formed the Northwest landscape? Hit the road to see this offbeat geology.

RUBY BEACH

US 101 south of Forks, nps.gov/olym

If one thing defines the wild Olympic coast, it's sea stacks—hunks of basalt that began their existence as lava flowed millions of years ago. Sculpted into current form by the gradual, relentless erosion of pounding waves against a rocky headland, these fascinating rock outcrops sit just offshore at several Olympic National Park beaches. Ruby Beach is a favorite for its variety of sea stacks accessible at low tide. An easy quarter-mile hike from the parking lot spills you out onto the pinkish sand beach, uniquely tinted from tiny crystals of garnet. A shallow creek bisects the beach—to the south, see the Hoh sandstone marine deposit in rock outcrops, and to the north rocks are more volcanic in origin. The largest sea stack, Abbey Island, is composed of volcanic breccia.

MOUNT ST. HELENS NATIONAL VOLCANIC MONUMENT

SR 504 and SR 503, fs.usda.gov/giffordpinchot

NORTHWEST FOREST PASS

On a quiet Sunday morning in May 1980, Mount St. Helens blew its top in the most disastrous volcanic eruption in US history. The lateral blast triggered a landslide down the north slope, and a pyroclastic flow of gas, pumice, and ash mowed down all in its path. What remained was a denuded moonscape with trees toppled like toothpicks, the ground singed to a crisp, and animal life erased. Drive through this blast zone to reach the Johnston Ridge Observatory, then peer into the gaping crater. Interpretive kiosks tell the eruption story and highlight signs of the ecosystem's gradual recovery. On the volcano's south side, descend into an underground world at Ape Cave (1.5 miles round-trip), a natural tunnel through which fluid basaltic lava once traveled during an eruption two thousand years ago. The path is rough in places, so sturdy boots and gloves make scrambling more comfortable. Dress warmly: the lava tube is always 42°F. Bright headlamps allow you to enjoy the dark cave.

STEAMBOAT ROCK

SR 155, Electric City, parks.state.wa.us

DISCOVER PASS

At the end of the last ice age around fifteen thousand years ago, an ice dam that held back giant Glacial Lake Missoula would periodically rupture, causing the Missoula Floods—several cataclysmic deluges that swept across Eastern Washington. Those floodwaters met ancient lava flows and carved out a patchwork of soaring basalt benches, isolated mesas, and wide coulees. One of those remnants is a hunk of columnar basalt, Steamboat Rock, sitting like the

Titanic on a reservoir called Banks Lake in the Grand Coulee. Hike to the top for a stunning view (3.2 miles round-trip, 760 feet elevation gain). Notice the granite boulders strewn about—these huge rocks, known as "erratics," were left by the receding ice sheet before the floods.

GINKGO PETRIFIED FOREST

I-90 at Vantage, parks.state.wa.us

DISCOVER PASS

Wonder what happens when a swampy forest gets flooded with lava? The trees turn to stone. About sixteen million years ago, lava spilled from giant fissures in the earth's crust and covered much of Eastern Washington, Oregon, and Idaho. These prehistoric basalt floods submerged whole forests, and with the help of silica-rich waters then transformed them into buried treasure—petrified wood—heirlooms of the tropical forest that once covered these parts. A 2-mile interpretive trail from the visitors' center features a few dozen species of these cool fossilized trees. Step inside to examine polished petrified specimens up close.

NATURE NOTEBOOK

Location: _____ Date: _____

Co-naturers: _____

Find some weird geology closer to home—it's everywhere! What did you find, and what's your hypothesis for how it was formed?

_____

_____

_____

_____

_____

_____

_____

_____

_____

MIMA MOUNDS

12315 Waddell Creek Road SW, Olympia

DISCOVER PASS

There's a mystery in the prairie. Behold a landscape of odd mounds of earth, the origin of which has sparked theories ranging from prehistoric gophers to glacial deposits. The neat pattern of natural domelike mounds could be the result of seismic activity, or perhaps they're actually wind-blown dunes. A popular geologic hypothesis says the Mima Mounds formed from the shrinking then swelling of wet clay soils. Ponder this mystery as you walk the 3-mile paved interpretive trail that weaves through the peculiar mounds.

OMAK ROCK

Omak Lake Road, Colville Indian Reservation

Precariously balanced rocks are among the weirdest geologic formations found anywhere, and prompt many questions: How did that rock get there? Will it fall on me if I touch it? (No.) Will it fall in an earthquake? (A big one, probably.) Omak Rock is a large, 40-ton glacial erratic boulder balanced on a smaller rock near Omak Lake in the Colville Indian Reservation, deposited in its current position by an ice sheet thousands of years ago. Interestingly, it remained intact through the 1872 North Cascades earthquake, estimated to be magnitude 6.5. Sacred to the Colville people, the rock represents a symbol of nature's perfection. The public is welcome to respectfully visit the rock.

COPALIS GHOST FOREST

Copalis Beach

The geologic story of this unusual landscape was pieced together over the past few decades. Near Copalis, a large stand of skeleton red cedars and spruce about a mile inland from the coast were killed by an infusion of ocean saltwater, but how? Through some detective work using tree-ring dating and records from Japan of an orphan tsunami, geologists pinned it on a mega earthquake on January 26, 1700, about 55 miles off the coast. The only way to reach this eerie terrain is by boat—launch your own canoe or kayak from Johnson's Mercantile in Copalis, then paddle upriver for half a mile.

BEACON ROCK

34841 SR 14, Stevenson, parks.state.wa.us

DISCOVER PASS

Hikers mob the trail to the top of Beacon Rock on nice weekends, a steep 1-mile climb up expertly engineered steps and switchbacks to an impressive panorama of the Columbia River Gorge. What many of them don't know is they're standing atop an ancient volcano, or at least what's left of it. Beacon Rock is a volcanic plug, formed eons ago when magma within a volcano vent hardened. When the Missoula Floods poured through, the volcano's softer outer shell was washed away. This 848-foot basalt monolith was a beacon to Lewis and Clark on their journey to reach the Pacific, and so it was aptly named by the explorers.

LEARN MORE

For many more paths to explore our state's weird rock formations, get the guidebook *Hiking Washington's Geology*, by Scott Babcock and Robert J. Carson.

HIKE TO FALL COLOR

GET OUTSIDE FOR BOLD HUES AND CRISP AIR

Larches and
needles near
Blewett Pass

photo by Kim Brown

AUTUMN IN THE Northwest is nirvana. Wild landscapes are imbued with flame red, bright orange, and soft yellow hues, a beauty that is both enrapturing and fleeting. Weird weather patterns may shorten the show—in years where a hard frost comes early, color formation in leaves can come to a crashing halt, and a windstorm may send them straight to the forest floor.

In Washington the prime window for hitting up peak fall color in the mountains is roughly mid-September through mid-October, snow level depending. Lower elevations with lots of deciduous trees and understory will show longer and likely boast the most variety of colorful foliage—deep auburn and marigold yellow on vine maple, russet and clay hues on Garry oak, bronzed willow leaves, and vivid yellow on big-leaf maple and aspen. Mountain trails show off meadows full of fiery red-and-orange huckleberry bushes and the glowing gold of larches, our only conifer that drops its needles.

Ever wonder how leaves know when to change color? We humans have a sense that fall is underway when the days start to shorten and the air feels cooler. Trees know it, too, and they stop photosynthesizing. As moisture and green chlorophyll slowly drain from their leaves, colors hidden before (like red, purple, yellow, and orange) emerge. Once leaves fall to the ground, these bold colors

fade to brown. Fall foliage is but one reason to keep your boots by the door. Enjoy loads more solitude on trail with the crowds of summer long gone. Hungry mosquitoes and pesky flies have all but disappeared. Wildlife are busy gathering food for the oncoming winter and may be more visible.

WHERE TO GO

Autumn weather can be unpredictable, so extra caution is essential. Pack lots of layers for warmth and a thermos of hot cocoa, and get ready to fill your lungs with cool, crisp air surrounded by a palette of fall hues. These spots are delightful.

YELLOW ASTER BUTTE, MOUNT BAKER

SR 542 east of Glacier
fs.usda.gov/mbs, (360) 599-2714
NORTHWEST FOREST PASS
7.5 miles round-trip, 2500 feet elevation gain

The best bang for your buck for a spectrum of fall color is right here, and there's a great chance of ripe huckleberries in September, too. If those are gone, thank a black bear and gain solace in the stunning glacier-clad peaks of Baker and Shuksan. This trail starts with nearly 2 miles of switchbacks through scattered trees and open avalanche slopes. Veer left at a trail junction and the path undulates along slopes and through multicolored fields of heather and huckleberry bushes. Then get ready for the final huff-and-puff ascent to the grand finale view on the butte's south side.

LAKE ANN, NORTH CASCADES

SR 20 at Rainy Pass
fs.usda.gov/okawen, (509) 997-2131
NORTHWEST FOREST PASS
3.4 miles round-trip, 700 feet elevation gain

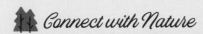

Connect with Nature

Collect and press fall leaves. Sandwich them in a single layer between sheets of newspaper, then place each of these flat between stacked heavy books. After a few weeks, your leaves should be flattened and ready for fall craft projects—arrange them with small pumpkins into a centerpiece, tuck them into greeting cards as a surprise autumn relic, or assemble them into a collage and frame.

The star attraction of this hike are flame-yellow alpine larch usually at their peak early to mid-October. It's one of the easier hikes to see larches turn in fall, so expect plenty of company on weekends. The hike shares the first 1.3 miles with Maple Pass Loop, a longer hike that rises and encircles the glacial cirque that cradles Lake Ann. A side trail leads to the lake and back again. Late-season huckleberries cling to blazing red bushes along the trail, and craggy granite scenery reminds you why you live in Washington.

TONGA RIDGE, STEVENS PASS
US 2 near Skykomish
fs.usda.gov/mbs, (360) 677-2414
NORTHWEST FOREST PASS
6 miles round-trip, 400 feet elevation gain
Perhaps the easiest ridge walk on the western slope of the Cascades, it's no surprise Tonga Ridge is also one of the most popular. Autumn affords you some solitude to enjoy the fiery huckleberry meadows awash in color like a painting. Hike through whole hillsides of sun-sweetened huckleberries—bring

NATURE NOTEBOOK

Location: Date:

Co-naturers:

Describe the wonderful, seasonal things that you saw, felt, smelled, heard, and tasted on your autumn hike.

URBAN FALL FOLIAGE

Lowland trails and city parks are full of great autumn walks to squeeze in after work.

MERCER SLOUGH NATURE PARK, BELLEVUE
This 2-mile stroll circles a real working blueberry farm with bushes that turn a deep auburn in fall. The trail loops around the largest wetland complex on Lake Washington, most of it on boardwalk.

SEWARD PARK PERIMETER LOOP, SEATTLE
The 2.6-mile, paved trail that parallels the shore is lined with lovely deciduous trees and bushes that turn burnt red and gold in autumn.

POINT DEFIANCE PARK SQUARE TRAIL, TACOMA
Walk the 4.4-mile perimeter loop of the park through old-growth forest with an understory of ferns and vine maple.

JOHN A. FINCH ARBORETUM, SPOKANE
Blazing gold and orange leaves of oak, maple, mountain ash, crabapple, and other deciduous trees dot these 65 acres of rolling hills in October.

a container to gather for home or forage your way up the trail. Hike to Sawyer Pass then turn around; for a climb, there's a spur trail to the summit of Mount Sawyer. Keep an eye out for black bear and deer as they fatten up for winter.

NACHES PEAK LOOP, MOUNT RAINIER NATIONAL PARK
SR 410 at Chinook Pass
nps.gov/mora, (360) 569-2211
NORTHWEST FOREST PASS
3.2 miles round-trip, 600 feet elevation gain
This lovely loop skirts the eastern boundary of Mount Rainier National Park through subalpine meadows carpeted with berry bushes. In fall, the meadows erupt with a psychedelic blast of red and orange, as if they're on fire. What could make such a scene even more stunning? The backdrop of the mountain. Hike the loop in a clockwise direction for the best views.

BLACK CANYON, CENTRAL WASHINGTON
L. T. Murray Wildlife Area near Ellensburg
wdfw.wa.gov, (360) 902-2515
DISCOVER PASS
7 miles round-trip, 1250 feet elevation gain
Central Washington's canyon country transforms into a fiery palette in fall—russet, burnt sienna, and banana yellow paint the leaves of deciduous trees and shrubs, illuminated against black basalt cliffs. Hike in morning or early evening for the best light. From the trailhead, climb gently up the canyon, with some orange cottonwood and yellow aspen leaves quaking in the breeze. Until a wildfire burned through a few years back, an old homestead cabin sat about a mile in among a grove of aspen, but little is left of it. The trail splits; head to the right and climb a bit higher into the open ponderosa pine forest, eventually settling atop Umtanum Ridge with a sweeping view of fall's glory and your turnaround spot.

HUNT FOR BEACH TREASURE

TURN A BEACH DAY INTO A SCAVENGER HUNT

The beach at Kalaloch invites exploration.

WASHINGTON'S beaches are brimming with treasures waiting to be found. Roam a sandy shore with a keen eye for the curious, useful, or unique. Unusual specimens of ordinary objects may strike your fancy—an oddly shaped stone or blasted piece of driftwood that slips easily into a pocket. Save the item for a craft project, place as decor on a windowsill, or discard on the beach later the same day.

Serious beachcombers collect particular treasures, like agates, fossils, or vintage glass fishing floats. Jewelry artists poke around for sea glass or jasper for their creations. Certain pieces of marine debris are popular with collectors, like a sake bottle from Japan, or one of the twenty-eight thousand rubber duckies that spilled from a Chinese cargo ship in 1992. Plenty of treasure washes up on Washington's coastline, favorably placed along the North Pacific Gyre—the clockwise circular pattern of currents that head our way after sweeping up the coastline of East Asia. The gyre is hit with fierce storms that push rocks, shells, and debris high onto the beach. About 20 percent of flotsam that drifts onto Washington's ocean beaches comes from Japan. Inland beaches on the Salish Sea are good for items that drift locally.

Comb for treasure on any beach, at any time. The best beachcombing, though, is after a windstorm as the tide heads out. Scan the sand in front of you as you walk along the tide line. Carry a backpack to stow your loot. A walking stick doubles as a prod to loosen sand or rocks around a submerged object. The more remote and uncrowded the beach, the higher chance you'll get first dibs on whatever washes up. Unfortunately, found treasure often sits alongside found trash. Bring along a garbage bag for the plastic you encounter, and pack it out—it's harmful to marine wildlife. The growing problem of ocean trash can only be solved if each of us does our part.

WHERE TO GO

Some beaches catch more treasures than others. The presence of driftwood is a good sign, as are foraging gulls and tide lines of surf and washed-up kelp. Tideland access is complicated in Washington—Pacific Ocean beaches below the high tide mark are open to the public except for tribal lands, but within Puget Sound only public beaches are fully accessible; heed private property signs.

DAMON POINT
Discovery Avenue SE, Ocean Shores
3.2 miles round-trip
Cross a narrow spit to beachcomb around tiny Protection Island. Take your time walking along the gravel bars and pebble beach—

LEARN MORE

Help protect the wild Washington Coast by volunteering to clean it up. The annual Olympic Coast Cleanup is in April around Earth Day (see coastsavers.org for details). Old tires, shoes, fish nets, and plastic bottles make up some of the many tons of trash the crews clean up on our beaches. After beachcombing on the Olympic coast, swing by John's Beachcombing Museum (143 Andersonville Avenue in Forks). Retired plumber John Anderson has combed Northwest beaches since the 1970s and displays his many tons of cool finds in this funky exhibit, including a totem pole made of fishing buoys.

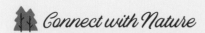 *Connect with Nature*

Make a beach memory jar. Comb the beach at low tide for a variety of items—a unique shell, beach glass, cool rocks, a sand dollar, or a bit of sea fern. Lucky beachcombers may find a glass float, agate, or a starfish skeleton. Gather a little sand into a ziplock, too. When you return home, assemble the relics in a large glass jar. First, line the bottom with the sand. Arrange the objects one at a time—be creative! The reliquary sand jar will look great on a desk or mantel to remind you of the beach every day.

agates and jasper may be hiding among the common stones or tangled in the seaweed.

GLASS BEACH
5800 Kuhn Street, Port Townsend
6 miles round-trip
There's a bit of a hike to access this beach, but it's worth the effort. Hike west from the parking lot at North Beach County Park at low tide along the beach for 3 miles to Glass

Beach, which is chock-full of tide-tumbled sea glass.

ALKI BEACH
2665 Alki Avenue SW, Seattle
3 miles round-trip
Amble along the stretch of beach from Alki Beach Park to Duwamish Head in West Seattle, keeping an eye out for frosted sea glass and shards of broken pottery.

NATURE NOTEBOOK

Location: _____ Date: _____

Co-naturers: _____

Crashing surf, salty air, and an endless sky—a walk on the beach is a sensory shower and a tonic for stress. Note the sensations of being at the beach (the sounds, smells, and feel) and describe some of them below.

_____

_____

_____

_____

_____

TREASURES TO FIND

UNIQUE SHELLS
Seashells are hand-held elegant sculptures, once homes to gastropods (one shell), bivalves (two connected shells), and chitons (eight interlocking plates).

SEA GLASS
These frosted jewels are real pieces of glass that began their life as seltzer bottles or ceramics, then were broken, tumbled, and weathered by sand and waves over the years. If you find a piece with edges still sharp, toss it back to the sea to be polished by nature for another few years.

DRIFTWOOD
All that driftwood piled above the high tide line usually comes from inland rivers, gets carried out to sea, tumbled in the surf, then washes up. Collectors turn it into furniture or sculptures.

AGATES
When you're walking along a cobble beach and something bright and shiny catches the sun, it might be this semiprecious stone. Agate is essentially quartz, formed in volcanic rocks. Hold them up to the light—an agate will be translucent. Many collectors polish this jewel of the sea in a rock tumbler.

SAND DOLLARS
Often mistaken for a seashell, the hard, white sand dollar is actually the skeleton of a sea urchin. If you find a live one (darker in color with tiny hairs on the underside that move) carefully set it back where you found it.

GLASS FLOATS
Once fairly common on Northwest beaches, these colored orbs aren't used by Japanese fisherman any longer. Still, modern beachcombers are always on the lookout because some old glass floats remain out there in the Pacific, just waiting for a big storm to push them in.

MESSAGE IN A BOTTLE
It's a rare treat to find a note inside a washed-up bottle, sometimes set sail from a distant continent many years before.

OBJETS D'ART
If one person's trash is another's treasure, there's plenty to be found on a nearby beach. Eclectic finds like a doll, unique bottle, or vintage sign might fit right in with your offbeat decor.

RIDE A MOUNTAIN BIKE

PEDAL THROUGH TWISTS, TURNS, AND HOPS

Biking near
Lake Chelan

photo by Jodi Connolly

RIDING A MOUNTAIN BIKE is a little like steering your own roller coaster through the woods. As you swerve around tree trunks, roll over roots, and drop down stair steps, your heart pounds and every muscle in your body is engaged. As is your mind, ever present as you navigate each twist and turn through the understory. If you like your nature with a side of adrenaline and lots of fun, mountain biking might be your new favorite hobby.

Some cyclists forgo the technical drops and twists of thrilling singletrack trail rides for long epic rides in the backcountry on wide, gentle paths dubbed doubletrack or even on dirt roads. Try combining a few miles of mountain biking with a day hike to cover more ground. As cherry-stem access roads into wilderness get washed out and can't be repaired for vehicles, bike the miles of old rough road instead of walking the remaining miles to the trailhead. A trusty commuter road bike won't do well on trails, however. Mountain bikes are designed for rugged terrain like mud, dirt, and gravel. The tires are fatter and have tread made for traction on loose soil and substrate, and impact is absorbed by a specialized suspension system. Flat handlebars keep you in an upright position while you ride for control and balance.

Start with a mountain biking class or guided ride to learn the basic techniques (body position, braking, cornering, climbing, descending), learn a little MTB lingo and etiquette (ring a bell around blind corners, shout "bike!" to alert hikers of your approach), and get comfortable riding on a trail. You'll find classes offered at your local bike shop, through REI, Evergreen Mountain Bike Alliance, or the Evergreen Crank Sisters—an all-levels women's riding group. Most beginner courses provide mountain bikes for students.

Mountain bike tricks and stunts aren't just for daredevils; they can be valuable maneuvers for dodging obstacles on the trail. The most indispensable trick (and the foundation for other complex stunts) is called The Manual. A lot like popping a wheelie, keep the front wheel off the ground while centering your balance over the rear wheel. Next up is the Bunny Hop: add it on to The Manual by jumping off the ground with the bike to clear small logs or other obstacles.

WHERE TO GO

Fewer trails in Washington are open to mountain bikers than to hikers and equestrians, and fewer still are designed specifically for them. Discover places to ride with the Evergreen Mountain Bike Alliance's map-based database of more than two hundred trails in Washington with trail stats, difficulty ratings, cool features, and rider reviews. Remember that designated wilderness areas prohibit all mountain biking and, with only a few exceptions, national park trails are off limits. Some state park trails popular among mountain bikers are open to them seasonally only, so read the fine print. Here are some great beginner-friendly rides to try out on both frontcountry and backcountry trails.

DUTHIE HILL MOUNTAIN BIKE PARK, KING COUNTY PARKS
26300 SE Issaquah–Fall City Road, Issaquah
kingcounty.gov
Beginners, start here. Duthie Hill in Issaquah is the state's most popular trail system for mountain bikers because all 8 miles of trails were specially designed and built for them, 6 of them cross-country and 2 miles of free-ride or flowy jump trails, with lots of skill-building features. Connect to Grand Ridge from here, another much-loved singletrack mecca.

PARADISE VALLEY CONSERVATION AREA, SNOHOMISH COUNTY PARKS

23210 Paradise Lake Road, Woodinville

snohomishcountywa.gov

Evergreen Mountain Bike Alliance and Snohomish County envisioned a new use for this old homestead near the King-Snohomish County line, and the result is 11 miles of beginner-friendly twists, turns, and roots on gentle up-and-down singletrack trail. Riders share the trails with hikers and runners, and some trails allow horses. The nearly 800 acres are home to deer, cougar, coyote, bear, lots of birds, and the salmon stream Bear Creek.

GALBRAITH MOUNTAIN TRAILS

Birch Street and Lakeway Drive, Bellingham

wmbcmtb.org

This large complex of free-ride and cross-country trails known to cyclists as "Galby" sits on private timber land, but access for cyclists is guaranteed by a recreation easement agreement brokered by the City of Bellingham and others, including Whatcom Mountain Bike Coalition (WMBC), who brought their vision to life here: over 65 miles of singletrack trails on 3000 acres overlooking downtown and Bellingham Bay. Built and maintained by volunteers, the fast and flowy loops and technical jump lines at Galby form the bedrock of Whatcom County's strong MTB culture.

LOWER BIG QUILCENE, OLYMPIC NATIONAL FOREST

Off US 101 south of Quilcene

fs.usda.gov/r6

NORTHWEST FOREST PASS

On the drier east slope of the Olympics is this beautiful lowland valley with one of the region's most-loved backcountry mountain biking trails. The 6.2-mile trail stretches from a lower trailhead to an upper one, which are also connected by a road. Most cyclists start at the top and descend 1200 feet to the bottom, enjoying the rushing river rapids and stands of towering old-growth along the way. Two trailside campsites make this a nice first-time bike packing trip.

ECHO RIDGE, CHELAN, OKANOGAN-WENATCHEE NATIONAL FOREST

Off US 97 near Chelan

fs.usda.gov/r6

NORTHWEST FOREST PASS

It's a popular Nordic ski area by winter, but after spring snowmelt, fat tires explore these

BUYING OR RENTING A MOUNTAIN BIKE

A new mountain bike is a pricey investment. The necessary accessories are similar to those required for road biking: a well-fitting helmet to protect your head, gloves to protect your hands, a water bottle, a light (important even if you don't plan to ride at night). You'll also need a way to transport a bike to the trailhead, either in your SUV or truck or on an external bike rack. Borrow a bike from a friend, or rent a bike and rack at your local bike shop. If you decide to buy, consider buying used at a gear resale shop. Mountain bikes get lighter and faster every year and that's to a thrifty buyer's advantage: last year's model gets sold to make room in the garage.

30 miles of interlooping trails around Echo Ridge above the Chelan Valley. The network of trails can be combined to form loops for every skill level—from easy flow trails along exposed ridge terrain to steep climbs and descents through open forest.

CARBON RIVER ROAD, MOUNT RAINIER NATIONAL PARK

Off SR 165 south of Carbonado

nps.gov/mora

NATIONAL PARK PASS

Here's one of the few national park trails in the Pacific Northwest open to bikes. This 10-mile-round-trip ride on the old Carbon River Road used to be a drive, but the road was severely damaged in 2006, when 18 inches of rain in two days flooded the valley. Now the road is closed to vehicles and has been converted to a wide doubletrack trail that leads hikers and mountain bikers through one of the finest, greenest old-growth rain forests in the Pacific Northwest.

Trees here are absolutely titanic: Douglas-fir tall enough to pierce the sky, western red cedar, Sitka spruce, and western hemlock. The old Ipsut Creek Campground (5 miles in) makes a lovely backcountry camp for a "bike-packing" adventure (get a free backcountry camping permit from the park first). Trails beyond the campground, including the half-mile to Ipsut Falls, are closed to bikes.

NATURE NOTEBOOK

Location: _____   Date: _____

Co-naturers: _____

After riding on fat tires through the forest, you'll never see a trail quite the same way again—every root, step, log, berm, and banked corner presents a challenge that turns your ride into an adventure and engages your mind fully in the moment. Describe the mind-body connection you feel while riding.

_____

_____

_____

FORAGE FOR FUNGI

NORTHWEST WOODLANDS STOCK NATURE'S PANTRY

Shaggy mane mushrooms in rural King County

IT MAY SEEM like an awful lot of work to hunt for chanterelles on your hands and knees on a drizzly fall day when you can just buy them at the farmers' market. But that's not as much fun. Get yourself some identification know-how, then venture into the wild and collect weird and wonderful fungi right out of the duff for your dinner.

The Pacific Northwest region is mycologically rich thanks to a mild climate and lots of moist, mossy forest—the preferred habitat of delicious king boletes and woody chanterelles. Not all tasty mushrooms require conifer woods, though—shaggy mane emerge in city parks and disturbed areas, and tasty morels flourish in forest recently burned by fire. In all, there are more than thirty species of well-known edible mushrooms in Washington's wildlands. To forage, you need a knife, basket, guidebook, and common sense. Some edibles have toxic look-alikes. A case of mistaken identity might give you tummy trouble—or much worse. Don't eat anything you can't positively identify. And until you're an expert, forage with people who are, or stick to easy-to-identify fungi.

A few days after a big fall soaker, mushrooms pop up everywhere—on fallen logs, tree trunks, the forest floor, and even your own grassy yard. To find them, you have to hunt. Wear clothes you don't mind getting dirty, because you might spend a significant amount of time climbing over logs or on your hands and knees peeking under tree limbs. When you find an edible mushroom, look for more nearby—many species grow in groups. What you see is the "fruit" of the fungus, a repository of spores set to disperse and reproduce. The rest is underground, a network of mycelium that has a symbiotic relationship with the roots of nearby trees. In fact, the whole forest depends on fungus,

and nutritious wild mushrooms are a staple in the diets of elk, bear, and lots of small critters. Identify first, then harvest by cutting the mushroom at or just above the ground.

You can legally gather mushrooms on most public lands in Washington for personal use; exceptions include some city parks and North Cascades National Park. Some national parks and forests require a free permit for mushroom foraging that you can get online or at a ranger station, while others don't require any permit, and neither do state parks. All public lands have a daily limit, ranging from 2 quarts to 5 gallons. If you don't know the foraging rules, call the land manager and ask.

FOUR FORAGABLE FUNGI

After you've taken a class or mushroom walk with an expert, hunt for one of these easy-to-identify edible fungi. Avoid finding random mushrooms and trying to ascertain if they're edible; instead, know which specific mushroom type you're hunting for that day and look in the right habitat (elevation, microclimate, forest type, indicator plant species).

KING BOLETE
On the coniferous forest floor, this large, meaty mushroom kind of looks like a lightly toasted burger bun atop a thick stalk that widens at the base. The cap, brownish-tan and paler at the edges, may be as much as 8 inches across. Under its cap are white to pale cream spongelike pores, not gills. Where there is one king bolete, there are usually many more, so keep looking and loading your basket. Kings have two seasons in Washington—spring on the eastern slope of the Cascades and after fall rains at lower elevations on the western slope and the Olympics.

How to cook. Brush the cap of a large bolete with olive oil and grill it like a steak. Known as porcini in Italy, sliced boletes dry well in a dehydrator for flavoring soups, risotto, and tossing with pasta throughout the winter.

GOLDEN CHANTERELLE

You can taste the woods in the buttery, earthy goodness of sautéed chanterelles. Novice foragers often start with chanterelles because they're so easy to identify. In the temperate rain forests of Western Washington, look for clusters of chanterelles growing out of the duff around Douglas-fir trees, thanks to a cozy mycorrhizal relationship with these mature conifers. The forked ridges that run down the cap and stem of this mushroom are not actually gills. There's a nontoxic but nontasty imposter in our forests known as the false chanterelle that has an underside of true gills that stop at the stem—learn this difference and you'll easily tell them apart.

How to cook. Slice lengthwise and pan-fry like a steak or chop and sauté to use in

A boletus mushroom on the forest floor

Photo by Milan Tmenović

a creamy pasta sauce or risotto, or eat atop pizza blanc.

CHICKEN OF THE WOODS

Also called sulphur shelf, which offers some clues, this bright peachy-orange fungus grows as fan-shaped shelfs attached to stumps, snags, or sometimes living trees. They tend to bracket in overlapping clusters, but you'll also find them as single shelves. The underside is pale yellow with tiny pores (no gills). Here's where the popular name comes in: these mushrooms have both the taste and texture of chicken with a hint of lemon. Harvest when they're young and succulent, late summer to early autumn. Look for them growing on downed logs and stumps in low- to mid-elevation temperate forests of the Olympic Peninsula and western slope of the Cascades.

How to cook. Eat them breaded and fried like chicken tenders with a tangy dipping sauce.

MOREL

Not all mushrooms wait for fall. This most-prized mushroom is in season for a few weeks in May or June, depending on elevation. They're not easy to find, but once you come upon one, there will be more nearby. The morel's elongated cap has a characteristic honeycomb appearance and attaches to

LEARN MORE

Puget Sound Mycological Society is the country's largest organization for fungi enthusiasts, and there are smaller such groups for Spokane, South Sound, Olympic Peninsula, Yakima Valley, and other cities. Connect with these groups for events, field trips, workshops, and recipes. Each fall, their Wild Mushroom Show features an exhibit with more than two hundred mushrooms.

North Cascades Institute offers mushrooming classes in the fall from their North Cascades Environmental Learning Center on Diablo Lake. For great descriptions and identification criteria, pick up the field guide *Mushrooms of the Pacific Northwest* by Steve Trudell and Joe Ammirati. Connect with other edible mushroom enthusiasts and get identification help on the private Facebook group, Pacific Northwest Mushroom Identification Forum.

the hollow stem at the base of the cap or close to it—these characteristics set a true morel apart from a false morel. Chefs love them because they're smoky, a little nutty, and

🌲🌲 Connect with Nature

Get crafty with fungi by making a spore print. Find a large, mature mushroom cap and separate it from the stem with a knife. Place it gills down on a blank piece of paper, then cover the whole thing with an upside-down bowl so it can sit undisturbed. A day later, carefully lift the mushroom cap and you've got a spore print.

SAFE SHROOMING

Start with a mushroom class or a guided walk with your local mycological club. Be 100 percent sure of your identification before you cook and eat a mushroom. If there's any doubt, throw it out. Never eat or even sample wild mushrooms raw—always cook them thoroughly.

When trying a new type of mushroom, eat a small amount and wait twenty-four hours for any allergic reactions. Identify a mushroom by comparing all characteristics; don't rely on pictures alone. Don't overharvest. Take only what you need, and leave enough

behind for critters and to spread spores. Check the local rules before you forage on public land, and get permission from the landowner on private land.

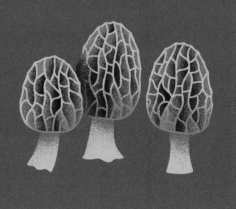

vaguely sweet. In the years just after a burn, a singed forest at mid-elevation can produce big flushes of morels, but they don't need fire. So-called "naturals" are morels that reliably surface in the same location year after year in woodsy or hardwood forests (one species is closely associated with cottonwood trees,

another with spruce); most morel hunters keep their secret patches tightly under wraps.

How to cook. Chop morels and sauté in butter with some diced shallot and a simple seasoning of sea salt, cracked pepper, and rosemary. Spoon onto toasted flatbread or baguette and enjoy.

NATURE NOTEBOOK

Location: _____   Date: _____

Co-naturers: _____

Try sketching a mushroom from your hike. Sketching the mushrooms you find will heighten your awareness of key features you might otherwise overlook, such as the color gradient and pattern on the cap, the presence of a fairy ring, or the girth of the stem. Use watercolors to fill in the sketch.

SADDLE UP ON A HORSE

GET IN THE SADDLE AND HIT THE TRAIL

Riding on
the Long
Beach
Peninsula

WHEN WAS THE last time you were on a horse? If it's been a while (or never), you may have forgotten what it feels like to hoist yourself up on the saddle, take the reins in one hand and a nice deep breath, then ride off into nature.

It takes courage to get on a horse for the first time. Learn the steps for mounting ahead of time to build confidence before your ride. Once the horse has been saddled and the cinch is just right, stand on the horse's left side. Take the reins in your left hand and grab the horn (the knob on the top-front of the saddle) with that hand. Put your left foot securely into the left stirrup and your right hand on the back of the saddle. Next comes the mount—push up onto your left leg like you're climbing a tall step while swinging your right foot over the back of the horse, all in one smooth motion. Your right and left hands will now be on the horn. Place your right foot into the right stirrup. You're on a horse! For an easy dismount, just do that in reverse.

Once you're riding, keep your posture upright instead of leaning forward or backward. If you feel nervous or wound up, the horse may feel nervous, too—they're intelligent, empathetic creatures who sometimes mirror human emotions and behavior. Deep breaths are key, and you can also try a calming mantra. Ask your guide for tips on relaxing if necessary—you'll have a smoother, more enjoyable ride if you and your horse are relaxed and calm.

WHERE TO RIDE

Washington is a beautiful place to ride, from a sandy beach to a fragrant Cascade forest. If you enjoy short rides at a local stable, you'll love a multiday guided horseback excursion in the wilderness—"horsepacking" is a lot like backpacking, except you're riding a horse who is carrying your gear. Here are a variety of adventures to get you into the saddle and out trotting on a trail.

WESTSIDE STABLES
21200 Westside Highway SW, Vashon Island
westsidestables.com, (206) 463-9828
Vashon Island has a robust equestrian community and a 43-acre public equestrian playground, Paradise Ridge Park, in the center of the island. Many other island roads and trails are horse-friendly. To experience Vashon from the back of a horse, call Westside Stables and set up a guided trail ride.

LONG BEACH HORSE RIDES
409 Sid Snyder Drive W, Long Beach
(360) 642-2576
Who hasn't daydreamed of riding a horse on a wild sandy beach with the salty breeze tousling their hair? Long Beach Horse Rides (also known locally as Back Country Wilderness Outfitters) leads horseback adventures on the beach—choose from a one-hour or two-hour ride. Ride single-file through tall grass over the upland sand dunes. Once you reach the wide sandy beach, the horses can space out a bit. The guide will show you how to use the reins and pull back if you'd like to try a short trot. The sunset ride heads south on the sand toward Cape Disappointment State Park then back to Long Beach while enjoying the sunset on the Pacific Ocean.

FLYING HORSESHOE RANCH
3190 Red Bridge Road, Cle Elum
flyinghorseshoeranch.com, (509) 674-2366
This slice of horse heaven is perfect for a weekend getaway and affordable enough for almost any budget. Stay in a rustic sleeping cabin (bring your own sleeping bag), then saddle up for a two-hour guided trail ride on

NATURE NOTEBOOK

Location: _____   Date: _____

Co-naturers: _____

Ready to use your imagination? Write about your horseback ride as a short story, but not from your own perspective—write it with your horse as the narrator.

_____

_____

_____

_____

_____

_____

_____

_____

_____

_____

_____

_____

_____

_____

_____

_____

horseback through the sunny pine forest of the Teanaway area. Private arena lessons are offered as well.

K DIAMOND K GUEST RANCH
15661 SR 21, Republic
kdiamondk.com, (888) 345-5355
This 1600-acre family ranch is nestled in the beautiful Okanogan Forest just south of Republic. Like many dude ranches, K Diamond K offers the all-inclusive "American plan"—a per-night fee includes lodging, three square meals, and the opportunity to take part in ranch activities, like grooming a horse or milking a cow. A stay here includes twice-daily guided trail rides on horseback. Riding lessons are available as well. At night, settle into your room in the log cabin–style lodge built of peeled logs from larch and fir.

SUN MOUNTAIN LODGE
604 Patterson Lake Road, Winthrop
sunmountainlodge.com, (509) 996-4735
Just outside the tiny old west town of Winthrop, take a ride into the open ponderosa pine–dotted hills of the Methow Valley led by an expert wrangler. Choose from a ninety-minute or half-day ride, or try the horseback lessons that are offered at the arena. The ultimate splurge is the Cowboy Dinner—it starts with a scenic ride on

horseback to an old homestead for a western BBQ dinner and live music.

DARWOOD OUTFITTING
Various trailheads in Methow Valley
darwoodoutfitting.com, (509) 997-0155
The Methow Valley ranks near the top for horseback riding in the Northwest, especially for guided backcountry pack trips into the gorgeous, palatial Pasayten Wilderness—there are several experienced outfitters in the area. One of them is Darwood Outfitting (previously called Cascade Wilderness Outfitters), who have shared their love of enjoying the backcountry on horseback for four generations. On a guided pack trip, you bring your sleeping bag and personal gear, and the outfitter provides the horses and pack mules, tents, food, fishing poles, the guides, and a chef. Join a scheduled pack trip, or they'll plan a custom backcountry adventure for your family or group of friends.

PICK YOUR OWN APPLES

HIT THE ORCHARDS, AND BRING A BASKET

Washington's apples are world famous: find out why.

IF FALL IN Washington could be tasted, it would be an apple from a local orchard that was sweetened in the sun and tree-ripened, then plucked off its branch with your own two hands. More apples and pears are grown here than in any other state, a testament to Washington's nutrient-rich volcanic soils and pure mountain water.

The epicenter of apple country is the Wenatchee River Valley, with a climate distinctly ideal for growing apples—sunny dry days and cool nights. The Wenatchee River plunges east through Cascade foothills flanked on both sides by rolling orchards that yield nearly 60 percent of the nation's apples—more than ten billion a year, all hand-picked. Varieties range from the ubiquitous Red Delicious, Fuji, and Gala to sought-after heirlooms like Maiden Blush, Winesap, Palouse, and Golden Russet. West of the Cascades, several small family farms and cideries tend apple orchards as well.

Picking our own fruit forges a connection to the soil that feeds us. It supports small, independent growers, and keeps fertile farmland from becoming pavement and sprawl. Most U-pick apple orchards are certified organic or grown without pesticides.

WHERE TO GO

Apples are ready for picking from late August into November, with the peak varying by the apple type and location. Pick enough for eating as well as for fall baking—tucked into apple pies, crushed into apple cider, and simmered into apple butter. To make your stash last into winter, store apples in the fridge crisper. Bring your own buckets or baskets to take your haul home. Prices vary but most orchards charge a modest few dollars per pound.

STUTZMAN RANCH
2226 Easy Street, Wenatchee
thestutzmanranch.com, (509) 669-3276

Pick your apples at this century-old family farm in fall if you're a fan of crunchy Fuji and bright Gala apples; they're ready for picking just as the Wenatchee Valley trees begin to turn crimson and golden. Gather some Bartlett and Asian pears as well. In early autumn, pick your own bunches of grapes, too. This farm has been passed down through generations.

FEIL PIONEER ORCHARDS AND FRUIT STAND
13073 US 2, East Wenatchee
wenatcheefruitstand.com, (509) 884-7570

The U-pick here is picking apples out of baskets at a fruit stand, but oh what a fruit stand. More than one hundred varieties of heirloom apples have been grown at the family's nearby orchard since 1908, when the family arrived in Washington. Persuaded by the Great Northern Railroad to go west, they grew fruit to be freighted back east. Select from hard-to-find varieties like Newtown Pippen, Spitzenberg, Winesap, Arkansas Black, Winter Banana, King David, and Empire. Mix and match them for fall baking or pairing with cheeses.

JOHNSON ORCHARDS
4906 Summitview, Yakima
johnsonorchardsfruit.com, (509) 966-7479

Pick Gala apples and Bartlett pears, then search out smaller stands of more unusual apple varieties at this orchard that dates back to 1904, one of the oldest in the state.

SKIPLEY FARM
7228 Skipley Road, Snohomish
skipleyfarm.com, (206) 679-6576

NATURE NOTEBOOK

Location: _____   Date: _____

Co-naturers: _____

Eating food grown and produced in your region supports local growers and reduces your carbon footprint. How can you incorporate more locally produced food into your life?

_____

_____

_____

_____

_____

_____

_____

_____

LEARN MORE

Find U-pick orchards and farms at pickyourown.org. Stop by the Washington Apple Commission Visitor Center (2900 Euclid Avenue, Wenatchee, [509] 663-9600) to learn all about the Apple Capital of the World and sample local varieties. Apple Days, one of the Wenatchee Valley's most popular fall festivals, is held in early October at the Cashmere Museum and Pioneer Village.

Connect with Nature

Make delicious apple butter in a slow cooker from a mix of ten to twelve heirloom apples (some sweet, some tart). Chop them into quarters, leaving the peel on some for natural pectin, then add a cup of brown sugar and half a cup of white sugar on top of the apples. Add half a cup of apple cider, and some spices like a few cinnamon sticks and pinches of ground cloves, allspice, and nutmeg. Give it a stir, put the lid on, and set the slow cooker to low for about seven hours, when the apples will be golden brown or darker and falling apart. Remove the cinnamon sticks and any chunks of apple peel. Use a potato masher for chunky apple butter, or an immersion blender for smooth. Refrigerate in jars or follow health and safety protocol for canning. Enjoy!

Tucked into the misty foothills in Snohomish, this cute farm grows many dozens of varieties of heirloom, organic apples for the picking (like Sansa, Elstar, and Fiesta), plus pears and fall grapes. It's close enough to Seattle to draw crowds on weekends, so opt for a weekday if you want to pick in peace.

APPLE CREEK ORCHARD
5367 Barr Road, Ferndale
(360) 384-0915
Throughout October, this pastoral orchard hosts U-pick for popular Jonagolds, a cross between Golden Delicious and the blush-crimson Jonathan apples. You'll also find Honeycrisp, Melrose, Gala, Mutsu, and Snow Sweet apples, plus some pears and pumpkins.

JONES CREEK FARMS
32260 Burrese Road, Sedro Woolley
skagitvalleyfruit.com
This rustic orchard nestled in the Skagit Valley is a U-pick favorite. If you visit one orchard in the valley, go here; it's the best place in Puget Sound to pick your own heirloom varieties of apples—more than one hundred different kinds. Also offered are U-pick Asian pears and pumpkins.

TRY GEOCACHING

GO ON A HIGH-TECH TREASURE HUNT

Could this be a geocache location?

photo by KV

WANT TO HUNT for hidden treasure on your next hike? Okay, "treasure" might be too grandiose for what you're likely to find in a geocache—think trinkets and doodads, action figures, beads, a coin of foreign currency, or a bit of poetry. A geocache is a hidden collection of small, offbeat objects, usually in a box or jar, placed in a publicly accessible outdoor spot for the purpose of being found. You've walked by them, over them, and around them without even knowing they were there. They're in your city parks. There's a geocache midway across the Tacoma Narrows Bridge, and on the summit of Mount Adams. People who hunt for them are geocachers, and they're often wildly addicted to their sport.

When geocaching was the hot new hobby for hikers in the early 2000s, you needed some hefty navigational tools and know-how—topographic maps, a compass, and for the gadget-obsessed, a pricey GPS unit. Nowadays, the gadgetry most of us carry in our pockets has everything you need to get started—a smartphone with GPS capability (standard on modern cell phones), and a free app. Launch your geocaching adventures almost anywhere—from a neighborhood park to the backcountry.

HOW TO FIND A GEOCACHE

To find a cache, navigate to a specific set of GPS coordinates, then try to find the container hidden there. To do this, download the free Geocaching app (available for Android and iPhone). Create a login, and with geolocation enabled, touch the "map" icon, which displays a map with your current location in the middle plus locations of nearby geocaches, represented by green box icons. If you're in a city, you might see these icons in parks, greenbelts, street easements, or on the grounds of a public library. In state parks and national forest lands, geocaches are found at trailheads, under downed logs or behind boulders along hiking trails, sometimes even far into the backcountry.

Start by finding a geocache near where you live. When you reach the location, chances are, you won't see the geocache container at first—because it's hidden! Tap the map's icon for that cache, and you'll get a cryptic hint where to look. For example, "a thorny affair" might tell you to look near some blackberry brambles (ouch!). "Be like a troll" means to look under a footbridge. Click through to the description of the geocache for more hints. When you locate the cache, open it and sign the log (bring your own pen). On your app, click the "Log" icon and mark it as found—from now on, that cache will appear as a smiling face on your map. Each cache page has an activity section where you can post a note, upload a photo, and read other geocachers' notes about their experience at that cache.

Wondering how all these caches got there? Geocachers created them, and you can too once you've gotten the hang of finding them. Always get permission from the land manager or landowner to hide a new cache. When choosing a hiding place, don't make it too easy or too challenging, and minimize impacts that geocachers will make on the landscape reaching the hidden treasure. Lastly, get a durable, waterproof container to house your cache, as these often remain in their hiding place for years.

If geocaching sparks joy, keep at it! Consider subscribing to the premium version of the Geocaching app—it opens up some fun challenges to reach caches that aren't accessible in the free version, like puzzles and riddles, and includes a map layer with hiking trails.

WHERE TO GO

YOUR NEIGHBORHOOD

Geocaching around your home turf gives you lots of excuses to take long walks outdoors. Gain a fresh new perspective on places you see every day, and notice cool features of your hood. Some urban parks are treasure troves—Point Defiance Park in Tacoma has more than thirty geocaches, and the Chuckanut Mountain area in Bellingham has more than one hundred. Some cities, including Seattle, discourage and may even remove geocaches from city parks if the locations aren't approved in advance.

YOUR FAVORITE HIKES

Add a fun twist to your day hikes and a novel motivation to push on another mile. Most well-trodden trails outside of national parks and designated wilderness will have a cache or two—some host many more. In the Columbia Gorge, hiking trails in the Catherine Creek Recreation Area hide a few

LEARN MORE

The Washington State Geocaching Association advocates for geocachers, working with parks departments to create beneficial relationships between land managers and the geocaching community. The Geocaching app's headquarters is in Seattle's Fremont neighborhood (837 N 34th Street, Suite 300), and they offer tours.

dozen geocaches. The Rattlesnake Ledges Trail outside North Bend has five caches.

FOREST SERVICE ROADS

What a brilliant idea to line long Forest Service roads with caches every tenth of a mile—it makes a fun day of caching by mountain bike. Popular roads for this are the Little Quilcene Road into the eastern slope of the Olympics and the Suiattle River Road in the Cascades out of Darrington.

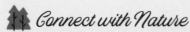 Connect with Nature

Learn to identify ten native trees. Geocache "hints" are laden with trees as markers, and you'll have more luck finding caches if you know a hemlock from a cedar. Examine a tree's bark, needles or leaves, cones or seed pods for clues about its identity. When acorns are underfoot, look for the lacy leaves of a Garry oak nearby. The bark of a Douglas-fir is deeply grooved, while a western red cedar's is stringy and peels loose in long strips. Ponderosa pine, common on the eastern slope of the Cascades, has long needles in bundles of three.

NATURE NOTEBOOK

Location: _____   Date: _____

Co-naturers: _____

What were the contents of the very first geocache you found? If you were to create a geocache, where would it be and what would you put in it?

_____

_____

_____

_____

_____

_____

_____

NATIONAL PARKS

Although geocaches were once banned in national parks (and rogue user-created ones still are), the park service creates and maintains their own geocaches for the public to enjoy in places that ensure protection of the natural and cultural resources of parks. Geocache icons within national parks often look different in the app, and they are different—they're called "earthcaches" and are interactive: you solve a puzzle or answer questions about the area's history or natural resources. All three of Washington's national parks have park-created geocaches.

HIKE IN THE RAIN

DRIZZLE BRINGS THE RAIN FOREST TO LIFE

Moss and mushroom on a Lake Quinault nature trail

IN THE NORTHWEST'S temperate rain forests, "hiking season" is a misnomer. These low-lying river valleys are at their most glorious when pelted with rain and shrouded in mist. Fall is when the rain forest truly comes to life—with bugling elk searching for a mate, the poetry of falling leaves, and the persistent *drip, drip, drip* that makes this place so magical. Tourists are gone, salmon are running, and the rain keeps falling. All you have to do is show up for this phenomenal nature show.

What makes a temperate rain forest? A lot of rain, at least 55 inches per year, although river valleys on the west side of the Olympics get up to three times that. A verdant matrix of mosses, lichens, liverworts, and ferns festoon some of the world's largest cedar, spruce, hemlock, and big-leaf maple trees. Their trunks and branches drip with beardlike tufts of spike moss and other epiphytes in tangled shades of green.

The Quinault, Queets, Hoh, and Bogachiel—take your pick. These four protected wilderness valleys in Olympic National Park are the archetypal temperate rain forests, with 140 to 180 inches of rainfall each year. Many forested valleys on the Cascades' western slopes also qualify as temperate rain forest, albeit less soggy ones. If you live in Western Washington, chances are there's a rain forest hike within an hour's drive of your house.

Dress for a day in the rain, with warm wicking layers (no cotton) topped with a rain coat, rain pants, and waterproof hiking boots with good traction—wet rocks, log bridges, boardwalks, and mud can be slippery. There's more risk when crossing streams swollen with swift, high water, so judge wisely if you should cross at all—use caution if you do. Keep an eye on the time because it gets dark by late afternoon in autumn, or even earlier under a dense canopy of trees.

WHERE TO GO

With the right gear and a keen sense of curiosity about nature, you'll find drizzly days are a wonderful opportunity to hit the trail.

QUINAULT RAIN FOREST NATURE TRAILS, OLYMPIC NATIONAL PARK

nps.gov/olym, (360) 288-2525
NORTHWEST FOREST PASS
5 miles round-trip, minimal elevation gain
If you like your rainy day hikes short, easy, and interspersed with mugs of hot cocoa in front of a giant fireplace, head to the valley of the giants. Several trails on both the south and north shores of Lake Quinault lead you under magnificent old trees draped with spongy moss. On the South Shore Road, the interpretive Quinault Rain Forest Nature Trail is under a mile; the Quinault Loop Trail is closer to 5 miles, allowing for a few good hours of easy hiking through this moist emerald paradise. Access to this looped trail system is from either of the Forest Service campgrounds (Falls Creek or Willaby) or from the historic Lake Quinault Lodge (in the lobby you'll find the previously mentioned fireplace). On the North Shore Road, don't miss the stunning Maple Glade Rain Forest Loop Trail / Kestner Homestead that departs from the Olympic National Park Quinault River Ranger Station and wends through a verdant boggy paradise for less than a mile.

BOGACHIEL RIVER, OLYMPIC NATIONAL PARK

US 101 near Forks
fs.usda.gov/olympic, (360) 374-6522
NORTHWEST FOREST PASS
8 miles round-trip, 400 feet elevation gain
Some might say the most spectacular rain forest hike is the Hoh River Trail in Olympic National Park. Maybe, but if you want the

beauty of the Hoh Rain Forest without the crowds, head to the Bogie, the rain forest river valley just north of the Hoh. The easy hiking is nearly flat as it meanders through this mist-shrouded forest. Begin amid second-growth trees and cross into Olympic National Park after 1.5 miles, where you'll see old-growth ancient trees tall enough to pierce the sky. Two stream crossings will get your feet wet (if you're not wearing waterproof boots). Once you've had your fill of lichens and fungi, turn around and return the way you came. A side trail, the Ira Spring Wetland Trail, can be added for a loop.

TWIN FALLS, NEAR NORTH BEND
I-90 to Exit 34, (360) 902-8844
DISCOVER PASS
2.6 miles round-trip, 500 feet elevation gain
Big-leaf maples add some subtle fall color to the old-growth conifer forest along this trail to two waterfalls that are fed by 60 inches of annual rainfall. Moss-draped trees flank the south fork of the Snoqualmie River over a ground filled with spongy moss, nurse logs, and ferns. Listen for the long, complex trill of the Pacific Wren or the jackhammering of woodpeckers. Then you'll hear the falls. At about three-quarters of a mile in is the first view of the falls. Another mile brings you to the trail's big payoff: a high footbridge over the river right between the upper and lower waterfalls.

OLD SAUK RIVER, NORTH CASCADES
Mountain Loop Highway near Darrington
fs.usda.gov/mbs, (360) 436-1155
6 miles round-trip, 150 feet elevation gain
The Old Sauk Trail just south of Darrington is an easy, flat trail that meanders alongside the beautiful Sauk River through an emerald mossy wonderland. Designated a Wild and Scenic River, the Sauk is protected critical habitat for spawning salmon and other critters, and the forest hasn't been logged for nearly a century. Fall and winter hikers are rewarded with large numbers of salmon-loving Bald Eagles who perch above the river where the living is easy. Autumn draws mushroom hunters in search of foragable fungi.

BOULDER RIVER, NORTH CASCADES
SR 530 near Oso
fs.usda.gov/mbs, (360) 436-1155
8.5 miles round-trip, 700 feet elevation gain
If pounding waterfalls and towering, mossy trees are your jam, you'll love the Boulder River trail. The lush out-and-back trail ambles through one of the few remaining low-elevation old-growth forests in the

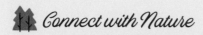 *Connect with Nature*

Have you ever been scrolling through social media and an image of nature grabs you? Brief visuals of nature can shift your perspective and elevate your mood when work or life gets too busy. Use your smartphone to capture images of nature on your hikes—from landscapes to close-ups, from a found bloom to a lost leaf. Enjoy the images when you need to lift your spirits, and share them on social media to lift others.

NATURE NOTEBOOK

Location: _____ Date: _____

Co-naturers: _____

Ponder all the ways nature benefits you. List them, with gratitude.

_____

_____

_____

_____

_____

_____

_____

_____

Cascades. Sword and deer fern cling to the ground at your feet, while fragrant red cedar and hemlock provide some shelter from rain clouds above. A handful of waterfalls plunge into the trail's namesake river from a cliff on the other side. At 1.25 miles is the trail's highlight, Feature Show Falls—a massive twin curtain waterfall that streams down a moss-laden cliff wall. Take a seat on the provided bench and gawk. The trail hugs Boulder River most of the way to the dead end.

BE A LIGHTHOUSE KEEPER

SENTINELS OF NAVIGATION DOT THE COAST

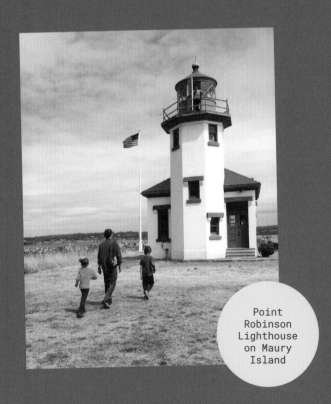

Point Robinson Lighthouse on Maury Island

LIGHTHOUSES REMIND US of the lesson we humans have had to learn over and over throughout history: nature cannot be tamed.

Before lighthouses, there were many shipwrecks. Hidden dangers like shifting sandbars and fog-shrouded sea stacks lurked up and down the rugged Washington coastline. In ferocious storms, a foreboding headland could smash a ship into driftwood. From the mouth of the Columbia River to Cape Flattery and throughout Puget Sound, thousands of vessels were lost to the sea. Lighthouses were needed to guide mariners to safe harbor.

Washington's first navigational light was the Cape Disappointment Lighthouse, built in 1856 to warn mariners of the treacherous river bar where the Columbia spills into the sea. This part of the coast was known as the Graveyard of the Pacific for its tendency to wreck boats. A year later on Tatoosh Island, the Cape Flattery Lighthouse steered ships away from its hazardous headlands and narrow coves. Soon more than two dozen lighthouses guarded the state's coastline; most remain in operation today, standing sentinel over the sea.

For many years, lightkeepers tended to these sentinels while living in a keepers' residence next door, sometimes with their family. Their work was isolating, exhausting, dangerous—hauling fuel up hundreds of steps, trimming the wicks, polishing every nook and cranny of the Fresnel prism lens, sounding the fog horn, and so on. Living conditions could be harsh, at times going months through stormy winters with no human contact. Their workplace—on the edge of sea and land—was invariably one of stunning beauty.

WHERE TO GO

Want to keep a lighthouse yourself? All lighthouses in the US are now automated with electricity. Still, a few remain staffed with volunteer keepers to tend the grounds, greet visitors, and give tours—caretakers for a piece of maritime history. Others have been converted into vacation rentals. Both experiences give you a taste of what it must have been like to be a real lightkeeper a century ago.

NEW DUNGENESS LIGHTHOUSE, OLYMPIC PENINSULA
554 Voice of America Road W, Sequim
newdungenesslighthouse.com, (360) 683-6638
This is the ultimate gig, tending to a historic lighthouse on a windswept beach surrounded by surf, boats, and wildlife. The lighthouse and keepers' residence are perched near the end of Dungeness Spit, a 5.5-mile-long natural sandbar with driftwood and seagrass that shields a bay and wildlife refuge. One of the Northwest's oldest, the New Dungeness Lighthouse has aided ship navigation through the Strait of Juan de Fuca since 1857. Volunteer lightkeepers serve one-week shifts as they have continuously since 1994, taking care of the property and giving tours up the seventy-four steps of the lighthouse tower. To report for duty yourself, join as a dues-paying member of the New Dungeness

LEARN MORE

The United States Lighthouse Society shares the maritime legacy of lighthouses and works to preserve them. Find lighthouses wherever you go at lighthousefriends.com.

NATURE NOTEBOOK

Location: _____   Date: _____

Co-naturers: _____

Describe what you think your typical day would be if you were a lighthouse keeper on the Washington Coast a century ago.

_____

_____

_____

_____

_____

_____

_____

_____

_____

Lighthouse Association, then check their calendar for availability and book your week. Lighthouse keepers pay a per-person fee. In the large keeper's quarters built in 1904 are four bedrooms, a full kitchen and formal dining room, a cozy living room, and two bathrooms. Downstairs is a rec room with Ping-Pong and laundry. Bring your own food for the week. A jeep transports you and your gear to and from the lighthouse along the slender spit at low tide, which in winter months is often by moonlight.

BROWNS POINT LIGHTHOUSE, SOUTH PUGET SOUND
201 Tulalip Street NE, Tacoma
pointsnortheast.org

The lighthouse, 34 feet tall and built in 1933, stands just above the tide line at the eastern entrance to Commencement Bay. Known for being shrouded in fog, Browns Point is a danger to ships but a lovely cloak around the austere and boxy art deco lighthouse, recently restored by the Points NE Historical Society. As lightkeeper you won't trim the wick or blow a foghorn (those operations have been automated for decades), but you will raise and lower the flag, keep the cottage yard tidy, and conduct tours on Saturdays. For downtime, cast a fishing rod from the shore or kick back in the historic keepers' cottage built in 1903 and watch passing sailboats eclipse the sunset. Rent the cottage on VRBO.com.

POINT WILSON LIGHTHOUSE, QUIMPER PENINSULA

Fort Worden State Park, Port Townsend
uslhs.org, (415) 362-7255

One of the region's most important navigational aids is at the tip of Point Wilson, the entrance into Puget Sound via Admiralty Inlet. Standing 51 feet tall and made of reinforced concrete, the current lighthouse dates from 1914 and is octagonal—a design intended to resist the wind. It still uses the original fourth-order Fresnel lens. Famously, the SS *Governor* sunk here in 1921 and still rests on her wrecked keel 240 feet beneath the water's surface. Rent the Chief's House—restored quarters for the Coast Guard—which sleeps up to eight in four bedrooms, with kitchen, dining, and living rooms.

POINT NO POINT LIGHTHOUSE, KITSAP PENINSULA

9009 NE Point No Point Road, Hansville
uslhs.org, (415) 362-7255

Bunk down in this cool relic of maritime history. Puget Sound's oldest lighthouse (built in 1879) still stands on the sandy beach at Point No Point, guiding ships of all sizes safely up, into, and out of Admiralty Inlet. Since the late 1970s, the light has been automated, but like all lighthouses it was originally manned by a dedicated keeper who tended to its operation—cleaning the fragile lens, replenishing fuel, trimming the wicks, and so forth. The historic lighthouse keepers' quarters, now a vacation rental, have a full kitchen, living room, dining room, two bedrooms, and a bathroom, all decked out in Victorian antique furniture and nautical-themed artwork. Take in the panoramic view of Puget Sound islands and Cascade volcanoes from its spacious porch, and keep an eye to the sea for seals, orcas, and migrating waterfowl. Beachcomb on the sandy beach at low tide. The property is also home to the US Lighthouse Society Headquarters and Museum, and lighthouse tours are offered seasonally on weekends.

POINT ROBINSON LIGHTHOUSE, VASHON ISLAND

3705 SW Point Robinson Road
Vashon / Maury Island, vashonparks.org

Stay for the weekend or a whole week at one of the two renovated keepers' quarters. The two residences share the beach with the lighthouse and other features of the historic light station. The current lighthouse, similar in style to Point No Point's but shorter at 38 feet, was completed in 1915. Sitting halfway between Seattle and Tacoma, it is a twin of the Alki Point Lighthouse across the water in West Seattle. Its fifth-order Fresnel lens is still in the tower's lantern room.

NORTH HEAD LIGHTHOUSE, SOUTHWEST WASHINGTON COAST

N Head Lighthouse Road, Ilwaco
washington.goingtocamp.com, (888) 226-7688

The lighthouse sits atop North Head, a rocky promontory just 2 miles north of Cape Disappointment and the mouth of the Columbia River. It lets southbound ships know they're approaching the river, and steers them off from the shipwrecking Long Beach Peninsula. First lit in 1889, the lighthouse is built of brick masonry with a cement plaster overlay. All three lightkeeper residences sleep six and are available as vacation rentals through the state park, each offering stunning ocean views, lots of Victorian antique decor, and books about lighthouses.

SOAK IN A HOT SPRING

WHERE NATURE MEETS NURTURE

Soaking at Goldmyer Hot Springs

THE PACIFIC NORTHWEST is geo-thermally blessed with steamy, natural hot springs. Indigenous peoples revered them as sacred places for restoration and healing, and hot springs are cherished for those same reasons today. The springs form when ground-water gets heated by magma or hot rocks deep below the earth's surface, then rises back up through cracks in the earth's crust called vents. Hot springs often form around areas of volcanic activity. The hot water may spring out of the ground or seep into a small pool or stream, mixing with cooler surface water. Several of these warm, wild pools can be found in Washington's mountains, so if lounging in a vat of hot mineral water becomes your new favorite thing, you live in a great region for it.

Northwest hot springs come in many varieties. Some are scenic, natural basins set deep in the woods. To reach them, one must get there on foot. Trails to wild hot springs are well trodden, as mobs of hikers come to soak in their relaxing minerals, so expect to be bumping elbows while you soothe your muscles, especially on weekends. In general, the shorter the access trail, the more crowded the pool (Baker Hot Springs). If the hike in takes a few days, expect blissful solitude (like Gamma Hot Springs). Many thermal tradi-tionalists prefer to dip au naturel (Scenic or Olympic Hot Springs). On the other end of the geothermal spectrum are resorts with in-ground pools or soaker tubs filled with hot mineral water piped in from a nearby source, often with on-site lodging (Sol Duc or Carson Hot Springs).

The temperatures of natural hot springs range from a warm 90° F to dangerously hot. A comfortable soaking temperature for most people is 100–102° F, although some veteran soakers prefer pools a bit hotter than that.

Hot springs resorts add the perfect amount of fresh water to hold a hot pool at a desired temperature, but the temp of wild hot springs may vary when there's an influx of cooling rain or snow. Check the temperature with your hand or foot before plunging in.

WHERE TO GO

Although summer draws the largest crowds, autumn and winter are ideal seasons to partake in a hot, restorative soak. Even with a serious chill in the air and snow on the ground, these mineral pools stay nice and steamy under a ceiling of skyscraping conifers.

OLYMPIC HOT SPRINGS, OLYMPIC NATIONAL PARK

Off US 101 west of Port Angeles
nps.gov/olym, (360) 565-3130
NATIONAL PARK PASS
20.8 miles round-trip, 1500 feet elevation gain of road cycling
⭐ *Best for: bikepackers*

This sweet series of hot spring pools along Boulder Creek in the Elwha River Valley were once easy to reach on a 5-mile round-trip hike. They will be again someday, once the washout of Olympic Hot Springs Road is repaired (currently slated for fall 2023). In the meantime, bike or hike the road beyond the washout just past the Madison Falls parking area—it's 8 miles and 1500 feet up to the Boulder Creek trailhead. Once here, leave bikes behind and backpack in. The hot springs comprise a dozen or so steamy soak-ing pools set in the misty rain forest, some hotter or more secluded than others. Temps range from 85° to 105° F. A spacious camp-ground sits near the hot springs (backcoun-try permit required).

SOL DUC HOT SPRINGS RESORT, OLYMPIC NATIONAL PARK

12076 Sol Duc Hot Springs Road, Port Angeles
olympicnationalparks.com, (888) 896-3818 or
(866) 476-5382

⭐ *Best for: soakers who seek soft beds*

Spend the night in a rustic cabin in Olympic National Park's Sol Duc Hot Springs Resort surrounded by towering, mossy conifers along the scenic Sol Duc River, just steps away from three steaming mineral hot springs pools of progressively warmer temperatures. There's a freshwater pool, too. Soak in the pools while listening to the sounds of the temperate rain forest. The resort has poolside dining and a small store, and is usually open March–October (weather dependent).

BAKER HOT SPRINGS, MOUNT BAKER

Off Baker Lake Road
fs.usda.gov/mbs, (360) 856-5700

⭐ *Best for: bang for your buck*

Don't be tricked by the rough forest service road into thinking you'll have solitude. The word is out about this place, so come on a fall weekday morning if you want a chance

---

NATURE NOTEBOOK

Location: _____   Date: _____

Co-naturers: _____

Mineral hot springs are thought to have curative powers—from boosting circulation and relaxing tense muscles to softening skin with minerals like silica and sulfur. How did you feel after a soak? How was your sleep different that night?

_____

_____

_____

_____

_____

_____

_____

at getting the soaking pool to yourself. This steamy pond sits in the forested foothills between Mount Baker and Baker Lake. From the parking lot it's under half a mile to the springs on a well-trodden, sometimes muddy path—follow the strong scent of sulfur. The pool is large enough to accommodate a dozen soakers and ranges in temperature from about 96° to 102° F, depending on rain or snow. Move around to find the good hot spots near the vents.

SCENIC HOT SPRINGS, CENTRAL CASCADES

West of Stevens Pass

scenichotsprings.blogspot.com

scenichotsprings@gmail.com *(for reservations)*

⭐ *Best for: privacy seekers*

The steamy springs fill three cozy soaking tubs (bathing suits optional) perched on a scenic cliffside on private property encircled by national forest land. You often need to make reservations months in advance, but a peaceful, rejuvenating day of soaking here is well worth the wait, especially in crisp, colorful autumn or snow-flocked winter. Get there in boots or snowshoes via a 2-mile hike that gains 1200 feet in elevation.

GOLDMYER HOT SPRINGS, CENTRAL CASCADES

Middle Fork of the Snoqualmie River near Snoqualmie Pass

goldmyer.org, (206) 789-5631

⭐ *Best for: soakers who want the crème de la crème*

Like Scenic Hot Springs, this geothermal utopia outside North Bend up the Middle Fork Road is on a private in-holding surrounded by national forest, requires reservations well in advance, and is clothing optional. Limited to twenty visitors per day to protect the

SAFETY AND ETIQUETTE

Keep in mind that wild hot springs on Washington's public lands are not regularly monitored or maintained and may contain bacteria. Use the pools at your own risk. Keep your head above water so you don't unwittingly take in water, and don't soak if you have open cuts.

Be respectful. Keep noise to a minimum if others are there to relax. Be welcoming and share the space with others. Leave no trace—if you pack anything in, pack it out. Soaking in the buff is common at most backcountry hot springs, even when not condoned by the land managers. If you choose to dip sans bathing suit, be modest. Use common courtesy if others are nude by not pointing or staring. Don't actually "bathe" in the hot springs—no soap.

fragile ecosystem and scenic beauty, these remote soaking pools are never crowded. The descending, stone-walled pools are fed from a waterfall that springs from the ground out of a cave and tops 110°F. Each pool is slightly cooler than the one above it, and there's a cold plunge pool for quick cool-downs. It's 4.5 miles to the hot springs on foot, snowshoes, cross-country skis, or bikes via the Middle Fork Road. There is primitive camping on-site for a modest fee.

BIKE TO WINERIES

SPIN, SWIRL, SNIFF, SIP

Harvest time at the vineyard

Photo by Tina Witherspoon

WHEN IT COMES to Washington wine, it's all about the terroir. Diversity defines the topography and climate of the Pacific Northwest, reflected in luscious reds and crisp whites. When you sip a merlot from Walla Walla or a sauvignon blanc from the shores of Lake Chelan, you're tasting Washington.

You'll find wineries on both sides of the Cascades, though the really ideal conditions for viticulture are on the east side, where hot, arid days of summer sunshine beautifully ripen grapes and bring out the sugars, while cool nights help balance acidity. Together, these climate conditions create perfect wine grapes, so it's no surprise that 99 percent of Washington's planted vineyard acres are east of the crest. To savor the terroir on two wheels, plan a self-guided cycle-and-sip tour through wine country. Several wine regions beckon cyclists with unfussy tasting rooms, moderate terrain, and country roads that crisscross pretty rolling vineyards. The rewards? Tasting local wine straight from the source, and maybe even a friendly chat with the person who made it.

WHERE TO GO

Come during the early fall harvest, when clumps of ripe grapes hang lazily from their vines, ready to be plucked and crushed. Later in autumn, most tasting rooms open their doors for Thanksgiving weekend when vineyards show off golden and amber hues on trellised vines.

WALLA WALLA VALLEY

More than one hundred wineries are scattered throughout the Walla Walla Valley in and around its same-name town, a favorite for touring by bicycle, especially if you love lush red wines like syrah (big, tannic, and a little spicy) and are a sucker for fall foliage. Wineries are clustered in five distinct areas—downtown (great for strolling and sipping), northeast of town by the airport (with flat terrain perfect for beginner cyclists), west of town (taste at a few of the region's oldest wineries), east of town (including Leonetti Cellar, the region's oldest winery), or south of town (the most scenic and popular with cyclists). Tasting rooms within each area are close enough to easily bike from winery to winery. For stunning scenery, head south where rolling hills are carpeted by vines with a serene backdrop of the Blue Mountains. Plan a cycle route at wallawallawine.com.

RATTLESNAKE HILLS, YAKIMA VALLEY

Riesling, merlot, and cabernet sauvignon grapes love to ripen in the long days of sunshine and arid air of Rattlesnake Hills. Cycling on the scenic country roads north of Zillah, you'll sneak peeks of Mount Rainier and Mount Adams between sips at some of Yakima Valley's oldest and most interesting wineries. Park and ride from the lot at Two Mountain Winery and create a small or large loop, depending how much you want to pedal and sip. Some must-stop tasting rooms are Paradisos del Sol, Bonair, and Hyatt. Plan a cycling itinerary at rattlesnakehills.org.

QUIMPER PENINSULA CIDERIES, PORT TOWNSEND

Trade grapes for apples and get your bicycle to the northern Olympic Peninsula. There's a centuries-old tradition in Europe of turning tart apples into hard cider, a craft that's had a renaissance in the bucolic countryside south of Port Townsend. All three cideries are within 10 miles of each other so start at Finnriver Farm & Cidery in Chimacum and taste the Orchard Series Ciders, fermented

NATURE NOTEBOOK

Location: _____ Date: _____

Co-naturers: _____

Keep tasting notes for the wines and ciders you try. Although wine is made from grapes, compounds are released during fermentation that create many other aromas and notes that hit your nose and tastebuds when you swirl and sip, from black cherry to pipe tobacco. What notes do you taste?

_____

_____

_____

_____

_____

_____

_____

_____

_____

from organic, estate-grown apples and pears, or botanical ciders infused with saffron, honey, or lavender. Next pedal north to Eaglemount, the first licensed cidery in the region, known for excellent standard varieties as well as some unique experiments with quince and ginger cider. Ride east for the last leg to Alpenfire Organic Hard Cider. Plan your cycle route at opciderroute.com.

LEARN MORE

Wish you had an interactive map with every winery and vineyard in the state to plan your own cycle-and-sip wine tour? You do—the Washington Wine Commission.

VINO VOCAB

Ditch your tasting room naïveté and get a little wine knowledge under your bike helmet.

Acidity. Too much acid means a tart or sour wine; too little acid and the wine is flat and boring.

AVA. In the US, designated wine grape-growing regions are called American Viticultural Areas (AVAs), distinguishable by geographic features, topography, climate, and official boundaries.

Estate. An estate-bottled wine means that 100 percent of the grapes used were grown in the winery's own vineyards.

Fermentation. To put it simply: yeast eats the sugar in the grape juice and makes alcohol.

Finish. The last flavor or impression a wine leaves in your mouth after you swallow (or spit).

Fruit-forward. With a fruit-forward wine, you taste fruit above any other flavors and nuances that may come from oak or terroir.

Full-bodied. A wine has complex flavors and evokes rich texture and robustness.

Legs. The term for the wine that clings to the glass as you swirl it around looking clever.

Oaked. Some wines are aged in American or French oak barrels, or alternatively oak chips are added during the fermentation or aging process. Serious oak exposure results in complex buttery, toasty, or vanilla flavors.

On the skins. How red wine gets its color and tannins: by fermenting on squished grape skins!

Residual sugar. The term refers to the amount of sugar in the wine that doesn't get turned into alcohol during fermentation; the more there is, the sweeter the wine.

Tannin. This compound found in grape skins, seeds, and stems gives red wine its texture and grip, as well as its staying power in a cellar. It's something you feel more than taste.

Terroir. This sums up the sense of place you taste in a wine—the soil, drainage, slope, sunlight, altitude, climate, and microclimate.

Vineyard. This is where they grow the grapes for making wine, though not all wineries have their own vineyard. Some vineyards sell their grapes to local wineries.

Vintage. The year in which the grapes were primarily grown and harvested.

SEE SALMON RUN

GREET THEM AS THEY RETURN HOME TO SPAWN

Salmon at the Ballard Locks

photo by Mary Metz

ONE OF THE most compelling mysteries in Northwest nature is the ability of salmon to return to the stream from which they spawned. They navigate to their native river, possibly using the earth's magnetic field as a compass, and seemingly using smell to remember their home tributary. After a lifetime (in fish years) at sea they return, laying their own eggs in the stream's gravel substrate. And then, they die. Their carcass decomposes over weeks and months, providing nutrients to their own eggs.

Most salmon species migrate to their home streams in the fall (late August–November), and that's when we can most easily watch them return, from the bank of a river in the wild Olympics to a Seattle city creek. Five species of salmon live in Washington's salty waters—chinook, coho, sockeye, pink, and chum. We also have steelhead, a seagoing rainbow trout (and the official fish of Washington State). Like salmon, steelhead trout return and spawn in their freshwater rivers, but unlike salmon they can survive spawning, return to sea, and return to spawn again.

To the Coast Salish tribes, salmon are life. Deeply embedded in their culture and identity, salmon are a symbol of prosperity and nourishment. One ancient Salish belief was that salmon are human relatives, and the runs of salmon were lineages. Some salmon must be allowed to return to their home rivers for those lineages to go on, assuring the preservation of human life.

It's a remarkable privilege we share to witness the salmon homecoming, not just on wild scenic rivers but in our cities and neighborhoods around Puget Sound. But they're not all thriving populations—many wild species of salmon, like the Puget Sound chinook, are dwindling under threats from overfishing, dams, sprawl development, dewatering of streams, pollution runoff, climate change, and habitat loss. Help recover these icons of Pacific Northwest nature by reducing pavement, gardening without pesticides, volunteering to restore stream habitat, and more. A great place to begin is by welcoming them home this fall.

WHERE TO GO

When viewing salmon, follow these tips: Move slowly and quietly, or salmon may think you're a predator and get spooked. Sunglasses reduce glare on the water. Don't step or wade into spawning streams—this could damage salmon eggs. Leave pets safely at home. Don't remove dead salmon carcasses—they provide important nutrients to the stream.

BALLARD LOCKS
3015 NW 54th Street, Seattle
Completed in 1917, the locks link Puget Sound with Lake Union and Lake Washington. Show up just before high tide anytime from late August (for chinook) through late September (for coho). Walk across the locks and marvel at the feat of engineering it took a century ago to connect our saltwater sea with Lake Union and Lake Washington, which was 29 feet above sea level at the time. While the locks get boats from one side to the other, the twenty-one-step fish ladder does the same for salmon as they leap up from one pool to the next. Don't miss descending to the underground viewing area. From the locks the salmon have up to 50 miles ahead in their journey home.

CARKEEK PARK
950 NW Carkeek Park Road, Seattle
Watch the return of hundreds of chum and coho salmon as they thrash their way through Piper's Creek in the late fall. On weekends

during the annual salmon run, volunteer salmon stewards mingle with visitors alongside the creek to chat about the salmon's life cycle. After spawning eggs in the creek bed, the salmon die, and the cycle begins all over again.

BUDD INLET

5th Avenue SW Bridge and Dam, Olympia

Did you know salmon pass right through downtown Olympia? Just before high tide, head to the 5th Avenue Bridge, which doubles as a dam separating Budd Inlet from Capitol Lake. See migrating salmon schooling below the fish ladder from late August through mid-September as they make their way from the salty waters of Puget Sound up to their spawning grounds, the Deschutes River. Most are hatchery chinook salmon. It's a bustle of activity as seals in the water, herons on the shore, and eagles overhead all vie to snag a bite.

CHUCKANUT CREEK IN ARROYO PARK

Parking on Old Samish Road, Bellingham

In October and November, Washington's most abundant wild salmon, chum, return to Chuckanut Creek. The short trails in this lovely park south of Fairhaven offer lots of

NATURE NOTEBOOK

Location: _____ Date: _____

Co-naturers: _____

List three things you personally pledge to do to help recover wild salmon populations in Washington.

_____

_____

_____

_____

_____

_____

_____

opportunities to see chum from the bank and from a footbridge across the creek. Watch with stillness and patience—you may observe a salmon digging a redd, the gravel nest in which a salmon deposits her eggs.

GREEN RIVER, FLAMING GEYSER STATE PARK

23700 SE Flaming Geyser Road, Auburn

Park near the old flaming geyser and walk to the riverbank—there are a few great vantage points to keep an eye on the water. Chinook salmon, exhausted from their long journey home, dig in the gravel to make a redd. A female chinook might lay around five thousand eggs before she dies. Three or four years later, only a handful of those offspring will survive to return all the way home to the Green River to spawn.

CHICO CREEK

3121 Chico Way NW, Bremerton

Kitsap County's most abundant salmon-bearing stream has been beautifully restored as prime spawning habitat for the chum salmon who call it home. Visit Chico Salmon Viewing Park from late October through

LEARN MORE

Save Our Wild Salmon takes action to restore wild salmon and steelhead to the rivers, streams, and marine waters of the Pacific Northwest. The Salmon Homecoming Alliance hosts an annual celebration of the salmon's return on the Seattle waterfront each fall.

November to watch them thrash and jump their way upstream. If you're lucky, you'll see some of the coho spawn right here in the cold, clear water and gravel substrate.

SOL DUC RIVER, OLYMPIC PENINSULA

6 miles up Sol Duc Hot Springs Road

Want to see salmon jump out of a river and leap their way up a gushing waterfall? This is the place. Native coho migrate through on their way to spawning grounds farther up the Sol Duc from late October through November. Peak run depends on rainfall; dry summers usually mean later runs.

ACKNOWLEDGMENTS

WITH HEARTFELT GRATITUDE, I want to thank all the wonderful friends who have adventured with me in nature throughout my life, sharing their knowledge, time, and support. My research for this book was born of my own experiences in the wild Pacific Northwest over many years, honing my outdoor skills with folks who were kind enough to teach me what they knew. Although there are too many generous friends to name them all, I am especially grateful to my dad for teaching me to fish, Susan Elderkin for preparing me for my first backpacking trip, Brian Hosey for building the best campfires, Shannon Harps (I miss you) for showing me the wisdom of Leave No Trace, Richard Smith for teaching me to paddle a kayak, Helen Ross Pitts for all of our fun birding excursions, Isaac for being my adventure buddy, and my mom for teaching me how to be a writer.

I'm grateful for the expertise and steady guidance of Kate Rogers, Emily White, and Mary Metz at Mountaineers Books as I developed this from a mere idea into a book. Thank you to Amy Smith Bell for your copyediting prowess and Melissa McFeeters for your beautiful graphic design. And I want to sincerely thank the friends who contributed their personal photos for this book.

Finally, I want to offer additional thanks to my incredible parents, Gary and Maria Braden, who have supported my interests and pursuits in every way; and a special thanks my best friends forever, my sister, Lesley, and brother, Eli.

RESOURCES

BOOKS

Some of the books below are out of print, but I've found them so helpful that I'm including them anyway. Most are readily available in libraries and used book outlets.

Babcock, Scott, and Robert J. Carson. *Hiking Washington's Geology*. Seattle: Mountaineers Books, 2000.

Barnes, Nathan, and Jeremy Barnes. *Washington Wildflower Hikes: 50 Destinations*. Seattle: Mountaineers Books, 2021.

Bauer, Alan L., and Dan Nelson. *Desert Hikes of Washington*. Seattle: Mountaineers Books, 2004.

Benoliel, Doug. *Northwest Foraging: The Classic Guide to Edible Plants of the Pacific Northwest*. Seattle: Mountaineers Books, 2011.

Bentley, Judy, and Craig Romano. *Hiking Washington's History*. Seattle: University of Washington Press, 2021.

Bradley, Laurel and Sam Demas. *Hut to Hut USA: The Complete Guide for Hikers, Bikers, and Skiers*. Seattle: Mountaineers Books, 2021.

Casali, Amber. *Hiking Washington's Fire Lookouts*. Seattle: Mountaineers Books, 2018.

Choukas-Bradley, Melanie. *The Joy of Forest Bathing: Reconnect with Wild Places & Rejuvenate Your Life*. Lexington, KY: Rock Point Publishing, 2018.

Fagin, Michael, and Skip Card. *Best Rain Shadow Hikes: Western Washington*. Seattle: Mountaineers Books, 2003.

Goldman, Peggy. *Washington Scrambles: Selected Nontechnical Ascents 2nd Edition*. Seattle: Mountaineers Books, 2014.

Hahn, Jennifer. *Pacific Feast: A Cook's Guide to West Coast Foraging and Cuisine*. Seattle: Mountaineers Books, 2010.

Hashimoto, Molly. *Colors of the West*. Seattle: Mountaineers Books, 2017.

Henderson, Dan. *Sea Kayaking: Basic Skills, Paddling Techniques and Trip Planning*. Seattle: Mountaineers Books, 2012.

Judd, Ron. *Camping Washington: The Best Public Campgrounds for Tents & RVs, 2nd Edition*. Seattle: Mountaineers Books, 2017.

Kruckeberg, Art, Karen Sykes, and Craig Romano. *Best Wildflower Hikes Washington*. Seattle: Mountaineers Books, 2004.

Link, Russell. *Landscaping for Wildlife in the Pacific Northwest*. Seattle: University of Washington Press, 1999.

Mass, Cliff. *The Weather of the Pacific Northwest, 2nd Edition*. Seattle: University of Washington Press, 2021.

Moskowitz, David. *Wildlife of the Pacific Northwest: Tracking and Identifying Mammals, Birds, Reptiles, Amphibians, and Invertebrates*. Portland, OR: Timber Press, 2010.

Nelson, Dan A. *Snowshoe Routes: Washington, 3rd Edition*. Seattle: Mountaineers Books, 2015.

Plumb, Gregory. *Waterfall Lover's Guide: Pacific Northwest, 5th Edition*. Seattle: Mountaineers Books, 2013.

Romano, Craig. *Backpacking Washington: Overnight and Multiday Routes, 2nd Edition*. Seattle: Mountaineers Books, 2021.

Sept, J. Duane. *The New Beachcomber's Guide to the Pacific Northwest*. Madeira Park, BC: Harbour Publishing, 2019.

Sibley, David Allen. *Sibley Birds West: Field Guide to Birds of Western North America*. New York: Knopf, 2019.

Thorness, Bill. *Biking Puget Sound: 60 Rides from Olympia to the San Juans, 2nd Edition*. Seattle: Mountaineers Books, 2014.

———. *Cycling the Pacific Coast*. Seattle: Mountaineers Books, 2017.

Trudell, Steve, and Joe Ammirati. *Mushrooms of the Pacific Northwest*. Portland, OR: Timber Press, 2009.

Washington Ornithological Society. *A Birders' Guide to Washington, 2nd Edition*. Delaware City, DE: American Birding Association, Inc, 2015.

Whitney, Stephen, and Rob Sandelin. *The Field Guide to the Cascades and Olympics 2nd Edition*. Seattle: Mountaineers Books, 2003.

ORGANIZATIONS

Alderleaf Wilderness College (wildernesscollege.com)
American Red Cross (redcross.org/swimming)

American Sailing Association (asa.com)

Backcountry Horsemen of Washington (bchw.org)

Battle Point Astronomical Association (bpastro.org)

Cascade Bicycle Club (cascade.org)

Cashmere Museum and Pioneer Village
 (cashmeremuseum.org)

Center for Wooden Boats (cwb.org)

Central Cascades Winter Recreation Council
 (snowrec.org)

Climate Solutions (climatesolutions.org)

Conservation Northwest (conservationnw.org)

Crank Sisters (EvergreenMTB.org/cranksisters)

Earthwalk Northwest (earthwalknorthwest.com)

Evergreen Mountain Bike Alliance
 (evergreenmtb.org)

Farm Stay USA (farmstayus.com)

Forest Fire Lookout Association (firelookout.org)

Geocaching (geocaching.com)

Gig Harbor Boat Works (ghboats.com)

Goldendale Observatory
 (goldendaleobservatory.com)

Great Backyard Bird Count (birdcount.org)

Human Nature Hunting (humannaturehunting.com)

JayHawk Institute (jayhawkinstitute.org)

Liftopia (liftopia.com)

The Mountaineers (mountaineers.org/courses)

Mount Tahoma Huts (skimtta.org)

National Weather Service (wrh.noaa.gov)

National Wildlife Federation (nwf.org)

NOAA Space Weather Prediction Center
 (swpc.noaa.gov)

NOAA Tides and Currents
 (tidesandcurrents.noaa.gov)

NOAA Washington Mountain Weather
 (weather.gov/sew/Mountainforecast)

Nooksack Nordic Ski Club
 (nooksacknordicskiclub.org)

North Cascades Institute (ncascades.org)

Northwest Avalanche Center (nwac.us)

Northwest River Forecast Center (nwrfc.noaa.gov)

Northwest Waterfall Survey
 (waterfallsnorthwest.com)

Olympic Coast Cleanup (coastsavers.org)

Orca Network (orcanetwork.org)

Puget Sound Mycological Society (psms.org)

Rendezvous Huts (rendezvoushuts.com)

Salmon Homecoming Alliance
 (salmonhomecoming.org)

Save Our Wild Salmon (wildsalmon.org)

Seattle Astronomical Society (seattleastro.org)

Seattle Ski Shuttle (seattleskishuttle.com)

The SLOW List (Standing Lookouts of Washington)
 (peakbagger.com)

Spokane Nordic (spokanenordic.org)

Stardate (stardate.org)

Student Conservation Association (thesca.org)

Summit at Snoqualmie (summitatsnoqualmie.com)

United States Lighthouse Society (uslhs.org)

University of Washington Astronomy Department
 (depts.washington.edu/astron)

Volunteers for Outdoor Washington (trail-stewards.org)

Washington Apple Commission Visitor Center
 (bestapples.com)

Washington Department of Fish & Wildlife (wdfw.wa.gov)

Washington Kitefliers Association (wka-kiteflyers.org)

Washington Native Plant Society (wnps.org)

Washington Ornithological Society (wos.org)

Washington State Department of Transportation
 (wsdot.wa.gov)

Washington State Geocaching Association
 (wsgaonline.org)

Washington State Parks (parks.state.wa.us)

Washington Trails Association (wta.org)

Washington Water Trails Association (wwta.org)

Washington Weather Chasers on social media
 (@WaWxChasers / #wawx)

Washington Wine Commission (washingtonwine.org)

Washington's Trout Unlimited (washingtontu.org)

The Whale Museum (thewhalemuseum.org)

The Whale Trail (thewhaletrail.org)

Wilderness Awareness School (wildernessawareness.org)

Wild Fish Conservancy (wildfishconservancy.org)

Wooden Boat Festival (woodenboat.org)

photo by Brian Hosey

LAUREN BRADEN is an outdoors and travel writer in Seattle and founded the local trip-planning website Northwest TripFinder. She is passionate about connecting Pacific Northwesterners to close-to-home getaways and outdoor adventures that nurture the soul. Her work has been featured in *Washington Trails*, *ParentMap*, *Outdoors NW*, the *Seattle Times* and the *Seattle PI*, as well as in books on travel, gardening, and citizen activism. Lauren previously worked as communications director for Washington Trails Association, as the advocate for wildlife habitat at Seattle Audubon, and as chair of the Seattle Women's Commission. Lauren lives in West Seattle with her beloved wildlife and veggie garden, husband Brian, son Isaac, and their golden retriever, Georgia. Find her at nwtripfinder.com or on social media @nwtripfinder.

ABOUT SKIPSTONE

Skipstone is an imprint of independent, nonprofit publisher Mountaineers Books. It features thematically related titles that promote a deeper connection to our natural world through sustainable practice and backyard activism. Our readers live smart, play well, and typically engage with the community around them. Skipstone guides explore healthy lifestyles and how an outdoor life relates to the well-being of our planet, as well as of our own neighborhoods. Sustainable foods and gardens; healthful living; realistic and doable conservation at home; modern aspirations for community—Skipstone tries to address such topics in ways that emphasize active living, local and grassroots practices, and a small footprint.

Our hope is that Skipstone books will inspire you to effect change without losing your sense of humor, to celebrate the freedom and generosity of a life outdoors, and to move forward with gentle leaps or breathtaking bounds.

All of our publications, as part of our 501(c)(3) nonprofit program, are made possible through the generosity of donors and through sales of 700 titles on outdoor recreation, sustainable lifestyle, and conservation. To donate, purchase books, or learn more, visit us online:

www.skipstonebooks.org | www.mountaineersbooks.org

SKIPSTONE

LIVE LIFE

MAKE RIPPLES

YOU MAY ALSO LIKE